LIMERICK CITY LIBRARY

Phone: 407510
Website:
www.limerickcity.ie/library
Email: citylib@limerickcity.ie

The Granary,
Michael Street,
Limerick.

This book is issued subject to the Rules of the Library.
The Book must be returned not later then the last date
stamped below.

PHIL DANIELS

CLASS ACTOR

MY AUTOBIOGRAPHY

**SIMON &
SCHUSTER**

London · New York · Sydney · Toronto

A CBS COMPANY

First published in Great Britain by Simon & Schuster UK Ltd, 2010
A CBS COMPANY

1 3 5 7 9 10 8 6 4 2

Simon & Schuster UK Ltd
1st Floor
222 Gray's Inn Road
London WC1X 8HB

www.simonandschuster.co.uk

Simon & Schuster Australia
Sydney

A CIP catalogue record for this book is available
from the British Library.

ISBN: 978-1-84737-620-6

Typeset by M Rules
Printed in the UK by CPI Mackays, Chatham ME5 8TD

For Jan, Ella, my mum, my two sisters,
Barbara and Brenda, and Anna Scher

CONTENTS

PREFACE

It's always a bit of a funny one, when people ask you what you do: to say you're an actor. 'Cos you know you're on a slippery slope then. All actors are. People will either say, 'Oh yeah, I remember you in this and that,' or, 'Well, I've never seen you – what have you done?'

Either way, you immediately have to justify yourself. And if they've not heard of you, it's always your fault. So you end up thinking, 'I can't be arsed to prove that I've been on the telly, or list all the things I've been in, just to back up the fact that I said I was an actor.'

Until now, I've often found it easier to say I was a caretaker or a dustman – just so I don't have to go through it. But hopefully I won't have to do that so much any more. Next time someone bursts out laughing when I tell them what I do for a living – and that has happened – I can just show them a copy of this book, and they'll have to believe me.

When I was younger I never really considered myself to be an actor, anyway. Acting was just one of the things I did, like playing football or being in a band. When I was on film or TV sets I kind of always related (early doors at least) to the crew more than I did to the cast. 'Cos I was from that kind of background, and they did the kind of things my dad did. But being very down to earth and 'not like an actor' – that can be an image you're living up to as well. I've probably fallen into that trap a few times, over the years.

It wasn't that I ever thought being an actor was something to be ashamed of. They're my second family, actors, in a way, because of all the jobs I've done with them. And on the whole they're great people. We're out on our own, in a certain sense, because we all know what it is that we do, and other people – we think – don't quite get it. It's kind of like being in a gang. And hopefully, if you read this book to the end, you'll have some idea of how that gang looks from the inside.

Not that all actors think about things the same way. The other week I was filming an episode of *Poirot* and David Suchet made a speech at the start about how Poirot was so far away from his real personality that he would have to stay in character all day. Now that's OK, because that's his style. But it's also a good example of what's called 'method acting', which basically involves doing everything in your power to actually *become* the person you're meant to be.

There's another, more old-fashioned view of acting: that it's all about being true to who you're not. When you went to a traditional drama school, it used to be that the first thing they'd do was send you down a kind of tunnel – tell you not to speak the way you did, try to change the way you acted – in the hope that you'd come out as a completely different person. They don't do that so much any more, because now there's a wider perspective on who can be an actor, and what acting really is.

She's never really got the credit she deserves, but I think a lot of the impetus for that change – certainly in this country – came from Anna Scher. She ran the theatre school in Islington that I went to from the age of twelve. And the way she taught me (and a lot of other people) to act was to use my own life experience to inform my performance through improvisation. It's almost like method acting turned inside out.

That's why my way of doing things is a bit more naturalistic. I can do all the other stuff (if I have to play a little Belgian, I can play a little Belgian), but Anna Scher taught me that whoever else you might be trying to be, you've always got to be true to yourself as well. People will have a go at you for that, but you've got to stick to your guns. And I always have done.

The differences between the characters I've played might be subtle, but they've been there. It's not like with John Sessions or someone, who has to be a completely different person for every part he plays, just to show how good he is. (Only joking, John.) The same applies with the whole typecasting thing. People often mention that to me with a derogatory implication, but don't try to tell me Sir Ralph Richardson or Sir John Gielgud weren't typecast. Of course they were. And it never did them any harm. In the end, you are who you are in this game. And that's just the way I like it.

PROLOGUE: CLOSE
TO THE EDGE

My first day's shooting on *Quadrophenia* was all that stuff on Beachy Head. Picking up Sting's bike and calling him a bell-boy was done another time.

The path they originally gave me to ride along the cliff top was a few yards in. But obviously I went nearer the edge and at one point I actually came off the bike. In the end, I remember Ray Corbett, the first assistant-director – a wise old owl who'd been in the business for years – going, 'Look, Phil, if you fell over the cliff, right, you'd be dead. They'd pay out straight away on the insurance, and some other geezer would be playing your part tomorrow. So let me give you a few words of advice: take it easy. Let the stunt-man do all that. You look after yourself.'

You can tell where they got the stunt guy to do it – 'cos of his terrible wig, and the tramlines you can see in the grass along the cliff top where I'd driven doing the first few takes . . . I don't think it really matters, though. There's an InterCity 125 in *Quadrophenia* at one point, even though the action is set in 1964. That kind of thing is part of the film's charm now.

It was September 1978, and I was nineteen years old. And if someone had told me that people would still be asking me about that day's work more than thirty years later, I probably wouldn't have believed them. The film turning out to be such a big deal wouldn't have surprised me, but the idea of me having the lead role in it took a bit of getting used to. The Who released the *Quadrophenia* album in 1973, but we didn't make the film till five years later, which meant I'd loved the record for years by the time I got the part of Jimmy, so I was almost like a fan stepping into the story.

For the moment, though, there was no time to think about the future. I was too busy trying to stay on Sting's ridiculous scooter. He could hardly ride that thing himself, 'cos it was covered in so much pointless silver shit that he couldn't keep his feet on it – he kept dragging them along the floor. Later on, when we did that scene where he rides along the seafront, you'd keep hearing them shout 'Cut!' because Sting had let his feet touch the ground again.

Although he wasn't yet famous, everyone still felt the urge to take the piss out of him. One day someone saw the name Gordon Sumner written on his call-sheet, instead of Sting. Prior to this some of the mods hadn't known what his real name was, and they all started singing the Jilted John single 'Gordon is a Moron', which had just been a hit that summer. They corrected that mistake pretty quick the next day.

He was always OK with me, Sting. When I told him I was in a band he said, 'Oh, so am I – do you fancy a jam?' Unfortunately I couldn't get there at the time he suggested; otherwise I could have been the fourth member of the Police. He wouldn't have wanted me, though: I'd never be sitting in the back for too long. Before he knew it we'd have been doing fifteen-minute songs with titles like 'Fresh Moroccan'.

One of the things that made *Quadrophenia* exciting was that none of us quite knew what we were going to be yet. We were all at exactly the right age to be in that film. Our destinies weren't set. Everything was up for grabs. And that energy fed back and forth between the actors and the characters we were playing. I think that's why it's so easy for people watching the film to relate it to things that happened to them when they were young.

The funny thing is, looking back now, you can see the way that the people we were on screen would help define who we were going to be in the future. It's almost like watching a documentary about a load of kids, and then afterwards getting to see how their lives turn out.

People are always surprised that we shot the final scenes first. I think someone had told the director, Franc Roddam, that it was best to get the most expensive set-ups out of the way early on, in case he ran out of money. But doing the last bit at the beginning was also really useful in terms of the acting side of things. Because that was the most emotional point, I could really let rip. Then, for the rest of the filming, I knew where I had to get to – and knowing I'd already got the ending in the bag gave me the confidence to build the performance up to that point.

By the time Jimmy is riding along that cliff top, he's meant to be in a right old state. His mum and dad have thrown him out. His mate's stolen his girlfriend. He's got the make-up on. He's all pilled up. Everything's gone wrong for him.

The story for the Who's original version of *Quadrophenia* – the one that came out on double-gatefold vinyl – was inspired by a mod who'd committed suicide. In Pete Townshend's ending . . . Well, I think Pete himself is the only one who knows exactly what happens, but basically Jimmy falls off a boat and drowns. It's all more sort of abstract, rather than something you can grasp hold of. Roddam's great coup is that the film starts with Jimmy walking back from the edge of the cliff.

Not everyone notices that, though. Either because they've missed the beginning, or they've had a couple of drinks, or they just weren't concentrating for the first few minutes. I often get people coming up to me and saying, 'You die in the end, don't you, Phil?' But when Franc and I used to talk about what might happen to Jimmy after the time-span of *Quadrophenia* ended, we always thought he could kind of turn into Alan Parker – go back and get another job in the advertising business, do a bit of this, do a bit of that, and come out the other side as a film director.

The way I played it is just that life has to go on: the bike goes over the cliff and Jimmy starts again. In a way, he conforms. But, in another way, he rebels against the idea of being a mod. Jimmy's got the sack for telling his boss to stick his franking machine up his arse, so when he sees Sting still carrying people's bags around, begging for tips, he realizes that the idea of him being this completely inspirational figure is just a sham: it's all bollocks.

That moment is like a glass shattering – all of a sudden he sees how his future would have turned out and he thinks, 'Oh fuck, I was gonna be riding round on a scooter on my own for the rest of my life.' And by saving himself but destroying the symbol of being a mod, Jimmy proves he's not going to be a victim.

The irony was that when Jimmy drove that scooter off the cliff, he might as well have given it to me to look after. For the rest of my adult life. Because from the day that film came out, everyone wanted me to be a mod. And when I wouldn't be one, people didn't like it. I remember there was a big hoo-hah once when my band did a gig at a pub and there was a parka thrust upon me. I refused to put it on and a huge row ensued about me not agreeing to wear this parka and being a 'traitor' – and I was saying, 'But we're not a mod band . . .!' It was all quite tricky, really.

It's never gone so far as me wishing I'd never done *Quadrophenia*, but there was a time when I wouldn't talk about it when I was doing interviews, because I wanted people to be interested in me for other things as well. Gradually I realized that if I was gonna carry it around with me forever, I might as well learn to live with it. I tried to shake it off but I couldn't, so now I embrace it.

Looking back, it's amazing how much of a turning point that film was for me. Everything else seems to revolve around it. Not just afterwards, but before as well. I put everything I'd learnt and everything that had happened in the first nineteen years of my life into that performance. The great thing about it was that while everyone thought of me as a newcomer, I'd actually been in the game a few years by then. So I knew what I was doing, but I was still young enough to make it look fresh.

As well as the beginning of my new life, *Quadrophenia* was also the end of my old one. Up to that point, I hadn't really got myself squared into a settled kind of existence. I hadn't even properly decided I was going to be an actor. I was enjoying myself: I had a few quid; I had my fingers in a lot of different pies. I enjoyed all that – I was an outgoing kind of guy. Still am, really.

But after *Quadrophenia*, even though I didn't realize it at the time, my world changed. The different things I did used to feed off each other in a positive way. Now, all of a sudden, the decisions I made began to have consequences. Doing one thing meant I couldn't do another thing.

I suppose that's what growing up is, really: it's about becoming what you're gonna be, not what you might have been. I'll go into the details later. But before we can send that particular scooter over the cliff, I think we'd better go right back to the beginning.

ACT I: BEFORE

1: WE AIN'T SOMERS TOWN, WE'RE KING'S CROSS

Saturday 25 October 1958 was a day very much like any other in human history. Chelsea beat Leicester City 5–2. The three-month US military occupation of Beirut came to an end. Oh yes – and I was born.

I made my entrance into this world at the Royal Free Hospital, Liverpool Road, which was in Islington, North London. It was just a hospital then, but it's flats now – nice, posh flats.

I have two older sisters. Brenda is five years older than me and Barbara is ten years older. I think my Uncle Bob (my mum's little brother), who was a bricklayer, looked after the girls while my mum and dad went to the hospital for the birth. They'd also had another child – a boy called Peter – before either of my sisters were born, but he had brittle bones, and died at three months old. I know that's what happened, but it was never really talked about.

By the time I came along, my family were living in Jessel House, which is on Judd Street, in King's Cross, just by the town hall. It was a private block and my dad was the caretaker, so the flat went with the job. He was actually head-caretaker of four blocks – Jessel House, Thanet House, Sandwich House and Queen Alexandra Mansions, which was just over the road. There was a guy called Mr White – 'Whitey', as my dad knew him – who was sort of my dad's henchman. He was the porter, that was his job title, and he had a flat in Queen Alex.

Judd Street is just to the south of Euston Road. The other side – the north side – we'd call Somers Town (and we ain't Somers Town, we're King's Cross). I'm not going to say anything bad about that place this early in the book, because I don't want the Somers Town after me, but it was very rough round there. There were a lot of kids hanging round on street corners; by the time I'd grown up a bit a lot of them were skinheads.

For the moment, though, number 9 Jessel House was our family home. Right at the end of the block, it was, on the first floor. When you came in through the front door, the first thing you saw was a corridor, with a place to hang your coats where the meters were. That led into the front room, which had a first bedroom leading off one way and a second leading off the other. Then there was a small scullery, with a bathroom on the end.

There are pictures from when I was really young with an open fire in the front room, but all I remember is an electric bar fire. We had a bureau as well – that was the big item of furniture. And in the kitchen there was a table with a yellow Formica top and some matching chairs. It was beautiful.

My parents were definitely pleased to have a son, but I think I was more of a surprise than a planned addition. Mum was thirty-six or –seven by the time she had me, which in those days was quite late to be having more children. And, because we only had two bedrooms, I didn't have a space of my own for as long as my sisters were still at home.

At first, I had to sleep on a camp-bed in my mum and dad's room. I can't remember much about that, except that it was a bit cramped. But I suppose they must have woken me up when they came in every night, because later on I slept in the front room – on a put-me-up bed – which I quite liked. In fact to this day I love going to sleep on the settee, which is probably a hangover from not having my own room as a kid.

Probably my clearest memory from childhood is my dad sitting in his overalls having a cup of tea with a newspaper under his arse to protect the chair. The thing about being a caretaker was that you were always on call. Obviously there weren't any mobile phones back then, so people would knock on the door to say their sink was blocked, and he'd have to go and fix it.

Jessel House wasn't like the blocks of flats on a council estate – it was much more middle class, like those serviced mansion-blocks you'd get in St John's Wood or Maida Vale. Some people rented their flats and others owned them. But the top-floor ones were almost penthouses. I remember an actress called Barbara Keogh who lived up there – she was very high and mighty, with big hair and even bigger hats. There was a guy called Harry Littlewood as well, who lived a bit lower down. He was basically a character actor and always seemed to have small parts in sitcoms.

Kenneth Williams was our biggest celebrity, though. He lived in Queen Alexandra, and his mum lived next door to him. Although he was one of the nation's favourites, my dad didn't like him. Dad had to go into his flat and fix stuff on many occasions and I think he was quite a demanding tenant. There was a fair amount of 'Oooh, Mr Daniels . . .' going on.

Stanley Baxter lived in Queen Alex as well, but I don't think he was quite so difficult. He was this very Scottish – almost Presbyterian – comedian and drag-queen, who was very big on TV in the seventies. I think he and Kenneth Williams had been friends and rivals for years. Apparently Baxter gets a lot of mentions in Williams' famous diaries. My dad doesn't, though.

Some people might say that this is why I ended up in show business – because on some subconscious level Kenneth Williams and Stanley Baxter and Barbara Keogh and Harry Littlewood had planted a seed – but I think that's a lot of old tosh. Life doesn't work out like that; there's a lot more chance in it.

When I look back at how big a part King's Cross has played in my life and my family's lives, I can't imagine coming from anywhere else. But me and my sisters were first-generation locals, really. My mum and dad only ended up there by accident.

My mum Edna's side of the family are all Geordies, and her maiden name was Newton. She had eight brothers and sisters and they grew up in Greenside, near Newcastle. My grandma Maggie used to take in people's washing. She didn't die till she was ninety-odd, so I knew her quite well. My granddad's name was William (which is my middle name) and he was a miner: quite a reserved sort of guy, apparently, though I never knew him. From what I can make out, they were very poor but quite respectable.

William had an allotment he used to grow flowers on, and when my mum was little she'd go out and sell them. Later on she worked as a mother's help for a family in a big house nearby. But then her sister Violet, who was a little bit older than my mum, moved to London and got a job as a maid in exactly the same part of Highgate where I live now. She wrote my mum a letter and – bosh – down she came as well, and started work in a house just round the corner.

It was the winter of 1937–8 when she left home, and she was only fifteen. My mum's eighty-seven now, but she's still really sharp: she remembers stuff. I asked her how things were in those days and she said 'a bit like a Catherine Cookson'. I'm not sure exactly what that means, but I assume it was an *Upstairs Downstairs* type of situation. Either way, there weren't any great expectations (if I can quote the title of another book, just to confuse matters).

Most of her family ended up coming down to London in the end – Auntie Violet, Mum, Uncle Bob and two more sisters, Irene and Gladys. The ones who stayed up North tended to be miners, like their father. In fact I think my Uncle Willie died of emphysema, which is the miner's curse.

My dad, whose name was Wilfred Ernest Daniels – although most people called him Bill – had been born in 1920; two years before my mum. He originally lived in Pudsey in Yorkshire, which is a no-frills sort of place, and where the cricketer Ray Illingworth came from. But my dad's family moved to London when he was eight years old, so he'd lost the accent by the time I came along. (He always sounded like a Londoner, and I've always spoken like my dad – maybe a bit broader, but basically I sound like him, and I am like him.) The weird thing was, their new home was about two streets away from where my mum ended up working; so, even though this wasn't where they met, there was already this funny kind of connection between them.

My dad's dad was a signalman on the railway, and they lived in one of those tied railwaymen's houses in Francis Place in Highgate, just at the back of where Gerry O' Boyle's pub, the Boogaloo, is now. I think it was a really nice place to live, with the woods all around. My dad had three brothers – Alan, Ray, and Bill – but they were very different from him. They were always quite quiet, whereas my dad was a bit more lively.

So anyway, after my mum had worked down in Highgate for about a year and a half, the Second World War broke out. She didn't like being in London with the war on, so she went home. There wasn't really any way of telling her family she was coming, so she just turned up on their doorstep.

Shortly after that she was conscripted and became an ATS plane-spotter. In 1941 she was sent to work at an anti-aircraft site in my dad's original hometown of Pudsey, which was another strange coincidence. Her job was to look for planes and then – towards the end of the war – doodlebugs. She never saw one of the latter the whole time she was there, until one came over on the day they were all due to leave; it was the biggest event of the year.

For my mum, the other big event of the war was meeting my dad. He was a sergeant in the army by then, and the first time they knowingly crossed paths was at the 101 Club in Leeds. My dad didn't stay a sergeant for long: he went out drinking with the boys one night and consequently had a stripe taken from him and was demoted to corporal. (Apparently he was in a regiment with a lot of Scotsmen, and I don't think he ever really forgave the Scots for this.) But, to cut a long story short – bomp, bomp, bomp – my parents got married as soon as the war ended, went on their honeymoon on a tandem (with my uncle tagging along on a bike), and moved back down to London to live with my dad's parents in Francis Place.

I think my oldest sister, Barbara, was born during that period; but one of my dad's brothers was still living at home as well, so it wasn't ideal. I know that on one occasion there was a bit of a falling out about a tidemark being left around a bath.

In the years immediately after the war, my dad learnt plumbing and electrics while working at a local firm called Flescher Brothers. But then the caretaker's job came up at Jessel House. It was a double position – caretaker for him and cleaner for my mum – and I don't think my granddad thought Dad should take it. Maybe he thought it was a bit beneath him – that's what I kind of got from my mum, although we generally tend to try not to talk about what's beneath or above or sideways – but my mum and dad needed their own place, so Jessel House it was.

After about a year of cleaning six floors of corridors, five days a week, my mum's back was going, but we had our feet under the table by then, so my dad stayed on as the caretaker while my mum did various other cleaning jobs instead. She worked at the British Medical Association for a while, and then at a dairy up in Kentish Town, and finally got a job with London Housing and Commercial Properties Ltd – the people who owned Jessel House – at their offices on Judd Street.

Initially she was their cleaner but then got another job, too, as their accounts clerk. She'd head off out of the flat early in the morning, clean the offices, come back home and make breakfast, get changed into smarter clothes, then go back to the offices to take in the rents with a ledger and all that. It was hard work, but my coming along meant she had three kids, and she wanted the best for us.

Next door to the London Housing HQ in Judd Street there was a sauna (don't forget this is King's Cross we're talking about). In the basement offices, where my mum cleaned, they had these big Gestetner machines – kind of like giant photocopiers, they were. There was also a door with a glass window which had at one time, before the two properties were separated, led through to the building that was now the sauna. Anyway, my mum went down there one morning to do her dusting and found some people from the massage parlour: they'd broken the glass, come in through the door and were splayed all over the Gestetner machines having a bit of a porn session. I think it was all a bit awkward, which was probably for the best. She wouldn't have wanted them coming back on a regular basis – God knows what she'd have been cleaning up.

My dad's job had a bit of a dark side to it as well – he'd sometimes be the first person on the scene to find a dead body. If someone hadn't been seen for a few weeks, he'd go in to check on them and find a corpse on the bed: that kind of thing. He went in to save an old woman from a fire once, and was invited to the town hall afterwards to get a bravery award.

What with him being the caretaker, and my mum doing the cleaning and collecting the rent, there wasn't much going on in those four blocks that they didn't know about. They were very discreet about everything, though, and would have never have gossiped to me or my sisters about it – more's the pity.

I suppose all this is a roundabout way of explaining that we were a typical working-class family, with no pretensions to being anything other than what we were. It's a strange sort of background for an actor to come from, really. But that's why I'm so grateful to Anna Scher – because she taught me a way to be an actor that was entirely consistent with it.

2: A BIT OF PAUL McCARTNEY'S HAIR

He was very good at knitting, my dad. I think this was because my mum was always doing it and he'd go, 'Give us that, Edna.' She describes him as 'a perfect knitter': if he made a mistake, he'd unstitch it all and start again. In later life he'd knit decorations for Christmas trees, and odd things like a wheelie-bin 'hat' (if you opened the bin there were three knitted rats inside). But when I was really young he knitted me a woollen football. I used to kick it up and down between the two doors at either end of the corridor, which in my imagination was Chelsea v. Arsenal.

I'd do that for hours on end – on my own, inside the flat. Although we lived on the first floor, there was a yard at the bottom with a good, straight wall that you could play football or tennis against. So when I got a bit older I spent a lot of time down there.

I always wanted to be outside, doing things, but the problem with Jessel House was that there weren't that many kids of my age there. The one other kid who lived in my flats was called Alan Slingsby. He always had a cold, but he became my mate anyway. There was another kid over the wall in the next block, called Adrian Gallagher, and I used to play with him as well. His mum was the school secretary, so she was quite posh. My mum liked his mum, so that relationship was encouraged.

Even though I didn't have many friends of my own age until I went to school, I was never backwards in coming forwards. I wasn't solitary or quiet. We had a lot of parties in our family – either at our flat, or at Uncle Bob or Auntie Gladys' places. I remember those big six-pint tins of Watneys Red Barrel turning up, and we had a tape recorder – one of those big old Grundigs with spools – that a Beatles tape might get played on.

We used to go away a fair bit, too. My Auntie Glad and Uncle Don and their two kids, Pat and Linda, lived in Kentish Town, and they had some kind of camper van (we called it a Dormobile but I'm not sure it really was one) that the whole gang of us would pile into and head off somewhere or other. I remember going to Llandudno once, and me wearing these smart little green shorts. What with my sisters and Pat and Linda, there were quite a lot of girls around, and then there was me. They were always playing with my ears, and I never used to like that.

At Christmas we'd go to my dad's brother Alan's house in Chelmsford. He was a bit more well-to-do than us – he was in insurance or something. I used to like going there when I was little, because he had two sons who were my age – David and Steven. They're still about, I'm glad to say, as there aren't all that many other Daniels left.

I used to enjoy going up North to see my mum's family as well, even though it took a good eight hours to get there. We'd get the bus up from the old King's Cross coach station (which was where the British Library is now), and stay at my Auntie Dolly's house in Ryton-on-Tyne, which is five or six miles outside Newcastle. They all thought I was posh because I came from London. And we always used to have pease-pudding – 'Pease-puddin' hot, Pease-puddin' cold . . .' – and then walk down to the river through the 'willis' (which I think is a Geordie term for 'woods').

I always liked it up there because they had pets – guinea-pigs and ferrets, that sort of thing – but I haven't been for years. The last time was twenty years ago when I was at the RSC in Newcastle. People start dying off after a while, and then it's all second cousins and you don't quite know who they are.

We never managed a ferret in Jessel House but we did have a few pets at various times, though my dad always ended up looking after them. A budgie called Ringo was the first one I remember (so, if your 'porn name' is taken from your first pet and your mother's maiden name, mine is Ringo Newton, which kind of works). My dad had tropical fish as well – the ones you've got to heat the water up a bit for. Those angelfish are the most beautiful creatures, but they're always tearing great lumps off each other.

I've always counted myself lucky that when I was little my dad was around more than most people's were. He'd be in having a cup of tea, then he'd be out, then he'd be back – waiting for something else to happen that he'd have to deal with. I suppose that was quite good preparation for life as an actor: you've got to learn how to have a cup of tea and watch the telly or listen to the radio.

The Archers was on a lot, and me and my dad always watched *Blue Peter* together. We were *Blue Peter* fans for years. I did get a Blue Peter badge: much later, when I was an adult, my old mate Peter Duncan gave me one. But I've done nothing to actually earn one in my whole life. Obviously *Blue Peter* portrayed quite a wholesome, middle-class idea of childhood, but I wasn't very politically aware at that stage – I just liked watching John Noakes make a fool of himself. It was only later in life that I'd look at these things and think: 'That's not how life really is.'

My dad did a bit around the house, but not an awful lot. Sometimes he'd do the breakfasts when my mum was off cleaning, and he would make a big cheese and Branston pickle sandwich at lunchtime. My mum did most of the cooking, though – egg, ham and chips was my favourite. Still, I really liked having my dad at home so much in the school holidays. It's been similar in a way with my own daughter, Ella. She's grown up now, but I've spent a lot of time picking her up from school over the years, and I've really enjoyed being more a part of her young life than a nine-to-fiver who just gets to see their kids when they're going to bed.

So the up-sides of my dad's job were the flat that came with it and the fact that he was often around. The down-side was that he was never really off duty. People could knock on our door at any time and he'd pretty much have to do what they wanted. Maybe on a Sunday they'd sort out a little rota – my dad and Whitey and this other caretaker called Fred would all muck in with each other – which meant my dad could go fishing. But other than that, his job was pretty much full time.

You're in an interesting situation, being a caretaker, because in one way you're the king of the block, and in another you're quite sub-servient. The way I saw it, there was kind of a funny line between the stuff that it was reasonable for people to expect him to do and the things that weren't part of the job. My dad would do some 'privates' – which was basically painting and decorating to earn extra money for holidays – but people would also try to get him to do that kind of work for nothing.

I can still see him sitting in his blue overalls with a bit of paint on them. Because he did a lot of decorating there was always a bit of paint on his specs as well. It's a badge of honour, that: paint on your bins.

He was very handy, my dad. And not just with the knitting, either. It was his job to look after stuff and make it work for a living, and he was good at it. Carpenter, decorator, electrician, plumber: he could kind of be them all. He was an all-rounder. Sadly, that wasn't something I inherited. I've never been much good with my hands. Later, at school, I was useless at woodwork and metalwork, but my dad never gave me a hard time about it.

I used to love going downstairs into the basement, though, where Dad had his own room full of tools. I really liked the smell of that place – all three-in-one oil and wood-shavings. It had a little trap-door that you could look up at people through.

There was one way I was able to help my dad with his work. I was really, really thin when I was little – so thin that my mum once took me to the doctor's to ask about it. He just told her, 'Listen, love, I wish they were all like him.' Being that skinny could be useful at times. The toilet windows at Jessel House would swivel outwards when you opened them, leaving a gap that was just big enough for me to squeeze through. When people got locked out I could slip through their open toilet window like some Dickensian urchin and let them in the front door. So I made myself helpful in that way: letting people back into their flats. It would be nice if I could turn this into a metaphor for taking on different people's characters as an actor, later in life, but I've not quite worked out how to do that.

I remember once there was a round-the-world aeroplane race, and me and my dad got up on the roof of Jessel House (this was before the penthouses were there, so Barbara Keogh can't have been in residence yet). We sat there and watched this Harrier jump jet taking off and landing at the coal yards, up by King's Cross station.

Other than the occasional Harrier jump jet, the biggest landmark on our horizon was St Pancras Station. That was a constant presence, looming grandly over us throughout the time I was growing up. It's a wonderful building, with the hotel at the front, and I've always thought of it as the cathedral of King's Cross.

We got to go into it once, when I was at primary school. It was designed as a hotel before central heating was invented, but then between the planning stage and the completion of the project, radiators came along, so it kind of died as a hotel because it didn't have the heating. It's got some beautiful staircases, though, and I'd like a flat in there now it's all been done up. So far the closest I've got to owning a bit of St Pancras was putting a picture of me sitting on the steps on the back of my album cover.

It's an odd one, WC1 – St Pancras aside. It's one of those places where you're kind of between areas. You never felt like you were North London, but you never felt like you were West End either. Obviously once I got a bit older I would just get on the bus and head off in one direction or another. But when I was little the nearest thing to that was going on Sunday walks with my dad around the City of London. It was absolutely dead, but it was very interesting to see how all the old buildings looked without any people around. The Lord

Mayor's Show was an important event for us Daniels as well. We always used to head out to watch that, in days of yore, as we loved a bit of a spectacle.

Generally Sunday was the big day for leisure. Sometimes my dad would go fishing, or he might go to the pub at lunchtime with a guy from the flats who he was mates with. He was very friendly, my dad, and he liked a pint down the Skinners Arms. But you never saw him drunk.

As well as the Grundig, we also had a record player – one of those box-things. It was only ever on Sunday mornings that my dad played records, and it'd probably be a bit of Andy Williams, or more likely Jim Reeves – 'The Gods Were Angry with Me for Loving You', that was one of his favourites. We played 'Distant Drums' at his funeral. It was a bit of an odd choice, I suppose, but it was quite romantic.

My eldest sister, Barbara, was the first one to bring any decent music into the flat. I remember that Beatles album that has them all leaning over a stairwell on the cover, and then *Rubber Soul*. I used to listen to that a lot. Plus she had a little bit of Tamla Motown. I don't think she got right into it, but when we cleared out the records I found singles like Stevie Wonder's 'Yester-Me, Yester-You, Yesterday' and Lee Dorsey's 'Working in a Coalmine'.

The Beatles were the ones she really loved, though. She had a bit of Paul McCartney's hair, which she'd ripped off his head and kept under a piece of Sellotape in a scrapbook. This big gang of girls had got a tip-off that the Beatles were gonna be somewhere, so they all went down there and dived on them, and Barbara managed to come up with a clump of his hair. McCartney was lucky to get out alive.

It was probably one of the first times there'd been that kind of mass hysteria. But a bit of mass hysteria is lovely when you're a teenager, isn't it?

Looking back, this was a real period of cultural transition (although obviously you never think about that kind of thing at the time). I remember the rat-catcher – who had two teeth that stood at the front, just like a rat's – telling us gruesome stories about putting a load of rats in a barrel so they'd fight till there was only one left. He came round less and less as the years went on, and it was the same with the rag-and-bone man. These staple characters of working-class street life were gradually vanishing from the landscape.

My dad used to smash pianos as well. It was a legacy of the forties and fifties that most flats had pianos in, but hardly anyone played them any more. People wanted to get rid of them, so they'd get my dad to take a sledgehammer to 'em. It's like sacrilege now, isn't it? The first one might have been a bit of fun, but after that it was hard work – after all, you've got to get 'em downstairs first.

But, even though the Beatles and all those kinds of sixties things were happening, the Second World War was still very much in people's minds. There were still remnants of Blitz damage around us as I grew up. I remember we used to play in a bombed-out church in King's Cross. The stillness of it all used to really give us the willies.

My dad had been shot in the war. He was jumping out of the window of a building that was about to be bombed when a great big nail went through his foot, and then he got shot in the arm. But, typically of people of that generation, he wouldn't talk about it that much.

I know he used to train people in unarmed combat. He'd never teach me that, even though I wanted him to. I suppose it was for the best, really, as once you know that stuff you can end up killing people – you don't just give 'em a whack. I used to have a lot of play fights with my dad, though. I was always initiating these little wrestling contests in the hope that he'd teach me something he'd learnt in the war.

As luck would have it, later on in life we discovered that my dad was actually from German stock. My sister did one of those genealogy things and found out that my great-granddad on my father's side was German, and his wife was Danish. You can see it in us once you know. My mum's got quite dark hair, but I'm the only one in our family who looks the way I do. Most of the others have got straight-ish hair. It's just me that looks like a Spanish anarchist.

I don't think my dad was all that keen on the Germans. I don't think anyone who'd been in the war was. They were 'the Hun', 'the Square-Heads', 'Nichts in the winkel', so my dad could have done without finding out he was related to them. Dramatic irony: I think that's what it's called – poetic justice, even.

3: AT THAT MOMENT, DAMON ALBARN'S EARS MUST HAVE PRICKED UP IN HIS MOTHER'S WOMB . . .

I went to Argyll Primary School, which used to be called Manchester Street. On the first day, we all had to wait in the hall. I was with my mum, and there was a kid there called Paul Fitzsimons, who later became a great mate of mine. Everyone was running round the hall, ringing the bell and being naughty, and I remember thinking, 'Blimey, this is quite lively . . .'

Of course I'd already been to St Leonard's nursery in Coram's Fields, so I knew the score, but still, it was a bit of an eye-opener. At nursery we always used to go for a sleep in the afternoon on these comfy canvas beds – to this day I still love to go and have a nap after lunch (if I'm not playing golf, that is) – but I could see that that kind of thing wasn't going to be happening any more.

Even though Paul Fitzsimons became my mate, he was also kind of my nemesis. He was always just that bit better than me at football. Later on, he was school captain when I was vice-captain. I was probably the second-best footballer in our year (although I did score twenty goals to his eighteen) and that's how those things were decided. Academic achievement was never really a factor. But Paul always came just above me in the marks, anyway. He was a bit bigger than me. And he was the best fighter.

My mum is quite small and my dad was too. In fact we're a small family. And on top of that, as I've already mentioned, I was very skinny. I think this is quite a common thing, but as a child I didn't ever really walk anywhere. I just ran. For years. I would always imagine I was in the Olympics and I was just beating the Russian to the line as I got home and won the gold medal.

I didn't have to do too much running away from trouble. I've been lucky in that department. I've had the odd scrap, but throughout my life I've generally managed to avoid major conflict. I don't know if I was funny when I was a kid, but I could certainly talk my way out of trouble from quite an early age. There were a few occasions in my childhood when I was going to get bullied – there was a little bit of that at Argyll, but it didn't last very long. I remember someone jumping on me once 'cos I was supposed to have said something to his sister, but it wasn't me.

By the time I got to secondary school I had a mate whose brother was a bit of a hard nut, so that was always useful. I don't remember having any fights at all, then. And I do wonder whether the parts I've played as I've got older have given me a false sense of confidence. People think I'm a bit rough because they've seen me knocking people about on the screen. In adult life I think I've surreptitiously put it about that you don't want to mess with me – just to keep people off my back – but at primary school I was probably as fearful of conflict as the next kid.

My sister Brenda is deaf. Not completely deaf, but she can't hear vowels, and we used to have special earphones for her so she could watch the telly. She had a lot of problems when she was young, with the deafness. Because you can't hear, your language develops slowly, and it took them ages to diagnose it – no one knew what was wrong with her.

There was a lot of prejudice in those days, so you had to fight to stay in school – that's what happened to my sister, basically. They had a lot of battles, my mum and dad, with various agencies. In the end, a wonderful lady called Miss Morley sorted it all out for them and Brenda ended up going to Haverstock School, which had (and I

think still has) a special class for partially deaf people. I don't necessarily think that helps, in some ways, because you're singled out, but
she did well there.

I remember there was this hearing place called the Nuffield
Institute, round the corner in Gray's Inn Road, and Brenda had
to go there to get a hearing aid. They were massive in those days –
like mobile phones were in the eighties. People would take the
piss. It was difficult for her. Had I been her older brother I would
probably have gone round hitting people, but being five years
younger made it a bit more complicated: you didn't quite know
what was going on, and there wasn't much you could do about it
anyway.

I think these kinds of things are probably dealt with much better
nowadays, but Brenda had more problems waiting down the line.
When she was older she trained to be a nursery nurse – passed all the
tests and got a job – but then the council kicked her out, because
they said she couldn't hear when a baby when was crying. She got
herself sorted out all right in the end. She's the secretary of Bracknell
College now, and a much-respected lady.

There was a lot of negative stuff that happened in those days if you
weren't quite the same as everyone else. And not just in schools. It's
strange when you're a kid, though. Because in some ways it's really
important to be the same as everyone else, but in others it's good to
stand out.

I remember when I was little I always wanted football shirts for
Christmas. I had a Wolverhampton Wanderers shirt and a West
Brom shirt. My Wolves one was the orange with the black, and
pretty recognizable. But how my mum got hold of the West Brom
one, I don't know, 'cause *no one* had a West Brom shirt. It was very
dark navy and white, with a white arm and matching cuff. It was
well tasty.

I think the sixties was maybe when fashion started to become
really important to kids as young as we were. You had to wear the
right clothes or you'd get the mick taken out of you for being a

'melt'. No one knew exactly what it meant – 'You melt!' – you just didn't want to be one.

I always liked my clothes when I was little. I think I had a few trendy green shirts which I was pleased with, and I know I had a pair of crushed-velvet trousers that my sister bought me – real big loons – but I'm not quite sure how they fitted into the historical time-line. I remember that the older I got, the less satisfied I was with other people's choices; I wanted to make choices of my own. That wouldn't have been a sign of any great individuality on my part, mind you. It was all about getting the chance to copy people, really.

At primary school, if someone else had something, that was it: you wanted it. We didn't have a uniform at Argyll – no blazers or ties or anything like that (I've never really liked ties, though I now have a Pucci one I'm very happy with). You could wear more or less what you wanted, and it was all about getting a Ben Sherman or a J-Tex (which was sort of a cheaper version), Levi's jeans or Sta-Prest trousers.

There were some kids with more money than others who had the full regalia, and that won them everybody's admiration. I remember I had a pair of permanent-press trousers once, which weren't quite Sta-Prest but were close enough. The first day I wore them I was playing football in the playground and I fell down and put a great big hole in the knee. But my mum put a patch on it, so I didn't care.

Once I'd started to make my own choices about clothes, I really wanted a pair of brogues. That was a big deal. If you had a pair of brogues, you could be seen as tough. Once I got old enough to be properly out and about on the streets, the fashion of the time was moving more in a suede-head direction. You weren't quite a mod, and you weren't quite a skinhead: the lines were still sharp, but a little softened. The ideal thing was to wear a crombie (though I never got one till my forty-ninth birthday) with red socks and a pair of loafers or 'smoothes', which were a bit like brogues, but with no indentations.

My clearest childhood fashion memory is of going to the cobbler,

Mr Christadolu, to get steel tips – or 'Blakeys', as we called them – put on my shoes: one on each heel and one on each toe. It did make your shoes last longer if you had leather uppers, but it was the sound they made against the ground that was important: you sort of had to have them. Your shoes weren't complete without a set of steel tips.

My dad was very practical, and smart enough in his own way – he'd buy a pair of Hush Puppies – but that type of thing was not something that would really have concerned him. Mind you, looking down at the Uggs I'm shamefully wearing today, the days of steel tips seem a long way off to me too.

When I finally bought my first pair of brogues, it was from a place called A&A's, at Chapel Market in Islington. I suppose they wanted to be first in the phone book. I say in Islington, but in King's Cross we considered Chapel Market as ours – going 'Up Chap' was just a quick hop up Pentonville Road on the 73 bus. On this important occasion my mum came with me, 'cos the brogues cost a fiver – which was a lot of money in those days – and she wanted to make sure they fitted me.

Now that I'm thinking about it, I'm pretty sure those brogues were bought as part of the new uniform I needed for going to secondary school. This means I've managed to race ahead to the end of six years of primary schooling without saying anything about what I actually did there. This probably gives you a fairly accurate impression of how much attention I was paying in lessons. It wasn't that I didn't enjoy it, just that nothing the teachers were telling us seemed to be very important.

How to grow daffodils: that was one of the useful lessons we learnt at Argyll Primary. You'd get given a bulb, and you had to take it home and get it to grow, then you'd take it back to school when it was done and, depending on how well you'd done, you'd get either a black-and-white or a colour picture of a daffodil.

I remember my dad put mine in the cupboard, which was definitely a good move, 'cos it needed darkness to shoot. But, even though it grew pretty well, when I took it in I still got only a black-and-white picture – which I can still remember being really upset by. So much so that I have decided to use this incident as an emblem of the unfulfilling nature of my whole experience of primary education, to register a protest against such inhumane treatment.

I did get hit a few times at school, and I always thought quite unfairly. The one I remember clearest was a bit of a class thing, I suppose. We were watching a schools programme on the big telly – you have to be a certain age to remember when they used to wheel the big telly out. The teacher asked us some question or other, and I went to answer it saying, 'Well, that geezer over there . . .'

I think that at that moment Damon Albarn's ears must have pricked up in his mother's womb, but the teacher didn't like it. He said, 'What is a geyser? It's something you light, is it not?' I cheeked him back and he gave me a bit of a slap for it. Then I got sent to Miss Buchan, the headmistress.

From quite an early age, for me, school pretty much meant waiting for playtime. I wasn't really naughty – we had special classes for badly behaved kids, and I never got put in them – but I was always more interested in football than I was in lessons. Towards the end of my Argyll career this approach began to pay dividends, when we won the Camden Primary Schools Cup for the first time ever.

We beat Toriano School 4–0 in the final, up at Market Road in Brecknock. My dad came to see it. I scored two and Paul Fitzsimons scored two, so we had parity then at least. Having said that, I scored twenty goals that year, so I still maintain I was the better goal-scorer. Paul and I went on to play football together for the Mary Ward youth club, but he had a bit of a bad cartilage at a very young age and had to have it operated on when he was twelve or thirteen. That curtailed his football a bit, which was a shame. He drives a black cab now, though, so he did all right in the end.

4: MY FIRST MEMORY OF ACTUALLY GOING TO A FOOTBALL MATCH IS OF THROWING SNOWBALLS AT THE FORMER ENGLAND CAPTAIN BILLY WRIGHT

Because all my mates at school were renting off the council and my family weren't, we were in a peculiar place in social terms. We weren't above, nor were we below; we were just different . . . More like in service, to be honest.

If you grew up in the council blocks – like Widborne and Midhope, which were down the road in Cromer Street – you'd be living next door to other families and constantly bumping into people. So you'd be forever in and out of each other's houses. Jessel House wasn't like that. (I suppose I *was* in and out of other people's flats, but only via their toilet windows.)

My mates did come round our house sometimes, but not as much as I used to go round to theirs. I suppose not having my own room was probably part of that. My mum will say I was a good boy. But we were kept on quite a tight rein as children, certainly compared to some of the Cromer Street kids who were allowed out on to the streets at a very early age. My parents didn't like kids hanging around on street corners, and if I went somewhere it would generally have to be within some kind of institutional framework.

This might be one reason why I got into performing at such an early age – because I enjoyed the freedom of it, and it gave me licence to express myself. Whenever we went on holiday to Pontin's in Margate or Camber Sands, or wherever, I'd always go in for the talent competitions. Even when I was really young: five, six or seven. I remember that on one of the first times I went in for a singing competition I did 'A World Without Love' by Peter and Gordon. I didn't play guitar then, but in later years I'd accompany myself, and for some reason I always found it easy to learn the words – I just liked the way one line followed on from another.

The first song I really loved was 'Puff, the Magic Dragon', which I'd probably heard on *Ed Stewart's Children's Favourites* on the radio. But it used to really upset me, 'cos of the ending . . . 'Jackie Paper came no more'. Dragons live forever, but not so little boys, so Puff was waiting for this kid to turn up but he never did 'cos he was old and dead: it was such a tragic song.

It wasn't just when we went to Pontin's that I'd end up singing. Often if we went for a family walk in Regent's Park I'd disappear for a bit, and they'd find me on the bandstand. I don't know what it was with me, really. My big sister Barbara was a very studious, very quiet girl – that's how she ended up becoming a librarian. And Brenda was kind of non-musical, because of her deafness (I think that was why she liked Engelbert Humperdinck). But she plays the guitar and sings now. Her party piece is 'Leaving on a Jet Plane', by Peter, Paul & Mary, which confirms her bad taste.

There was no history of people being musical in the wider family either, so I don't know where it came from. I was just keen, I suppose.

We did have a guy living next door to us who was a French-horn player with the Royal Philharmonic Orchestra. His name was Nigel Munasami. The Munasamis were a really lovely Indian family – I wonder if he's still about? Either way, his example wouldn't exactly have encouraged me in a musical direction, because he used to drive my whole family bonkers with the scales. They don't ever do a tune, do they, proper musicians?

Anyway, as I was saying before that brief musical interlude, my mum and dad were great believers in organized leisure. That's why I had to join the Cubs. I don't know exactly how long that lasted, but at least they had a football team. I don't think we ever went camping or anything. I just remember having a uniform and learning how to do knots. But I never became a Scout. Don't ever say I was a Scout.

The same building the Cubs used to meet up in – King's Cross Methodist Church, just by Euston Road – was also where Sunday school happened. It made me laugh that my mum and dad used to pack me and my sisters off to Sunday school when they didn't even go to church. I reckon maybe Sunday mornings was when nookie happened . . . Which would explain my dad putting the Jim Reeves records on – to set the mood.

I scored 99 per cent in a scripture exam there once. Then again, they're so keen on encouraging you to believe in God that you could write your name backwards and wrong and I think they'd still give you 99 per cent. At Sunday school there was a section of glass ceiling with grass growing over it from outside, and I thought that was where heaven was. In fact it was just a skylight with a load of old weeds growing where no one could get at them. I'm sure Richard Dawkins would have something to say about that . . . But Sunday school must have had some kind of impact, because my sisters are quite religious even now.

Barbara's got a house in Sandhurst, where the military academy is, and Brenda lives near my mum in Bracknell, so they're all quite close but both my sisters still go to church. Barbara's got this archetypal trendy vicar – Revd Phil – who wears leather trousers and is quite cool. He did the ceremony when my niece got married, and when my dad died, and if I needed anything else God-related doing I'd definitely go to him. Who's that writer who died recently . . .? J.G. Ballard. Revd Phil is the sort of vicar who would be in one of his books.

My sisters being girls, my dad was very reluctant to give them too much freedom when they were growing up, because of the nature of

King's Cross as an area. There was a lot of evidence around of the way things could go wrong. Argyll Square was just round the corner from us and was the centre of the red-light district. There were a lot of prostitutes and alcoholics hanging about, and a lot of action went on in the hotels around the square.

I remember there being quite a few times when my sisters were five or ten minutes late home and my dad put his coat on and walked down to the station – just to be about. I've taken that kind of anxiety on board with my own daughter. Until recently if she wouldn't phone, or was half an hour late and still had to walk home down the road, I'd get my coat on and go and find her. Now she's at university it's not so bad, because she's up in Manchester and there's fuck all I can do about it.

Although my dad was basically an upbeat individual, he was also quite sensitive and prone to worrying; I think I've inherited that. My mum's a bit of a worrier too, so it was probably inevitable that I'd end up that way. In fact, now I come to think of it, most of my family have got that trait. It's just one of those things you can't help, 'cos it's in your nature. It's nice to know that people care enough to be worried about you. And, if you're wise and you know what goes on in life, you are going to be a little anxious about two young girls out on the streets of King's Cross.

Luckily for me, there were a few less restrictions on boys doing what they wanted. And what I wanted to do was watch football. From a very early age I was obsessed with sport in general and football in particular. Of all the big historical events of the sixties – Churchill dying, the two Kennedys being assassinated, us getting our first colour TV – the only one I remember really clearly is England winning the 1966 World Cup. We were on our way down to Paignton in Devon on the day of the final, and when we arrived the town was dead. We got to the guesthouse where we were staying and everyone was sat around the telly watching it. From then on I was hooked.

My first memory of actually going to a football match is of throwing snowballs at the former England captain Billy Wright. I was seven or eight years old and my dad had taken me down the Arsenal, which was obviously the local ground. They were playing Sheffield Wednesday, but the game got abandoned 'cos there was too much snow, and we were all throwing snowballs at Billy Wright, who I think was Arsenal's manager at the time. I don't remember him being too bothered: it was just a bit of a laugh.

I never got the Arsenal shirt to go with the West Brom and Wolves ones, though. Generally when people ask me how I ended up supporting Chelsea I tell a story about getting on the wrong 14 bus – it went to Highbury in one direction but Stamford Bridge in the other. But the real reason was that my dad was never that bothered about football – fishing was more his thing. Whereas my mate Graham Hughes had another mate called Johnny Sheehan, and he and his dad used to go to Chelsea in the car every other Saturday. All of a sudden the three of us became mates, and me, Johnny and Graham would go to Stamford Bridge with Johnny's dad.

My mum would give me my pocket money – ten bob, or whatever it was – and then bomp: off we'd go off to see Chelsea play. He was great, Johnny Sheehan's dad – Harry, his name was. He used to let us wind down the car windows and scream and shout at everyone ('Oi mate, you wanker!'). He was very liberal in that sense, which came as quite a surprise to me given how strict my parents were.

The first game I ever went to see at Stamford Bridge was Chelsea v. Fulham. I think there were 50,000 there, and it must have been 1968 or '69, something like that. Arsenal weren't a very good team, then. They certainly weren't winning as much as they have in recent years, and they weren't very glamorous either. Pretty much all I can remember of the times I went to Highbury is that they always had the scores round the side of the ground on these little hoardings. Then there was that big clock, and that was more exciting than the football, to be honest.

Chelsea was a different matter, though. It was the late sixties and Peter Osgood had just turned up on the scene. Bobby Tambling was already there. The kits, I think, were also important to me. I liked the blue shorts with the white stripe. Celtic had style as well – they had numbers on their shorts but not on their shirts, and I liked that. It was just what everyone was into: being a goal-hanger in the school playground, and coming out on top in 37–22 victories.

On the home front, I made London club scrapbooks, which are probably still around somewhere, and I had a picture of Jimmy Greaves, who was the most lethal striker in the history of London football. I was really into statistics as well. I used to do the whole FA Cup with a dice. I'd draw all the teams out of a hat, write out the matches and then do each round, one after the other. I used to cheat for Chelsea so they always won. Very occasionally, though – maybe one time out of seven – I'd be fair and knock 'em out, just to see who else won. I had Subbuteo, which I used to play with my dad. And Subbuteo cricket I liked as well, which Johnny Sheehan had, with the little bats.

There was nothing scary to me about Stamford Bridge at that time – I was blissfully oblivious of the underlying threat of violence. Once, when I got a little bit older – about fifteen – I remember going up the North Bank at Highbury with Paul Fitzsimons (who was an Arsenal fan), and sort of half pretending to be a hooligan. I remember the Man United coming into the North Bank and people throwing punches at each other, and me briefly being kind of involved, but that was a one-off.

When you're smaller, people leave you alone anyway. We used to get to the ground by about half past one to get ourselves behind a barrier so we'd be in a good position to see the match. And we'd be standing there for an hour and a half before the game started. We always used to go to the same place – not in the Shed end, but in the one that's called the Matthew Harding stand now.

I can't remember what its old name was. I've forgotten a lot of the stuff I used to know about Chelsea because I got fed up with learning it to go on *Celebrity Mastermind* (I did pretty well in the specialist round – I think I only got one question wrong – but my general knowledge was always going to let me down, and in the end I came second to that comedian who is Jeremy Vine's brother). But since I was a kid I've sat or stood pretty much all around the ground. And I still recall the excitement of getting my first Chelsea shirt. In those days if you had a number your mum would have had to sew it on. When I played I was always on the wing, so when numbers finally did come into my life – in my teens – I would have worn 7 or 11.

5: SCHOOL OF ROCK

At eleven years old, when the time came for me to change schools, I went for an interview at Owen's Grammar, which would later become notorious for spawning Spandau Ballet. My friend/nemesis Paul Fitzsimons got in there, but I didn't.

I also went (and how I managed not to qualify for this shit-hole I simply do not know) and had an interview at Highbury Grove with Dr Rhodes Boyson, who was the headmaster at the time, and later became Margaret Thatcher's education secretary. What a wanker he was. I never got in there, either.

The place I really wanted to go to was William Collins, which was the local school, up in Somers Town. But that was where all the 'erberts went, so my mum wasn't having that. Then she found out that my friend Adrian Gallagher – whose mum was school secretary at Argyll – was going to Rutherford Comprehensive. That was presumed to be a better school, and I got in there, so that was where I went.

I remember going to John Lewis with my mum to get myself all kitted out with the uniform and the sports shirts. Unfortunately, Mrs Edna Daniels wasn't an MP buying expensive curtains, so she had to pay for everything with her own money, rather than getting taxpayers to stump up for it.

Rutherford Comprehensive is in north Paddington, on Penfold Street, near Church Street market. I'd get on the tube at King's

Cross and get off four stops to the West, at Edgware Road. My big sister Barbara had got into Raines Foundation Grammar school, which is way over in East London, in Poplar. She used to get the 77 bus and it took her ages. While Rutherford wasn't as far away as that, I was definitely going to a different area.

This was a bit of an opportunity for me, in a way. I soon made new friends at Rutherford, but I didn't really spend much time with them outside school hours. I went home and hung out with my old mates from King's Cross instead. That gave me a bit of extra mystique back at school, because King's Cross and Somers Town were considered tough places to come from. And of course I never did or said anything to dispel that idea. I think this image of myself – as a bit of an outsider who you wouldn't want to take liberties with – must have been one I quite liked.

When I was growing up there, King's Cross was a very white area. There was one road-sweeper who was black, and my mate Chris O'Cory – who played in the Cubs football team with me – was the only black kid I knew of my own age.

Edgware Road was a different matter: it was pretty much half and half. I don't remember this being a shock at Rutherford, though. You got the odd black guy doing the black-guy thing, and the odd white guy who didn't like it, but apart from that everybody just kind of mixed in. Racism never really seemed to be a problem at all until I left secondary school. That was when I realized that things weren't quite the way they ought to be.

My early memories of secondary school are bound up with really starting to get into music. This was the time when you used to go and buy singles for 50p, or however much it was, and I think the first one I came home with was 'Lola' by the Kinks. The record shop was in Chapel Market – Up Chap – near to A&A's, the home of the brogue, and I think it was called Al's. (Clearly your shop name had to start with an A if you wanted to be taken seriously as a retailer in those days.) My great mate Miles Landesman – 'Moose', we called him – who I ended up being in a band with, he worked in that shop for years.

I didn't understand exactly what the lyrics of 'Lola' were about – it took me decades to work them out – but that probably just added to the intrigue. I got hold of T-Rex's *Electric Warrior* album around that time as well, which I really loved (I loved it so much that I ended up buying *Romantic Warrior* by Return to Forever as well, but that was later on – in my jazz-rock phase). Max Romeo's 'Wet Dream' was also a big thing around that time, because it was a bit sexual – 'Push it up! Push it up!' And I remember buying one of those compilations of Judge Dread stuff too, which was an essential component of any young man's education in the very early seventies.

It was around this time that my sister Brenda left home, which meant I could finally have my own room. It was considerate of her to move out at quite an early age. I do remember it was a bit of a battle to put any pictures up – that was considered an abuse of the flowery wallpaper – but I did in the end. Nothing too controversial like Jimmy had in *Quadrophenia,* though. (Years later, when my daughter was growing up, I let her stick whatever she wanted on her walls.)

Being able finally to lock myself in my bedroom left me free to indulge in such solitary adolescent pleasures as getting into Santana. Yes were a really big band for me, too, especially *Close to the Edge.* And I liked the hippie group America a bit (who were best known for the song 'A Horse with No Name'), but I reckon that might have been when I was a bit older, because I liked a bit of a smoke by then as well.

Even more important to me than listening to music was the prospect of making it myself. As I've said, I'd always gone in for singing competitions (my mum says that at the end of one of them, instead of singing 'Boom Bang-A-Bang' I shouted 'Chelsea!') and I often used to stand up and sing at home for my aunts and my uncles. But I couldn't be an a cappella act for the rest of my life. At school there was a guy called Pedro who (as you'd expect) played Spanish guitar, and he told me about this guitar teacher who came to Rutherford one day a week.

This was good enough news in itself. But it turned out that you could get out of a school lesson if you went and had a guitar class. So one day a week – I'm pretty sure it was a Monday – I managed, with a little help from people who were very clued up on such things (i.e., Pedro), to tell every teacher that I had to go for my guitar lesson. That meant I could spend the whole day learning to play the guitar.

The teacher was an old boy called Mr Skinner, who would be one of the leading lights in my education. He wasn't pushy, and he didn't try and teach us the notes – just gave us the G, C and D chords we needed to play 'On the O-hi-o', and off we went. I think he felt that, with us being people who weren't that interested in being taught conventional academic subjects, there wasn't much point sending us back to class. So we'd just stay in these two weird offices he'd been given, playing 'On the O-hi-o' all day. And for me that was the start of thinking that there might be something more to teaching than bullying kids into learning things that didn't interest them.

The first guitar I got was out of a Janet Fraser catalogue. My mum was an agent for them: all my aunties got their clothes off her, and she got a small percentage as commission. So I got money off the price of an Eko acoustic guitar, which I had for years.

Mr Skinner was quite old, but he was really into Segovia, and he could play all this wonderful classical Spanish guitar. If I could have sat down and applied myself I could really have learnt something, but we just wanted to play 'Get It On' and 'Ride a White Swan', so we learnt them instead. It was basically rhythm guitar, rather than lead – 'Stairway to Heaven' was too hard when it came along a few years later. But I was into Neil Young and learnt to play 'Heart of Gold' quite well. 'The Needle and the Damage Done' stretched my technical ability to its limits, but I still gave it a go.

At one point, me and my mate Gary Callard (who I used to bunk off lessons to play guitar with) put a band together for a rehearsal. In my mind, the band was called Borax Flux, which is a kind of joining agent. I saw it in metalwork once and thought, 'That's a great name for a band.' We had a chance of getting a church hall to do a gig in as well, but it never quite materialized: we had one rehearsal and that was it. When I eventually managed to form a proper band, I ended up playing a Guild Starfire semi-acoustic. That was the first guitar I had that you could actually plug in. I was destined to perform, so it was only a matter of time.

The rest of school wasn't a complete wasteland. There were some teachers and subjects that were all right. I liked English. I can't remember the teacher's name, but I know it begins with an M. Mr Mahey, I think it was. I'd be tempted to write 'Don't quote me on that', but I realize that's not really an acceptable phrase to use in an autobiographical context. Anyway, in my first year, we had to write a story about a monster and Mr M didn't tell me off when I wrote a poem instead. He told me he really liked what I'd done, which might be one reason why I can still remember it:

> 'Look out!' he cried.
> 'It's still alive.
> Kill it,
> Kill it quick.'
> As its vulgar fingers touched my face,
> I felt like being sick.
>
> What was this thing from outer space
> Its green hands hot with rage?
> I stabbed it once, I stabbed it twice
> Then everything went black.
> The monster left me in the rain,
> Lying on my back.

OK. It's not exactly T. S. Eliot, but I'm sure you'll agree that the rhyme scheme is quite innovative. And, after getting that bit of encouragement from the teacher, I started writing little bits and pieces of poetry on a fairly consistent basis. Maybe it was laziness that made me not want to write an actual story . . . But I think poems probably do stick better in your brain (at least, they do in mine) because they're written to be remembered and said, rather than stored on the page.

My geography teacher, Mr Sterno, was another important figure for me. He was a drummer in a band himself, with my history and social-studies teacher, Mr Meehan, who's still about. By which I mean that we've corresponded over the years, and I bump into him occasionally through mutual friends.

They had a band called Tarot who once did a gig at the school hall, which really encouraged my ambitions as a performer. Mr Meehan had a big old Baldwin bass and he used to give electric-guitar lessons after school. I went to them, too, and we'd play things like 'Sunshine of Your Love' by Cream – der der der der, der der der, der *derrr* der.

Mr Meehan had long hair and wore some sort of black Afghan coat. He and Mr Sterno were both examples of that elite breed of teacher who were a bit rock 'n' roll. Out of the school environment these guys were heroes to me, but within school it was a different matter. Mr Sterno was very strict, and he once did the dirty on me.

The whole school had gone on strike because we didn't want to wear uniforms. I think the deputy-headmaster had caned someone for no reason – at least, no reason that we were willing to accept as sufficient – and there was this kid who was in the sixth form at the time. His mum worked with mine at London Housing, as it happened. He had red hair and was a bit of a revolutionary, and he started shouting: 'No more uniforms!' 'No more this!' 'No more that!' And it kind of caught on.

Everybody gathered in the playground and we all decided to go on strike and march to County Hall. (This was the early seventies, remember, and Britain was much more susceptible to political radi-calism back then.) Loads of us went; and afterwards, when we came back, there was a kind of amnesty where we were all assured that our parents wouldn't be told we'd bunked off all day. For some reason, though, Mr Sterno wrote a letter to my mum and dad and told them.

So he was an odd mix: a hippie, but also very strict. Looking back now, it seems fair enough. I prefer it when people are solid in that way, and don't give too much ground.

It was funny, that march. As far as I remember, we got a certain distance away from the school and everyone just melted away into the West End – all thoughts of revolutionary action forgotten. (I doubt that the red-haired kid's mum was very happy, though: I think he got suspended or even expelled.)

I used to do that a lot in those days – melting away into the West End. I used to virtually live in the British Museum 'cos it was warm if you'd bunked off in the winter; you got no hassle from the security people, because there were always school parties around and they'd think you were just a wayward straggler. I used to like going on my own to see the mummies: they were all powdery and it gave you nightmares to look at them. I was a bit of a mummy's boy in that way, I suppose.

I did do a fair amount of bunking off. And not just for guitar lessons. I picked up the important skill of turning up for the register and then hopping out. Never let anybody find out what your actual timetable was, that was my secret – 'I'm not doing your subject any more, sir, I'm doing French now.' At the time I thought it was strange that no one ever knew what you were meant to be doing. You always thought all the teachers were after you, but looking back now I suppose they just thought, 'If he doesn't want to come to school, what's the point?'

We were CSE fodder and academic attainment wasn't really on the menu. It's no coincidence that almost everyone from my school who anyone's heard of ended up in the music industry. Courtney Pine, he was at Rutherford at the same time as me. As was Paul Hardcastle. Gary Crowley, he was in the year below. And the lovely Steve Walsh, the big soul DJ, was in the year above me and kindly took me under his wing when I first arrived at the school.

6: A NEW DAWN

Anna Scher used to be a teacher at a primary school near Essex Road in Islington. I think it was called Rotherfield. She wanted to teach drama as part of her English lessons but the school authorities wouldn't let her – they said, 'No, you can only teach English in English.' Then she started doing a little bit after school, but they wouldn't let her do that, either, for some reason.

A little way further up Essex Road there's a block of flats, called Bentham Court, and in the middle of that block is a community hall. So Anna hired that out twice a week and the kids went there straight from school and did a bit of drama. It was all improvisation – nothing else but that. She'd tell them, 'You're the mum, you're the dad, and you're late home from school, and the first line is, "Why are you late home from school?"' And then, bomp: they'd be off.

Even though her own school wouldn't do anything to help her, Islington and Camden councils were obviously quite interested because they started to send her round the schools in the summer holidays, running these drama classes as something for kids to do. It was like a holiday play-scheme, really. They used to have one of those at the Holy Cross Church in Cromer Street. They gave us the downstairs and we painted it orange and did creative things in there with youth-leaders who were much more liberal and attuned to a freer way of thinking about things than the teachers at school were – they let us smoke, I remember that much.

Anyway, one summer – it must have been at the end of my first year at Rutherford, because I was twelve going on thirteen at the time – Anna turned up at Argyll, my old primary school. My friend/nemesis Paul Fitzsimons' little sister was going to the classes, and one day he had to go down there to pick her up, so a load of us went along for a laugh. I remember going into the hall and seeing all these kiddies doing drama – walking round pretending to be monsters or whatever.

This was actually one of the key moments in my life, though I didn't know it at the time. Being a bit older, we all thought we were it, but somehow Anna got us all up and having a go. We were trying to take the piss at first but she knew that letting kids think they're getting away with stuff is one of the best ways of getting them involved in things.

Other motivations were starting to make themselves felt at that age, too. I remember at primary school thinking that Pauline Patricks was lovely. And I definitely played kiss-chase with Josephine Benson and Jackie Owens a few times. But that was all when I was very young. Everything had gone a bit quiet on the girls front for a while after that, and there was more of a focus on blokey stuff. Then suddenly you're in your early teens, and that's when you really start to go on the sniff.

One of the most important things I noticed about Anna's drama class was this: whatever was going on in that room, boys and girls were doing it together. The story I always tell (in fact I've told it so many times that I've started to feel like I might have made it up, even though I know it's true) is that I saw this beautiful mixed-race girl called Dawn Jerraud there (I'm not exactly sure how her surname was spelt, but I remember there was something sophisticatedly French-ified about it) and thought, 'She's for me.' Dawn was definitely a big part of what kept me going back to Anna Scher's once I'd started going up the hill from King's Cross to Islington.

Also, I think I liked the fact that you didn't have to go to Anna Scher's if you didn't want to. Not to psychoanalyse myself too much, but the thing with me is that if I've gotta do something, I'm fucking loath to, whereas if I get the choice, and I fancy it, then there's no stopping me.

Either way, Anna took an interest in me, and before the end of the week, when she moved on to the next school – which I think was in Gospel Oak – she gave me the address for the Anna Scher Children's Theatre (which is what she was calling the Bentham Court community hall by that point). So, when the holidays ended, I started jumping on the 73 and going up there every Tuesday and Thursday, paying the princely sum of 10p a lesson.

I think one of my mates came with me the first time, but after that I went on my own. Some of my King's Cross boys might have thought it was a bit girly, but I'd already picked up the guitar by then, so I knew it was possible to do something outside the group without it causing too many problems.

Anna Scher is an Irish Jew. Her father was a famous Dublin dentist, and she's this amazing blonde woman with the Irish gift of the gab, who is also Jewish – which is a pretty potent combination. I know she was an actress for a little while and I think she'd maybe lost her nerve a bit, but she was never short of confidence with us. She was quite young and kind of nice – we all liked the look of Anna – but you wouldn't want to take the piss too much. Messing around was fine up to a point, but then: bang.

From the first time I went there, I just wanted to be good and do everything well. God knows why. I suppose because it was obvious from early on that I was someone who could do it; so, when the time came to pick people out to do things in front of the group, Anna often used to give me the nod.

I think she picked me so often because I was quite imaginative. I used to watch some of the others doing improvisations and they just seemed a bit square, so I would try to take things in a different direction. I think being in a band helped, too, later on, because that helped give me even more confidence to do things my own way.

My school reports over the years tended to say that I didn't concentrate and was too ready to muck about. And acting was a good
way of making the mucking about work for me. I still find that. It's
often the scratching around at the edges of a character that works
best for me professionally. So mucking about is kind of my job, now.

In those days, though, I just enjoyed getting up and doing my bit.
Pretty much the first time I went to Anna's I met this kid called
Noddy Bush (at least, that was what we all called him, even though
his real name was Terry). He became my mate, the person I'd mess
about with at the back during the warm-ups.

First off when you got there Anna would have you reciting the
'three Ps': punctuality, professionalism, and, well, I forget the other
p. (Phuck knows what it was . . .)

Then she'd get you all down on the floor and say, 'Listen to the
noises in the room. Now listen to the noises outside.' We'd just play
the sorts of games that directors might have used in the sixties. I think
Anna's since had a book out that includes all the exercises that she
uses with young children.

Once a session had properly got going, we'd do lots of things in
groups. You'd shut your eyes or put blindfolds on, and then you'd
have a girl and a boy in the middle of a circle going, 'Where are you,
Adam?' 'Here I am, Eve.' Or she'd get us all to line up in order of
how tall we were (people always think they're taller than they are).
That was how it all started off, really.

Anna had a partner as well – a guy called Charles Verrall – who'd
been there from the word go and had helped her set the whole
thing up. They were a couple, and later on they had a son called John
together.

It was funny doing drama in Bentham Court, because after us lot
they had bingo up there. At first all the old dears used to turn up for
their bingo right at the end, but gradually they started coming earlier and earlier to watch the kids doing their acting; this was good,
because it meant we got used to doing it in front of an audience.
Then, as things progressed, and people found out about the work

Anna was doing, we'd get directors coming and sitting at the back – looking for kids to be in productions.

Although Anna Scher would become renowned for encouraging a particular kind of – usually working-class – actor, the kids who went to her drama classes were an interesting mix, socially. For example, Islington council would send her troubled kids to see if she could do anything with 'em; and with her help a few of those people went on to make acting their profession. But there was always a healthy contingent from the Islington bohemian bourgeoisie there as well.

There were girls like Tilly Vosburgh – who would end up acting in lots of things with me over the years, including *Meantime*. She was the daughter of Dick Vosburgh, who was a top writer at the time. Zanna Hamilton was there as well, who also became a top-class actress, and you can tell from her name what kind of family she came from. But Tilly and Zanna were every bit as much the children of Islington as Kathy Burke was. That's kind of the point of the borough: it's quite posh and quite rough at the same time. The two sides tend to be quite strictly segregated, but the great thing about Anna Scher's was that anybody could go.

Nothing ever developed romantically between me and Dawn, sadly, though I did really fancy her. She came from Woodbury Down estate and she went to Anna's for years. Even though she wasn't initially that brilliant at the improvisations, she really stuck at it. I never had a chance with her. She was a bit out of my league, and I was pretty shy with girls at that time.

One key fact about Rutherford Comprehensive which I've previously neglected to mention was that it was a horrible, repressive, buttoned-up boys' school. Anna Scher's was different. Not just because there were girls there, but also because there was a bit more freedom generally. On reflection, it probably was the girls being there that was the most important thing. You got to work with girls, act with girls and just *talk* to bloody girls – people who were of the opposite sex and had different ideas.

Ideas were not the only thing on my mind, obviously. I've never admitted this in public before – and I hope it won't do permanent damage to my 'hard man of acting' image – but around the time I first started going to Anna's, and fell helplessly in love with Dawn Jerraud, Donny Osmond's 'Puppy Love' came out. Such was my stage of emotional upheaval that I bought it and played it maybe twenty times in a row. Donny spoke to me about this whole love thing. I bought 'Crazy Horses' too, a bit later on – oo-*waah* oo-*waah* – but that wasn't a bad track. And I'm still a Mormon to this day (joke).

7: SPITTING AT THE
ACTON HILTON

I hadn't been going to Anna Scher's for long – a couple of months at most – when I got my first professional job. The BBC was doing a TV version of the opera *Falstaff*, with Sir Geraint Evans. There's a bit where he's having a nightmare and all these gnomes are jumping over his back (I think they were fairies really, but at that stage I was happier calling them gnomes, or imps, or goblins) and about five or six of us from Anna's got the parts.

We had to go to the BBC rehearsal studios – 'The Acton Hilton', they all called it. It was a really big building with a huge spiral staircase going down through the middle of it. If you stood at the top you could see down about fifteen floors. So obviously we were all up there spitting. Unfortunately someone saw us doing it and we all got told off by Anna for bringing her into disrepute.

I remember this young choreographer showing us how to leap over Sir Geraint Evans' back. Sir Geraint was very nice to us, and the whole thing was a bit like a day-trip to another world. I wasn't fazed by it, though. Acting is one area of life I've never really felt inclined to worry about, and there weren't any lines to learn. We were just brought in to do our rehearsals, and then the chaperones got us out of the way as quick as possible, so as not to subject our impressionable ears to the fucking rattling on of the actual opera.

Not long ago, when I was advertising my football DVD (which is still available from all good internet retailers), I went on *The One Show* and someone in their archives had found a clip of me as an imp (OK, a fairy, but old habits die hard) in that opera, and made a still of it. Good job that wasn't at all embarrassing.

I got £16 for that job (*Falstaff*, not *The One Show*), and on my mum's advice I opened a Post Office account to put it in. In my mind's eye I can still see the first page of that blue account book, with '16' written in the right-hand pounds column. From the age of thirteen, then, I started making money, on and off, from my acting. And I was lucky that my mum was good at keeping tabs on the financial side of things (it was her job, after all), because she helped me keep my feet on the ground in that respect.

In those days, child actors had to have a licence to get time off school to do any parts they got. That meant going to County Hall for a medical every six months to make sure you were fit and healthy to work. I'd started smoking at that time, even though I was barely into my teens. My mum and dad didn't know (at least, I didn't think they did), and I always dreaded those medicals 'cos I was sure the doctor was somehow gonna find out and tell them.

My dad smoked like a trooper till he was about fifty – I was always popping out to get him twenty Navy Cut from the shop down the road – then he gave up. Those un-tipped fags had given him a terrible bloody cough. Later on he used to say that he gave up smoking so I could start, so maybe my efforts to keep my new habit a secret weren't as successful as I thought. The cigarettes got him in the end, sadly, but I suppose something's gonna get you.

Anna Scher's had been going a couple of years before I got there. One kid called Peter Newby had already been in a film, so you knew that kind of thing was a possibility. But in terms of a lot of people getting professional work, ours was probably the first generation that really came through.

Quite a few of the kids in my class got work quite early on and went on to be well known. Pauline Quirke and Linda Robson for a start; while Ray Burdis, John Blundell and Johnny Fowler were all in

Scum with me. Gary Kemp was there, too. Obviously he was in Spandau Ballet later on, which some people might think of as his greatest role, but really the highlight of his career was singing a duet with me.

It was before either of our bands had really started. We used to play guitar and sing together a bit, and we did this duet once on an ITV programme called *You Must Be Joking*, which Ray Burdis hosted with a guy called Elvis Payne. It was a kids' show, with a band called Flintlock playing on it every week. And Gary Kemp and I went on there in our Brutus jean-shirts and sang 'Sandman' by America. 'I understand you've been running from a man/That goes by the name of the Sandman', that was the chorus. I think it was a song about drugs, but luckily no one realized that at the time.

When it came to negotiating the deals for these kinds of extracurricular activities, Anna and Charles would act as our agents. We were all new to the game together – it was the first time for her and the first time for us – so there was no collusion between her and the TV companies.

Some of the other theatre schools that would be established later on (in the wake of Anna's success) were more like production lines for getting people on TV. But with her it wasn't a career thing; it was a teaching method. I suppose it was what would be thought of now as theatre in education, but it was very significant for me at the time.

I don't mean just in terms of supplying me with the kind of stimulus that school couldn't give me, but also in teaching me something about myself, helping me find ways of expressing myself that didn't involve any kind of compromise. What Anna would never do was try to change you: there was never a sense of her wanting you to be anything other than what you were.

I'm not sure where she got this idea from – I'd like to ask her, one day – but I think one influence might have been Joan Littlewood. The interesting thing was, once we got out into the business, we were a bit harshly treated as not really being 'proper actors', or so I often thought, because we used a lot of our own personalities in what we did. But doing so made our acting a lot more real. And our sense of not quite getting a fair crack of the whip gave us even an extra edge, because we were always fighting against that too.

Obviously not everyone from Anna's went on to star in *Birds of a Feather*. The place wasn't set up as a drama school, so there'd be forty other kids there who never did one professional job but who still got a lot out of it. Anna would divide maybe sixty kids into pairs, give us our starting line – something like, 'Why are you late home from school?' or 'You're my best friend; why are you going out with my girlfriend?' – and then we'd all be up arguing, and she'd wander round the thirty couples, watching us do our thing, before picking out a few to get up and do their piece in front of everyone.

We had all these red boxes as props, and sometimes there'd be a phone that would ring and you'd have to answer it. She'd give you the first line and you'd have to improvise one half of the conversation that followed.

These were the kinds of professional skills that would come in very useful later in life. In *EastEnders* people are forever on phones, as it's the easiest way to get people from one place to the next when you can't be bothered to write a proper scene. That's one of the reasons I ain't hanging around in Albert Square no more, but we'll get to that later.

One of the great things about Anna and Charles was that, because they were quite worthy and left wing, when you did get a job you never felt like you were just doing it for the money (even though the money was nice, obviously). We weren't allowed to do adverts until we were sixteen. And by law we had to have chaperones till we were that age as well.

The chaperones were usually the mothers of some of the kids and I think they got paid a bit. Grace Cook, who was Dexter Fletcher's grandma, she did a lot, and his mum did a bit as well. Dexter was another one of my contemporaries. He's managed to carry on looking like a little kid for most of his adult life (how does he do it?), but he's always been a really good actor.

I think my mum came to sit up the back at Anna's once, and she used to take me to County Hall for the medicals, but she never got involved with the chaperoning. Generally it was the mums from Islington who did that, and this was an activity I got on the bus to go and do, so it didn't feel like something she would need to be a part of. Plus I suppose I was always quite independent-minded, so I tended to keep my home life separate from the other things I did from quite an early age.

It wasn't that my parents weren't supportive, though. I remember being on holiday with them at some distant Pontin's or other when I'd been chosen to throw some spaghetti over someone in the film *Bugsy Malone*, and my mum and dad never complained about having to come home early so I could be directed by Alan Parker.

I had another blink-and-you'll-miss-it cameo in *The Naked Civil Servant*, the life story of Quentin Crisp. I had a scene with this guy Mark Burdis (Ray's brother; he's still an actor now, and he compères the Frank Warren cards on *Friday Fight Night* – he's the bald geezer going, 'Ladies and gentlemen . . .'), where we're sat round a pond in a park, and we go up to John Hurt and say, ''Ere mate, if you don't give us twenty quid we'll tell someone you've been fiddling with that kid over there.'

Then he says, 'I defy you to do your worst – I am the only stately homo left in England', or something along those lines. It was my first delinquent role, and the first of many times my mum would sigh and say, 'Why can't you play a good boy?' But on the up-side I did get paid £60. And that wasn't the end of the story. A cheque for an extra £3.26 came through from *The Naked Civil Servant* just the other week: I think that was my proportion of video sales over the years.

People think you just get paid once and that's it, but in fact they buy you out for only so long, and then you usually get repeat fees – although obviously they try to do you out of them if they can think of a reason. That's what's so good about *EastEnders* – you get paid once when it first goes out, and then you get 80 or 90 per cent again for the Sunday omnibus; so if you're in all of them you can get paid for up to eight episodes a week, which is a real money-spinner. If you can stay in it long enough you end up as a millionaire, like Adam Woodyatt must be by now.

The golden days of hanging out with Adam Woodyatt and the Albert Square mob were still a long way off for me at that stage. But one of the first jobs I got a bit of real reflected glory from was a thing called *Places Where They Sing*, which I did very early on in my career. It was a little half-hour drama on the BBC about an inner-city choir. Gordon Jackson was the choirmaster, and I think I was a bit of a rough boy – Billy Idiot – who was giving him (and everyone else) a bit of trouble.

I'd not thought about this for years, till I was watching a rerun of *The Professionals* on some satellite channel a few months back. I saw Bodie and Doyle and then bosh: Gordon Jackson was on the screen, and it all came back to me. My character was called Neville, and I was only thirteen or fourteen, in my little white chorister's ruff.

It was about kids but was more of an adult drama, the first proper grown-up TV I'd been in. I remember my mum was very impressed, 'cos Gordon Jackson was in *Upstairs, Downstairs* and had been in films as a young actor. My family definitely watched it with a slight air of ceremony. We wouldn't have splashed out to the extent of a cup of tea or a biscuit – we didn't go crazy – but it was certainly a bit of an event: seeing me in my angelic glory, and nearly playing a good boy.

8: EXIT, PURSUED BY AN ELEPHANT

The first two really big bits of acting work I did were both in dramas for kids. *The Molly Wopsies* was a six-part ITV series about a young evacuee in the Second World War who'd been moved away from London to the Oxfordshire countryside. It was the very first outside-broadcast drama series made by *Thames TV* – I remember seeing all these lorries with scanners in the back, and thinking they looked quite futuristic.

I had to live away from home for the duration of the filming, so Thames packed me off to stay with the parents of one of the girls in the show. She was about twelve, and the name of her character was Dottie Minton. They were really nice people (I remember her dad taking me to the speedway in Oxford, once), but I felt a bit like I'd been evacuated myself. Maybe that was the idea – to get me into the character – but I really wanted to be with the other actors, so after about a week I asked if I could stay in a hotel with the rest of 'em.

The idea of the show was that each week my character, Dottie Minton and another kid called Dinkey Dunkley would have some kind of adventure with a policeman. It was a romp, really, a bit like *The Famous Five*. They were all locals and I was the Michael Aspel among them. His story is quite fascinating. I think he got evacuated with his brother and they didn't go back home for four years; when they did go home their dad had changed – he'd gone completely military (he had been in the war, so I suppose we can't really blame him for that).

Some parents didn't want the kids back at all, and I guess some of the kids felt the same way. If you were from the mean streets of Wandsworth, and you went to stay with some professor and his family in Banbury who were really nice to you, you might not want to go back, might you?

Even though the filming was really enjoyable, I was happy to go home to King's Cross at the end of it. It wasn't quite on a Michael Aspel level, but when I got back to school some of the teachers' attitudes to me had definitely changed. I'd had a month off school. Their criterion for what I should be was a student, so if I wasn't at least nominally in the building, then something was very wrong.

You know how it is in this country. If a kid bunks off forever they won't really take any notice. But if I get the chance to pursue a career as an actor, or nowadays if I ask the school to let me take my daughter on holiday for two weeks in term time, I have the social services round. I think that if I want to take my child on a trip that she's always going to remember, I should be entitled to do that without any person from any authority interfering.

Education should be in the eye of the beholder, not in the eye of the state. It's a bit like cricket, I think: it should be about observing the spirit of the law, rather than the letter of it. That's why Geoffrey Howe talked about cricket in his resignation speech that finished off Mrs Thatcher – because it's a good game for getting similes and metaphors out of. Everyone should be able to get a bat, whether or not they score any runs.

People think football is the only sport I care about, but I've always really enjoyed cricket as well. I've been to the Oval a lot over the years – I've even played there – and I used to play a lot in the summer, as a kid. I really liked the statistics, and I had an uncle called Arthur – my Auntie Irene's husband – who was Durham's wicket-keeper for a while, when they were a minor county. He had to give it up in the end, because in those days it was still gentlemen and players, but I based myself on him a bit when I used to play. I was a wicket-keeper/batsman, which meant I came in at number 7 and was a bit of a dasher – I could get 19.

As a child actor you could have only sixty days off school a year to do paid work. I say 'only', but obviously sixty days is quite a lot and I don't think I ever quite used up my formal allocation. What I did do, though, was develop a very good way of pretending I was always acting – in effect I extended the guitar-lessons scam to include my new profession. I got found out once, when my mum phoned up to get me out of school to go for an audition and I wasn't there. But generally it worked OK.

Anna Scher was very good at minimizing the stress of the auditions process. Generally it would just be a director sitting at the back with the old women waiting for their bingo, watching us do our improvisations, then he or she would pick a few of us to go back the next day to do another audition with the director leading us.

I got a job for the Children's Film Foundation that way, which I dragged back into my head the other day. I don't know if it's ever been shown anywhere in the last thirty years, but it was called *Anoop and the Elephant* and it was about a circus.

Some baddies were trying to steal the elephant, and me, Linda Robson and this Indian kid called Anoop were the heroes who had to save it. Jimmy Edwards, he was the baddy. Julian Orchard was in it as well, and a woman who looked like Julian Orchard. We had to go to Darlington to film some of it and the rest was done at Denham Studios in Buckinghamshire, which I don't think are there any more. We would've stayed in hotels, which I can't remember much about; I do remember that the chaperoning was pretty loose, so long as you basically behaved yourself.

Of course I fell in love with Linda Robson – 'La Rob', as Anna Scher called her – but then everybody did. At the age of thirteen she was the perfect embodiment of everything a woman could be to me, but I was never big enough or mean enough for her: she always seemed to go for tougher guys.

Luckily for me there were a lot of extras around as well, who were mostly girls from a local drama school. One of them was a bit older than me and had brilliant tits that stood right out. We were in this tent together and all of a sudden she let me have a little feel. I remember being called to do my scene while my hands were in her bra, and having to struggle to get out of the tent in time because I had the horn.

Another time, Linda Robson and I had to do this scene with a donkey in it, and the donkey got the horn so badly (I suppose he was in love with La Rob as well) that we had to stop filming because we were both giggling so much. And that was only the beginning of the animal interference in the making of *Anoop and the Elephant*.

They'd hired an elephant from a circus and its owner used to wear this red cloak and looked like an old witch. She'd talk to it in Italian, which I think is the universal language of the circus – it was '*destra*' for right and '*si'nistra*' for left.

I was sitting in the tent one time (with my hands on that girl's tits) when the elephant went a bit mad and broke loose. Someone screamed 'Elephant! Elephant!' and we had to dive out of there before the elephant took the tent with it. Luckily this incident does not seem to have done me any long-term psychological damage (at least, I don't think so). These were my first real sexual encounters, after all. La Rob certainly went out of the old brain after that, but I think the elephant's name was Ella – which, strangely enough, is what I ended up naming my daughter years later. (Though I think she would want me to emphasize that I didn't name her after the elephant.)

As exciting as these formative on-the-job experiences were, they didn't stop me playing my full part in the teenage life of my own community. There was a youth club called the Mary Ward I used to go to, which was over by Coram's Fields, more on the Holborn side. Basically there was nothing to do there and yet one week, all of a sudden, we got all these woodwork tables and this, that and the other 'cos Prince Phillip – the patron saint of youth clubs – was coming to visit.

By the time he turned up we'd all been put in this woodwork group and were meant to be making a cupboard. You don't want to really do that at a youth club, do you? It's meant to be about playing table-tennis or snooker and listening to records. Anyway, Prince Philip arrived and had a go on the pinball machine (he knew how to enjoy himself). Then he walked round with all these dignitaries and asked everyone, 'What are you making?' My mate Johnny Sheehan said, 'A coffin for you', which got a laugh out of him. A few centuries previously he'd've been in the Tower of London for that.

I think Mary Ward herself must have been some sort of caring type, because there's a Mary Ward Centre up in Tavistock Place as well, where they do lots of art courses. I worked there for a while as a sweeper-upper when I was a bit older, but only 'cos a mate said they did life-drawing classes and we were trying to get a view of some nudie. I think we did have some success in that area, but the job only lasted about a week, so it's possible the authorities got wise to us.

The big youth club in King's Cross was the Tonbridge Club. I think it was something to do with Tonbridge public school, but you never saw the headmaster or posh boys in blazers there. It was much more free-form than the Mary Ward, and a lot rougher. I don't think I was really allowed to go there but I still did – all my mates used to hang around outside, and if the Old Bill came we'd go inside and play table-tennis, or skin up in these little cubicles they had.

It was open pretty much every weeknight and you could take your records there and dance to Dave and Ansell Collins. At this stage the hippie thing hadn't yet quite got me. Fashion was still all about looking smart and finding your own balance between mod, suede- and skinhead – they're all kind of interrelated anyway, so it's OK to mix them up a bit.

This old guy called Tom Hibbert and his wife used to run Tonbridge from their lofty perch upstairs. Years later I got a letter from her, inviting me to his retirement do, but I was never that keen on him so I didn't do anything about it. You're a bit hard on people in authority when you're young: he might actually have been OK. But the thing they had at the Tonbridge that was a bit weird was this really big karate class for grown-up blokes who'd come in their cars and who paid to attend.

To me the whole place had a bit of an air of charity about it, and I felt a bit resentful about that. Nothing ever seemed to be that organized – we never had a football team or anything – and if they were so fucking charitable what were they doing making all this money out of karate? We reckoned we should have all the facilities, but we used to get kicked out of the little gym for the karate blokes. Us 'erberts upstairs used to shout at them out of the window, and then they'd chase us down the road. If you got caught, you really got kung fu'd.

The Tonbridge Club was still a regular haunt of mine, though, and from the age of fourteen, right through to nineteen or twenty, I still popped my head in pretty often. By the time I was fifteen or so it wasn't my scene so much, as from then on I was basically stuck in basements playing guitar all the time. And once my band got going we did some of our first gigs at the Tonbridge. There was a girl who was some kind of a youth leader . . . Well, I don't know how I managed it, but I got hold of her somehow.

9: GOD GAVE
ROCK 'N' ROLL TO ME

Me and my dad saw the rock band Argent by accident once. We were walking past King's Cross Town Hall – I can't remember where we were going – when we heard this music coming from inside the building. I said, 'Come on, Dad, let's go in.'

They must've been playing a while as there was no one on the door by the time we arrived, so we just walked straight in and there were Argent singing 'God Gave Rock 'n' Roll to You'. We just stood there and listened. It was one of those great moments in life where you feel like you're in a film (as opposed to *actually* being in one, which tends to be a much more structured and less spontaneous experience).

There's a wonderful bit of footage of them doing that song on *The Old Grey Whistle Test*. At first you see Russ Ballard playing an acoustic guitar, but then he gets to the 'rock 'n' roll' bit, and all of a sudden he's got an electric. Two takes! Fantastic.

I'd always wanted to do things, musically, even before I saw Argent. I once came second in a singing competition at the railway club my mum and dad used to go to in Kentish Town. By that time I was playing guitar as well as belting the tune out, and I think I did 'On the O-hi-o' – that old favourite from Mr Skinner's guitar class. The girl who won was a good singer, whereas I was more like Bob Dylan reincarnated.

What I really needed was a band and, once it became apparent that Borax Flux was just an idea in my mind (it still is, really), there was only one way to make that happen. As luck would have it, during the very week I'd first encountered Anna Scher at Argyll Primary, I'd also met up with a guy called Peter-Hugo Daly; in the years to come I ended up doing a lot of different things with him – writing and performing music, and being in plays and films (he's the drummer who's a bit nutty in *Breaking Glass*, for a start).

We started going to Anna Scher proper on pretty much the same day, I think, and being new boys together we instantly struck up a friendship. Peter's a couple of years older than I am, and he became a big influence on me. He went to St Ignatius' Catholic College, and in the academic sense was a lot brighter than I was. He came from a normal family, though. (His name wasn't double-barrelled, the Peter and Hugo were two first names – I think he used them both because there was already a Peter Daly in Equity, the actor's union.) The thing we had in common was that we both liked to do things differently from everyone else.

After we'd been going to Anna's for a while, we had a big chat one day about music and he said, 'You play the guitar, don't you? I've got these two mates, Barry Neil and Miles Landesman, and they want to get a band together.' So we went to this guy Barry's house up in Stoke Newington and rehearsed in his bedroom, and I basically joined the band from that moment. At first I think both Miles and I were singing, and maybe there was a bit of conflict over that – but nothing massive. I had too big an ego to be anything other than the front-man.

As a band we had very odd taste. There was a lot of Who about, but Pete has five brothers and as a result was into a lot of the weirder, more 'progressive' things he'd heard the older ones listening to, like Gentle Giant and Sassafras. I was, well, not quite a three-chord man – I was a bit better than that – but Pete had a great grasp of music as a whole. He was a very, very talented keyboard player, who could read music and knew a bit of theory, and it was his idea that we should be called Renoir.

I was never quite clear on the concept of 'Impressionist rock' – whether we really were trying to capture the magic of Impressionist painting though our music, or whether it was just Pete being clever and coming up with an *NME*-type headline describing what we wanted to be. But don't be too hard on us: you've got to remember that all this was happening in 1973.

Barry Neil lived on Burma Road – one of those compact Victorian terraces in Stoke Newington. He and his mum lived downstairs, and a guy we always called Mr Twitman lived upstairs. The more electric we got, the less he liked it – which I couldn't really understand at the time, but now the memory of myself stamping on those effects pedals leads me to have a little bit more sympathy for him. And it can't have been easy going through life being called 'Mr Twitman', either, whether or not that was actually his real name.

At some point in the early/mid-seventies we finally took heed of his protests and relocated to the Landesmans' house in Duncan Terrace in Islington, where Miles' mum and dad (who were ex-beatniks) kindly let us take over their basement. The room was quite long and full of all this pop art. I remember there was a smashed-up piano artistically mounted on one wall (if only my dad had known it was possible to get people to pay for them), and on another was a kind of mattress that had been sculpted into a giant vagina. Basically, it was the perfect place for teenage boys to hang out.

From that point on, we effectively lived down there. It was really good of them to let us have our gear set up the whole time, but that was only the beginning of the influence Miles' parents would have on the way Renoir developed. His dad was (and is) quite a character. If you want to read about him, Miles' older brother Cosmo (who grew up to be a journalist for *The Sunday Times*, and was married to Julie Burchill for a while) wrote a very funny book about his family, called *Starstruck*, a few years back, which was basically about how much they all wanted to be famous.

He's a funny bloke, old Jay Landesman. He was a bit literary, but he was also a nightclub owner who had a white Bentley that he used to hire out for weddings on Saturdays. He also had this old hippie bus which we used to drive around in. And after a while he ended up becoming our manager. Well, he sort of did and sort of didn't, but we'll come back to that a bit later on.

If anything Miles' mum – Fran Landesman – had an even bigger impact on us. She's quite a well-known poet; and when we first started trying to come up with songs for Renoir to play, we set a few of her poems to our music. I think she enjoyed us doing that and it worked surprisingly well: her poems made really good lyrics for songs. And in terms of me eventually coming up with my own original stuff, singing hers first certainly helped me to advance as a songwriter.

It was obviously quite an unusual set-up. Fran's a wonderful poet, but hers were very much the lyrics of a middle-aged, middle-class woman – they're all about her love life and lost times from the past – and they tended to come from quite a world-weary perspective, so it was quite strange to have a cocky sixteen-year-old boy from King's Cross singing them. It kind of worked, though, because it gave us a different point of view.

I remember we did one song called 'Decline of the West' – 'All the good tunes have been written/All the good songs have been sung/Somewhere a promise was broken/Long ago when we were young'. Probably our heaviest number was based on a poem of hers called 'The Rope' – 'I can't go on/ I cannot cope/ To end it all/ I choose the rope'. We were Islington's answer to Joy Division before Joy Division had even happened.

The first gig we ever did was at a kind of left-wing, gay-rights resources centre in Hackney called *Centerprise*. Because it was a bookshop, I think maybe Fran stood up and did some poetry first and then we played acoustically. It was all a bit performance art, but we were just in a nice place, doing what we wanted to do. That was a really magical time for me – very hippie-ish, but really free.

Fran didn't write stuff specifically for us. We'd look through her poetry books and pick out the ones that looked like they might work, then Peter would come up with a musical setting. As time went on I started writing more and more of the lyrics and the basic songs in conjunction with Peter-Hugo and then he would kind of flower 'em up musically.

At first the words I wrote were slightly influenced by Fran, but gradually they became more fully my own stuff. Our music was still quite a strange mixture, though, because Pete was the real musical brains of the operation – he had a Fender Rhodes and some kind of early synthesizer – whereas the songs I wrote were a bit more straightforward, even a bit punky. When punk eventually came along we didn't really like it much. (It didn't like us much, either.) After 'Anarchy in the UK' we did a song called 'Anarchy in the KP', because we thought it was nuts.

Before that, though, when Renoir were just getting going, what happened was that a load of the Cromer Street boys kind of became our following. You always need that when you first start as a band, I think – a bit of a gang behind you. I'd known most of them grow-ing up anyway, then we did a couple of gigs at the Tonbridge Club and they liked us.

So, when we started playing on Friday nights at the Old Red Lion in Islington, it was only natural that the King's Cross boys came up to see us. The Old Red Lion is south of the Angel, where Roseberry Avenue goes down towards Sadler's Wells. It's a theatre pub now, but it was a real Irish boozer back then. We'd been in and chatted to the landlord, this geezer called Mick, who said he'd give us a regular spot.

On one occasion a few of the local boys from round the Islington area were there too and it all went off. What was particularly unfor-tunate was that this was the night my mum and dad had chosen to come and see us. So the gig ended with my mum hiding under the table while everyone was throwing bottles at each other and fighting. I don't think she came to see us again.

At that time the young ladies of Camden Girls' School loomed quite large on the radar of young men in our area; a couple of them went to Anna Scher's. There was a band around then called Hope, which Miles had been in once: they were working-class boys, but a bit more bohemian than us – and they were shagging a lot more Camden girls than we were.

Their singer was a guy called Danny Wright, who is dead now, sadly. He was quite charismatic but they were kind of our competition, so we weren't mates. (It's a shame the way that happens with rivals – you're never mates, are you?) Anyway, their exploits gave us ideas, and a few liaisons definitely happened between some of these middle-class Camden girls and the young working-class chaps of the Renoir fraternity.

I remember someone telling me a story about how he got off with one of the Camden girls when he was about fourteen. He couldn't believe the fact that she took him home to her house, he stayed the night, and her mum brought him a cup of tea in the morning. So there were a few different principles going on, but there was no harm in it and everyone was enjoying themselves. The Camden gang that we were involved with all seemed to be related to – who was that sex-god painter . . .? Lucian Freud. It seemed like he'd sired most of the Camden school for girls. Now that's what I call a Freudian slip.

10: FROM 'THE COURT' TO THE COURT

When I first started to get out and about on the streets with my mates, while I was still at primary school, there was a little gang of seven or eight of us, and we called ourselves 'the Court'. At the back of King's Cross, by the big blocks of flats, Widborne and Midhope, there are these pedestrianized areas – pavements that are quite wide and go all the way down, with bollards at either end. You can easily make a pitch out of them, and we all learnt our football there.

Just up on Cromer Street was a block of flats where Stan Flashman had his offices. He later became chairman of Barnet FC but at that point he was a famous ticket tout and, since his place was only round the corner from where we used to play football, we used to hang around there to see the famous players who went down there to flog their complimentary tickets.

Some top footballers whose names I won't mention would emerge from Stan's front door to find us waiting there with our autograph books. Sometimes they'd send us away with a flea in our ear, because even though it wasn't illegal, it wasn't something they particularly wanted people to know they were doing.

It wasn't that there weren't any parks near us. We had Coram's Fields to play in, Bramber was another a bit of green – 'Shit Green', we used to call it – and you could get in over the fence to Argyll Square if you wanted to. Or we'd just climb into the school playground – although the caretaker would always kick us out. Of course we'd just run away and climb back out over the fence again, but it's funny how when you're little that kind of thing feels really important.

Some of childhood's less visible barriers would prove much harder to get over. The Cromer Street boys – who in the previous chapter were establishing themselves as Renoir's answer to the Barmy Army – lived on the other side of a very clear social divide. Jessel House was on Judd Street, which is the main road going south from St Pancras Station, and Cromer Street cuts across it at right angles. It's a long old street, leading down to Gray's Inn Road, and I later wrote a song about it called 'The Cromer Aroma'.

At one end, Cromer Street has all these roads leading off it, one of which – Tankerton Street – has a kind of courtyard in it. That was where we hung out (hence 'the Court'). And the Cromer Street boys used to lurk about at the other end. It wasn't quite that never the twain would meet, because we'd all been to the same primary school and were all King's Cross boys at heart. But everyone knew which group they belonged to.

Essentially the difference between the two groups was that we were better behaved than they were. Most of the Cromer Street boys came from slightly rougher backgrounds than ours, and they were more into having fights. We were a bit more gentle, really. We just wanted to go round each other's houses and play football, whereas some of them were real scrappers. None of us really got nicked much as youngsters, whereas they were always getting their collars felt (or would have done, if they'd been wearing them).

It wasn't that we weren't mates with them – I played in loads of football teams with 'em over the years, and some of them were really good footballers (especially Ray Houghton, who went on to play for Liverpool and the Republic of Ireland) – but there was always a bit of a gap there. And, as time went on and I started really getting into music and acting, and they started getting into other things, those differences were magnified.

What we all had in common was King's Cross. And the one thing people really associated with that area was prostitution. We used to see 'the girls' around some of the private squares, but we never really used to follow them about. We'd be more likely to follow the geezers who were out looking for the prostitutes so we could tease them – throw things at them or whatever – but you were taking your life in your hands a bit doing that, as they were often quite mean sorts of people. It was all a bit depressing, really, so over time we sort of learnt to just let it go. You'd see the odd used Johnny lying around at the back of the flats, and that was about it.

Up by Euston Road was where the Palace of Varieties cinema used to be. When I was very young we used to go up there on Saturday mornings to run amok in the aisles, and sometimes watch cartoons or the forerunners of the Children's Film Foundation's timeless classic *Anoop and the Elephant*. But when they demolished that lovely old building and put up the new town hall in its place, they also built this terrible little pond there.

The pond was meant to be ornamental but it ended up just being where men took prostitutes for a shag. 'It's dying by the town hall/In ruin and decay/Where the picture palace stood/Now it's like an old ashtray': that was one verse of a song I wrote (aptly titled 'The Pond'). In fact, as I began to escape from Fran Landesman's influence and come up with more songs of my own, I found that a lot of them were about King's Cross.

Because that was where I came from, and because I was always the inquisitive type, my gaze roamed and alighted on things I could write about. It wasn't that King's Cross was all I knew. I've always had a bit of an eye for what it is about places and people that make them what they are. Basically, I'm nosey: I like looking out of my window.

Had I lived in the suburbs I'd probably have been twitching at the net curtains all the time; but because I grew up in the middle of London,I was always noticing particular ways that people spoke or behaved. And later on I'd use these behavioural details in my acting as well as in my song-writing.

If you looked at the kids who grew up where I did, for example, there was us lot – King's Cross – and then there were the Holborn, who were slightly more Dickensian than us. In fact they still are. A lot of fruit-and-veg boys come from down there, and they're much more sort of 'at it'. There are a lot more thieves and ticket touts.

You probably wouldn't pick up on these subtle distinctions unless you were a native, but they were definitely there. It's like this side of the river and that side of the river. People who come from north and south of the Thames are very different, but if you're not a Londoner you probably won't understand why. I'm sure New York's probably the same – or any other big city or town, for that matter.

As acting and music began to lead me away a bit from my original gang of childhood friends, I was always careful to make sure I didn't get isolated. When I first started at Anna Scher's it was just for an hour and a half after school on Tuesdays and Thursdays, so I'd probably come home and go and play football with my mates anyway. There might've been a few comments made, but no one ever really had a go. I never got victimized: it wasn't *Billy Elliot*.

As bigger things started to happen for me – in my mid and late teens – I made sure I kept a place in my own community. That relationship went both ways, too, because there was always a place in my acting for the people I lived with, whether this was a question of noticing specific things about someone I knew and then putting them into a characterization, or just a generalized sense that the work I did had to be true to where I came from.

When people ask me what was the first really serious acting job I ever did, it's probably not a coincidence that the one that springs to mind didn't even involve being on a stage or in front of a camera. There was this kid at Rutherford called Christopher Hartstone, and he had a few quid. I'd seen him wearing this jacket that was kind of made of denim and leather at the same time. I took a real shine to it, and I wanted to buy it off him for a pound or thirty bob or something.

I got the money off my mum, but the day the deal was meant to go down I was late for school, and for some reason I went to this café that had pinball machines instead, and somehow I did the whole thirty bob playing them. By the time I'd spent all that money playing pinball I was *really* late for school. So when I finally got there I went to see my house-master and told him that this great big Scottish bloke had robbed me – 'I had thirty bob to buy this jacket and he took the money off me, blah, blah, blah . . .'

Anyway, he sent me to the police station – presumably to test my resolve. So there I was, sitting in the cop shop with a fucking CID guy, telling him this same made-up piece of shit. He kept saying, 'You are telling me the truth, aren't you?' I was going, 'Yeah, yeah', till in the end he goes, 'Right, we'll investigate it – what's your telephone number?'

I never told my mum and dad when I went home, but I was waiting about three months for him to call. I got that jacket off Christopher Hartstone in the end and owed him the dough. I probably paid him, but I might not have. Anyway, I always thought of that as my professional debut: a nice bit of perjury that went a bit too far.

As far as more respectable acting assignments went, I did a play called *Penny Whistle* by an ex-*Guardian* writer called Laurence Dobie at the Hampstead Theatre. He was a funny old git, God rest his soul. It was kind of a child's-eye view of the world – a bit of a romp – and a gang of us from Anna Scher's were in it. There was also a play called *Heroes,* which was one of Stephen Poliakoff's early works.

That was a really interesting one to do, because it was upstairs at the Royal Court. I was dressed as a Glaswegian bus conductor, with spiked ginger hair even though this was before punk. It was Poliakoff predicting things, in a way, at the same time as doing something that was a bit like Berlin in the thirties – he was clever in that respect. It was a weird play, though. People were getting electric shocks for kicks, and I was this subversive boy who kept turning up and being a bit wild.

It wasn't a very big part – I was in only about three or four scenes – but it's a wonderful theatre, upstairs at the Court, and I was very excited to be doing a play there. David Dixon and Jonathan Pryce were in it as well, and I remember watching them and thinking, 'I'd like to do this'. I particularly admired Jonathan, and he kind of took me under his wing (I was only about fourteen at the time).

We must have rehearsed in the daytime but I can't remember alternating between doing that and going to school, which suggests that I might have used this high-profile theatrical engagement as an excuse to spend a bit more quality time with the mummies at the British Museum. A few of the teachers at Rutherford had definitely started to pick on me a bit at this point – they automatically assumed I thought I was the fucking bee's knees, just because I'd done a few things.

Heroes turned out to be the perfect preparation for my real theatrical breakthrough, which was Nigel Williams' *Class Enemy* – again upstairs at the Royal Court, but a few years later. Nigel does lots of arts shows on TV now, but he'd taught in various schools in southwest London before he started writing plays. This one was about a class with no teacher. There were six of us – five of us from Anna Scher's and one other guy, Michael Deeks (or 'Deeksy', as I knew him) – and our characters were all kind of lost in the world of education. Sort of like *The History Boys* in reverse.

Each one of the kids gets up in class and gives a lesson. One of the lads does one about immigrants stowing away on boats, another kid does one about his mum and dad being blind, and bread-and-butter pudding, and Perry Benson's guy tells a story about cats pissing and shitting in window boxes. Then the teacher comes in for the last five minutes and everything goes haywire. I haven't read it for years, but it's a fantastic play – they did it at drama colleges for years afterwards, because there were six really good parts in it. And the director, Bill Alexander, really got the best out of us.

He had a lot of influence on me, Bill. He was a very unusual type of guy for a director. He'd have this old mac on, he smoked all the time and he never combed his hair. It was a scripted play, but Bill gave us an enormous amount of freedom with it. He'd take us out for drinks after rehearsals and encourage us to do it however we wanted as long as we made sure that whatever we did we really practised hard.

Nigel Williams had written the script phonetically. One of the guys (who will remain nameless, but was a lovely fella) had learnt the whole thing exactly as written before he'd even come to the first rehearsal, so we had to put him straight. If I've got to play a Glaswegian – bus conductor or otherwise – I might write my part down phonetically, but it's something you should only do for yourself. You don't need a writer to do it for you.

Over the years, I've seen a lot of bad attempts at phonetic writing; and in this instance there was a bit of an argument about Nigel Williams using us as a middle-class mouthpiece. I couldn't really see that, though. We all live in one country, after all – it's not like the middle class and the working class live that far away from each other (especially in Islington). And Nigel had written that script at just the right time for us lot to jump on it.

Class Enemy was a huge leap forward for me (as well as giving me the title of this book). Tipping spaghetti over someone's head in *Bugsy Malone* was sweet FA, really. But this was me becoming an actor – taking the stuff I'd learnt at Anna Scher's to the British stage. This was us showing everyone that there were some new kiddies about. Not in a big-headed way, but our aggression was real, and we wanted everyone to know that we meant it. At the end of the play we smashed all the desks up, and we never used to care if chair legs flew into the audience.

The game with us kids from Anna's was that we were disciplined – we could make it look like we were having a free-for-all but still do the play and get all the nuances. That's what Bill did, really – taught us how to do that: not to just shout our way through the whole thing. And us lot posturing about and smoking joints on stage was just what the Royal Court needed at the time.

The production transferred from the small theatre upstairs to the bigger one downstairs, and it was the first time in donkey's years that this had been done. My mum and dad came along (though obviously there was a bit too much swearing for them). And I wore that jacket on stage – the one I'd got from Christopher Hartstone. Looking back, this seems like a pretty good example of life and art keeping each other honest.

After it finished its run at the Royal Court, *Class Enemy* was remounted at the Young Vic with a young guy called Mark Wingett playing my part. This was the first time he'd stepped into my shoes, but it wouldn't be the last.

11: OUT OF MY BRAIN
ON THE TRAIN

With all the exciting things that were happening in my life at that time, I never stopped to think about how lucky I was still to be alive to enjoy them.

I've mentioned before that when I was little there was a railwaymen's social club in Kentish Town which my mum and dad were members of. It was the scene of one of my earliest public singing performances. Dad had family connections to the railway – that was how we got in there. It had a ballroom and a bar and a kiddies' room round the back, where we could hang about all night while they danced the foxtrot, played bingo and had a few drinks. We used to go there a lot.

The main reason the railway club was such a big deal for my dad was that there was a fishing club affiliated with it. My dad was really into his deep-sea fishing. He loved to head off down to Folkestone and go out and catch cod and congers and all that sort of thing. One day he came back with an eel that was as long as he was tall.

I once went out deep-sea fishing with him, when we were on holiday in Brixham, but I didn't really take to it: I never enjoyed putting the worms on the hook. My dad and his mates loved it, though. They'd plan the trip like a military operation: they'd get up to Kentish Town for four or five in the morning, then this guy called Tug would drive them down to the Kent coast in a minibus, and they'd head out into rough seas in the middle of the Channel – the boat would be bouncing all over the place and they'd be sat there with silly grins on their faces. It was none of this beer fishing: you had to be committed and careful to do it.

My dad would get home at about six on a Sunday evening (in good time for *Songs of Praise*). There was always dogfish – which he used to do up for my auntie's cats – and usually cod and plaice. I never understood why we didn't eat the dogfish, which is quite a fashionable fish now. OK, it's a bit of a bottom feeder, but hold up – aren't prawns and lobsters?

You don't cast when you're on a boat, you just hang the line off, but a bloke forgot once, swung his rod back to cast and embedded his hook right in my dad's head. It was like a very English version of that scene in *There's Something About Mary*. After it happened, they were all ready to go back to land, but my dad said, 'No chance.' So they finished off their day's fishing before taking him to casualty, where they had to cut his head open to get the hook out.

Apart from the singing competitions and the fishing trips, the railwaymen's club also used to organize an annual day-trip. We never had a car (though we'd often go away in Uncle Don's camper van, and sometimes squeeze into my other uncle's Ford Anglia) so we always went on it.

One year – I think I was thirteen or fourteen at the time – we went to Margate. My sisters had left home by then, so it was just me and my mum and dad. We set off in the morning from Kentish Town. Because it was a railwayman's beano, we had our own train – a special. We had the day down in Margate on the funfair. There were loads of kids there and it was really good fun. But on the way home the driver was going too fast.

There's a steep turn on the track at Eltham, in southeast London, and he just ploughed straight into it. There was this whole thing afterwards about him having been pissed – apparently he was waving at people on the platform of the last station we went through.

Anyway, the train derailed. I was with a load of other kids in one of those old-fashioned carriages that have a corridor with a little door to a booth with six or eight seats. Our carriage was on its side, so I couldn't get out of the door, but I managed to climb out of the window. As I got down to the ground, I saw someone with blood coming out of their mouth.

When you looked back at the train, it was like World War III had happened. At first everything was eerily silent, but then really quickly we heard all these sirens coming towards us and people were looking for each other. 'Cos it was a beano, a lot of the parents were a bit pissed, and they were all trying to track down the kids they'd sent off to play with their mates.

I was scared that my mum and dad were dead, and obviously they were scared that I was. I always say that when we finally found each other, my dad clipped me round the ear'ole – 'Where've you been?' – but I'm not sure whether that actually happened or I just made it up to make what had happened seem less traumatic.

Either way, several people got killed and a lot of others were hurt. The secretary of the club died and left a wife and three kiddies behind. Apparently at the time of the impact he was walking up the train to tell the driver to slow down. I remember a kid called Jason lost his leg as well . . . It was a proper train crash, and probably the only blemish on my childhood, really.

I think I blotted the whole thing out of my mind at the time. Of course going to the railway club would never be the same, but I was probably kept out of the way when it came to attending the funerals. All I remember was that it affected me not so much on the day after it happened, but a bit more on the next day, and a bit more on the day after that. So I had only one day off school initially, and went back too soon, but then had to stay away a bit longer. I think that's often how shock works, isn't it?

It's hard to recall exactly how I felt – just a bit frail and weird, I suppose – but looking it up on the internet to check I'd got my facts right brought the whole thing back to me. The Eltham Well Hall train crash took place on 11 June 1972 and 6 people were killed and

126 injured. It was seeing the black-and-white photos of the after-math that made me think, 'Fucking hell!' Because I knew which carriage I'd been in. It was one of the ones that were over on their sides but still kind of upright, whereas a lot of the others were all bent up and broken.

The whole scene had faded into being some little thing that I never thought about, but looking at the pictures it was pretty hard to ignore: that train was *mashed*. And suddenly I could remember it all a bit more clearly – not being able to open the door, then climbing out of the big window. And I think the lady I saw bleeding on the ground was the wife of the club's steward; so, though she probably didn't know it at the time, she'd lost her husband.

The other thing that was a bit weird was seeing the reports of the investigation afterwards. I hadn't realized how pissed the driver was. Presumably 'cos it was a railwaymen's club, he thought it was a day out for him as well. It turned out that he'd had several pints at lunchtime, gone back home and drank sherry, then had another pint, then on the way back actually stopped off and got out of the cabin at a station to get more booze. Apparently he had spirits with him in the cab when they found him. He'd got so drunk that he killed himself and five other people.

I suppose it was probably a mercy that he was one of his own vic-tims, as anything else wouldn't have been very easy for him – or anyone else – to live with. You were probably allowed a couple of pints before driving a train in those days. You could see how toler-ated that kind of thing was by the fact that the inquiry ended up putting down alcohol as a 'secondary cause' of the crash. A second-ary cause?! Apparently the primary cause was going too fast.

Obviously I might not be the best judge of this, but I've never seen what happened that day as having had any major long-term effect on me. I know I didn't like going on trains for a long time afterwards – I always thought they were going too fast – but that was just common sense.

Two subsequent events would seem to confirm the suspicion that, when it comes to me and rail travel, discretion should probably always be the better part of valour. And I'm not talking about that eyeliner I had to wear in the sequence in *Quadrophenia* that's cut to the Who's '5.15', nor getting off with Hazel O'Connor in a sleeping compartment in *Breaking Glass*, neither.

When we were filming the original TV version of *Scum* – it says 1977 on the DVD box, but I'm pretty sure it was the year before when we actually made it – the lads and I used to have to get to the set in Redhill and back on the train from Charing Cross every day. There were no chauffeur-driven cars for us back then.

We were in another one of those carriages with a sliding door and six seats when another terrible thing happened (it's no wonder I found it so easy to look out of my brain when I had to sit in one of those again as Jimmy two years later – people always ask if I was actually stoned in those scenes, but that performance is free of all chemical enhancement: it's called acting). I don't want to incriminate myself or anyone else, and I'm not quite sure what the statute of limitations is when it comes to youthful indiscretions in train carriages, but let's just say we were messing about.

There must have been ten of us in there – and, before the tabloids start ringing me up, I can't remember if Ray Winstone was among us; it might just have been the Anna Scher gang. Anyway, everyone was mucking about.

Given what I'd been through not that long before, you'd think I'd have known better than to join in, but maybe it was a way of showing I wasn't bothered. We all kept fucking around and pretending to open the door, and then one of us actually did.

At that exact moment an express train came the other way, and somehow (I still can't work out how this happened, as the gap between the two sets of tracks would have been much wider than one door – maybe a load of idiots on the other train had an open-door policy as well) it ripped off first the door and then half the side of the carriage. Both the trains carried on along the tracks OK, but there was a gaping hole in the side of ours and a load of windows were cracked as well.

If you were making a comedy film featuring this incident (which of course you wouldn't, as that would be much too irresponsible) the best scene in it would have been the ten of us squeezing out of the little sliding door to escape the damaged compartment and then all guiltily getting off at the next station. It seemed like an absolute disaster. I remember getting home at about five to ten and waiting in a state of total paranoia for the ten o'clock news to come on.

Luckily there was nothing on the news, either that day or the next. No one seemed to have got hurt, and we could all go back to our normal lives as respectable young actors. Acting in the soon-to-be banned TV version of *Scum*.

The memory of this incident still alarms me to this day. There's a funny bit on a DVD extras commentary I did a few years back. *Scum*'s original producer, Margaret Matheson – to whom someone, in a bid to salve their conscience, must have confessed – keeps going, 'Tell them what happened on the train, Phil . . .' and I won't say anything 'cause I don't want to incriminate myself.

I think I've probably done that enough for the moment, so I'll save the last rail-related horror story for a bit later on. I don't want anyone thinking there's some kind of underlying theme of my personal journey through life, though.

The funny thing is, I never got into trainspotting when I lived in King's Cross – as a kid I went up the station once or twice, and saw the *Flying Scotsman* a few times with my mate Adrian Gallagher, who was really into it. It never really caught on with me, trainspotting, but I like it much better now. Where I live at the moment I've got the North London line at the end of my garden, so I can watch the trains to my heart's content. And I've even seen the *Orient Express*.

12: IN THE BASEMENT, WITH PETER PURVES AND TOM WAITS

The Boot, which was the main pub people from King's Cross used to frequent, was right next to the Tonbridge Club. We went there sometimes, but the Skinners Arms – conveniently located right underneath Jessel House – was my dad's local and the place he took me to have my first pint, when I was fifteen.

A lot of the early times I went out drinking with my mates, it was to the Lord Nelson in Holloway Road. We used to go and watch a band there later on – I can't remember if it was Be-Bop De Luxe or Ducks Deluxe, but it was definitely one or the other.

Trying to get served in pubs was a bit of a nightmare at that age, 'cos I looked young. God, did I look young. But there was a pub round the corner from school where they used to let us in at lunchtime, even though we were wearing our school blazers. I remember Christopher Hartstone got in trouble once, 'cos the religious-education teacher smelt booze on his breath. Perhaps he'd been drinking to forget the fact that I now owned his jacket.

The first time I ever had a bit of puff was probably a few years earlier, because I remember at that point the music I was into was maybe T-Rex and a bit of early Status Quo ('Pictures of Matchstick Men': when they were good). But the power of the herb opened my mind to a kind of music I wasn't usually into. My mate Graham Hughes had an older brother called Brian – Bruin, we called him –

and one day Bruin got me and Graham stoned and put *What's Going On* by Marvin Gaye on the record player. And man, it blew my mind – it was unbelievable, it was brilliant.

When the effects of the marijuana wore off I found I still wasn't that big a Marvin Gaye fan; but, even now, every time I hear that album it takes me back to Graham's brother's bedroom. And this formative experience set the tone for the way we used puff to enhance our enjoyment of music. Put it this way, it would have been much harder to appreciate the transcendent greatness of *Close to the Edge* by Yes without it.

Even though it was generally accepted among my peers that this was the way things were, my mum and dad would have been horrified to find out about it. Things were very different at the Landesmans'. Everyone there smoked dope in front of each other. Fran had some slimming pills that we thought were all right as well – 'Go and nick some speed off your mum, Miles,' became a bit of a mantra – and Jay certainly wasn't too bothered by the prospect of his sons and their friends experimenting with mind-bending substances.

Not much was done besides puff, though. I only took LSD about twice, but I didn't like it much 'cos I was never really willing to let myself go. I remember that on one of those occasions we were sitting round the table at the Landesmans', our eyes out on stalks, and Jay came in, sat down and went, 'El Trippo!' He knew what we were up to and didn't turn a hair.

There were things to be said both for and against these two different parental approaches. On the one hand, there was me with my mum and dad – whom I loved dearly – breaking away a bit to live a slightly different kind of life because they were old-fashioned. On the other, there were Cosmo and Miles with their mum and dad driving them round the bend because they let them do whatever they wanted. I suppose I probably had the best of both worlds, really – messing about in the Landesmans' basement, then going home to King's Cross for a bit of stability.

I more or less lived at Miles and Cosmo's house, though, and it was a very exciting place to be at that time. Georgie Fame had set some of Fran's poems to music as well, so he'd turn up every now and again and do a bit on her piano. Then there was a guy called Craig Sams, who used to run Ceres Grain – the first health-food shop in Notting Hill. I think later on he ended up starting Green & Black's chocolate. He was all right, too. I knew Craig's son Gideon a bit, who wrote the first punk novel (called, logically enough, *The Punk*). He unfortunately died really young.

Anyway, Craig brought some of the Notting Hill bohemian lot in with him, so you'd get them mingling with the Islington bohemian crowd. It was all quite glamorous, and Renoir were like this troupe of teenage entertainers in the middle of it all. When the Landesmans had parties (which they did a lot) we'd do gigs in the basement for 'em, and people would come down to smoke a joint and watch us.

I remember walking down the corridor once and seeing Peter Purves with one of those Afghan coats on, and a big joint in his mouth. As someone who'd watched *Blue Peter* with my dad through-out my early childhood, I was shocked. Obviously it was OK for us to have a joint, but you don't expect to see Peter Purves sucking on a big fucking J.

We met Tom Waits at one of those parties, too. He came down and sat with us while we played. He'd only done one or two albums by then. I just remember him coming down with his bottle of whisky in his hand and being very friendly, then disappearing back upstairs again into the hippie party.

It wasn't just the Landesmans' celebrity friends who had a big impact on Renoir. They were connected with all these American underground theatre people as well, from the San Francisco People's Theater – some of whom kind of latched on to us. That led to some funny incidents. Like when we played Enfield Town Football Club dinner and dance.

How they ever booked Renoir for that one, I do not know. Ray Burdis's band were top of the bill. They were a bit more conventional than us and did mostly covers, and I suppose we'd agreed to support

Age ten in a Terylene shirt

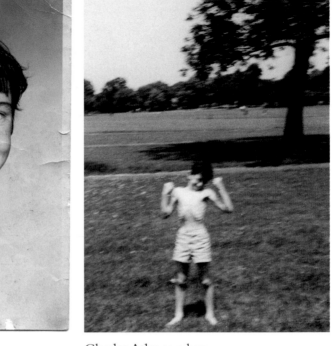

Charles Atlas as a boy

Camden Primary Schools Cup Winners 1970. Me with ball

Mum and Dad on honeymoon with Uncle Ray (the one not on tandem). Two's company, three's a crowd

Me (dark hair, in front) aged two with my two sisters and Cousin David, Christmas 1960

Dad in Jessel House after a day deep-sea fishing in Folkestone

Me and Ray Burdis in *Four Idle Hands* for ATV, 1976

I save the world from nuclear power: *Raven*, 1977

Me in my 'Renoir' days with all my axes, Sept 1979

Quadrophenia: The Ace Face and his mates,
Brighton seafront circa 1964

Sting's scooter was a
pig to ride. Lucky I
didn't kill myself

Out of my brain on the train

Left: Me and my hero Pete Townshend during filming of *Quadrophenia*

Below: Me and Alun Armstrong in *Billy the Kid and the Green Baize Vampire*, 1985

Me and Perry Benson on a quiet night out

The Fool in *Lear*: me
with my coxcomb

Scum, 1977

Me and Jan backstage at a Maxi Priest gig, mid-eighties

Me and Jan on good form

Right: 'Who's he think he is, Ernie Wise?' Mark Pollack from *Meantime, 1984*

Below: The Pollack clan minus Mavis (mum), aka Tim Roth, Jeff Robert and me

them just to get a gig. Jay was sort of managing us at that point, and he wasn't as focussed as he might've been, so we were grateful for any booking we could get.

By that time, there would usually be a couple of the San Francisco people with us who would come on stage and dance while we played. One of them was this guy called 'Apollo Paul'. He was actually South African – I think he'd been a merchant seaman for a while, before he dropped out and became a hippie – but he always dressed like Superman, for some reason.

Anyway, when he came out and started writhing about in front of us, the punters from Enfield Town Football Club were staring at him doing this weird dance, and they were shocked and outraged. I remember one of the club officials coming on to sell raffle tickets in the middle of the set and refusing to leave the stage until the last one was sold. So there was a bit of a clash of cultures.

The funny thing about Renoir was, even when we played at more appropriate venues, we never quite seemed to fit in. Like the time we drove down and played the Stonehenge Free Festival in Jay's old Reading bus – this kind of half-sized coach he had, that a whole gang of us could cram into.

It was the summer of 1976 – the really hot one. I was seventeen at the time, and I remember people were 'making love' (I think that's the terminology they would have used at the time) under the stage. But the ones who really got into Renoir were the army. I'm not quite sure what a load of soldiers were doing at a hippie festival, but presumably they'd sneaked over from Salisbury Plain when they should have been on manoeuvres.

The music we played was initially coming out of progressive rock, but there were other elements to it as well. I'd always liked a song with a good tune, and I suppose my singing was quite punky, in a way, because I'd always sing in my own voice – I'd never try to do an American accent or anything like that. So we were already a funny mix of different things, and being called Renoir probably didn't help. It seemed like a good idea at the time but, looking back, I think we might have gone a bit further with a name that suited us better.

The thing about Renoir I'm most proud of is that we were quite original. We'd play for hours and then listen back to what we'd done on the tape-recorder. And the point of the whole thing for me was not having any obvious influences. I wasn't interested in what anyone else had done: I had no heroes in that way. I didn't want to sound like Carlos Santana or anything.

That was kind of what I was trying to do as an actor as well. I didn't want to go off and live it in a different way for each role: I just wanted to be living it anyway. After *Quadrophenia*, some people suggested that I was like an English version of Robert De Niro. Obviously I was flattered by that on one level. But not on another, because I wasn't trying to do that whole American method thing. I wasn't really into Lee Strasberg. I wasn't like Daniel Day-Lewis.

Dan's a really innovative actor, and he's been lovely to me. He happened to be there a few years later when I broke my leg really badly playing showbiz football, and he wrote me a great letter afterwards saying how funny it was that when they gave me the oxygen mask I kept saying, 'This stuff is amazing – why ain't anyone else having any?'

I never saw any distinction between being an actor and being in a band (I suppose Apollo Paul and his mates might've had something to do with this as well). In fact, to me the two things were actively complimentary, because I would write songs about the plays I was in.

I wrote one called 'Class Enemy', about the school in the play, which was called 'Ballsache High'. 'God made things that creep and crawl/Ballsache High employs 'em all': those were a couple of lines in it. 'Deprivation, masturbation – something you know all about' was another one.

None of the other Renoir boys thought there was anything strange about me using my theatrical experiences in this way. When you're in a band you're always pleased if someone's written a song.

And given that Peter-Hugo was an actor as well, and our drummer Micky Dolan ended up going out with Tilly Vosburgh for a long time, this world wasn't exactly foreign to them.

All these things – the stage acting and the TV and the music – were separate, but they were all happening at the same time and there didn't seem to be any reason why they shouldn't go on doing so. I remember one day, while *Class Enemy* was on, I was off filming something else in the morning, then we did the play in the evening, and then afterwards they let Renoir do a gig at the Royal Court. It was certainly a lot more fun than going to school.

13: GOODBYE TO
BALLSACHE HIGH

I've never been flash about what I've got. At least, I don't think I have. Partly because of my background, and partly because I've never had much money anyway. Plus, when I was starting out – in my early teens – some of the stuff I was doing wasn't exactly the sort of thing you'd advertise at school anyway.

I mean, in *The Molly Wopsies* they gave me a pudding-basin hair-cut and made me wear short trousers. I was the evacuee from London who went off to have adventures with Dinkey Dunkley. That was hardly going to make me king of the playground in the days of Slade and Peter Osgood, was it?

Strangely, the first time my showbiz tendencies had any kind of negative impact on my life was on the football pitch. At the school-team try-outs in my first year at Rutherford I tried to score a cocky goal and it didn't come off, and this teacher called Mr Johnston took against me. From then on he thought I was a flash bastard. And, even though I'd played for Camden Schools and was one of the top players in Camden at primary level, he wouldn't pick me once I got to Rutherford.

His father was Harry Johnston, who was chief scout for Blackpool FC, and he picked people who were big but not especially good – a real English tradition. As the season went on I did start to get chosen for the school team . . . And this next bit is actually quite upsetting for me to remember, which shows how seriously I took my football. At the time, if you'd asked me my ambition, I'd have probably put playing for Chelsea before being a rock 'n' roll star, and certainly before being an actor.

Anyway, I got a few goals for the school team, but I was offside a lot and Mr Johnston always seemed to have it in for me. I scored the winner in the quarter-final of the West London Cup, and then we won the semi. But, come the final, I was on the bench. This is what I just can't understand a man doing to a kid: we were 5–0 up in the final with twenty minutes to go, and he didn't put me on. He just left me sitting there.

We'd got let off school that morning to play the final. I'd got a plaque for winning even though I hadn't played, and – to add insult to injury – in the afternoon I was showing it to my mate in a maths lesson when this teacher called Mr Dillon (who I never liked) came up and whacked it out of my hands. The little crest thing on the plaque came off and I got sent out of the class. It was one of those days when I realized that life can be shit sometimes.

Over the next few years my football suffered a bit. I was in and out of the school team. Mr Johnston caught me smoking once as well, and that didn't help. I think he didn't like it that I was an actor, either, 'cos he did a bit of amateur dramatics himself. Sometimes he was nice to me, but I never really knew where I was with him. It was a difficult time for me, really, because I was good enough, but he kept putting people in who were shite.

Even though I was in and out of the team, I scored a lot of goals. It was when the west London trials happened that I really saw the way things were going, because it was Mickey Bird and Jeff Chandler who got sent up for them; I didn't get a sniff. I think Jeff Chandler ended up playing for Blackpool – Mr Johnston liked him, so he got him in there. That was kind of it for me, then. I just thought, 'Bollocks to this,' and jacked the school team in: it was guitar time from then on.

I kept the football up outside school. Adidas Santiago were some of the first football boots I had, so you could see the South American influence was very important. Obviously which brand of trainers you wore was very significant. I liked Gola – Gola were big – and Puma (so four letters ending with an 'a' seemed to be the winning formula). Puma Mexico or Puma All Round, that's what we'd wear for playing on the Astroturf at Coram's Fields. I see people wearing those now – apparently they're 'classics'.

I was still playing for the Mary Ward, and there was another local team called Western Towers (which were the big flats at the bottom of Islington) that I used to play for sometimes as well. Plus, when I was about thirteen, I met a geezer through still playing for Camden Schools and went up to play with him in Barnet for a while. But it was never the same after not getting a game in that final.

At least the casting directors weren't leaving me on the bench.

The two acting jobs that really changed how people saw me were *Raven* and *Four Idle Hands*. I don't think I'd been seen on TV very much before then, and you're not exactly going to get recognized in the street for being in a play upstairs at the Royal Court. But *Raven* was something that really got me noticed.

It started out as another of those fish–out–of–water narratives, with me playing an inner-city orphan who'd moved out into the sticks to live with some old professor. He was a lovely guy, Michael Aldridge, who played the professor – we both loved cricket, so we used to talk about that a lot between takes. The way the story progressed was that a nuclear power-plant was gonna be built in that part of the country, and the professor was against it, and I was against it, and all of a sudden I sort of turned into King Arthur reincarnated, and ended up saving the world from nuclear power.

Raven was only a six-parter, but it really gave me a chance to act. The two guys who wrote it, Jeremy Burnham and Trevor Ray, were both actors and I think that helped with the script. My character was quite oikish at the start (I wasn't trying to play him like one of *The Tomorrow People* – Mike Holoway and all that lot: they really were from another planet) but that worked really well when we got into the more mystical bits. The whole thing was definitely a one-off. It was quite left wing, for a start, which was unusual for a kids' drama on ITV.

The same was true of *Four Idle Hands*. It was another six-part series, but this time with me and Ray Burdis playing two guys who left school with no qualifications, and each week went to the job centre and got a different temporary job. We were more or less the same age as the kids we were playing – I think we were fifth years at the time – which helped a lot, and the writer John Kane did a really good job of making the dialogue seem authentic.

The comedy in the story was us struggling to get to grips with all these different jobs: one week we'd be skin-divers, and the next we'd be working in a factory. And after work we'd meet up in this café (I think George Innes played the owner). Obviously it was a little bit contrived, but the underlying theme was quite serious – it was about kids not having proper jobs to go into after leaving school.

People really loved *Four Idle Hands*, but ATV said they weren't going to make another series because the subject matter was 'too depressing' and because that kind of thing would never happen. Jim Callaghan was prime minister by then, and mass unemployment was starting to become a reality, so they were way off the mark there. I suppose it was even more ironic than that: Ray and I did too good a job of putting across the reality of short-term employment, so we got made redundant.

A lot of the people whose work I was performing at that time – from Stephen Poliakoff and Nigel Williams in the theatre to the writers of *Raven* and *Four Idle Hands* on TV – seemed to have sussed out that there was trouble ahead. But for me the looming clouds of social and economic turbulence definitely had a silver lining. I was certainly getting a lot of good parts out of them.

It wasn't exactly a stretch for me to play someone leaving school at sixteen without any qualifications, as that was definitely the way I was heading. Once I'd done a couple of TV series I sort of forgot about school, really, and just treated it with contempt. My reports would always say, 'His extracurricular activities are not helping his schoolwork,' but to me at that time going to school was an extracurricular activity.

I was in a band, I was acting in plays – those were the things I wanted to do. I remember having to go and see the careers officer and telling him, 'I've already got a job, mate.' I was on the West End stage (well, not quite, but as good as).

There was a bit of drama done at Rutherford, but it was more kind of am-dram. The best thing we did was making a film called *Superkid*, which we shot on a Super 8 camera in Regent's Park with my old friend Mr Meehan. 'Mass media', I think that class was called. It would probably be called media studies now, but either way it was the perfect subject for me. He was a very progressive teacher, Mr Meehan. I think he's high up in the education authority now – still doing sterling work for young people.

If you had told me at that point that I was going to end up being a professional actor, I'd still have been quite surprised. I wasn't the class actor in the way that you have a class clown – the kid who everyone thinks is going to end up a comedian (though most people who actually are comedians will tell you that they weren't the class clown, either). If I didn't make it as a footballer, or a rock star, I probably had the idea of being a social worker lurking somewhere in the back of my mind 'cos I was a bit of a leftie.

That last option really was a bit of a long shot, as by the time exams came along I just wasn't interested any more. My English CSE is the only one I can actually remember turning up for. Once I got there I just wrote some massive poem instead of the essay I was supposed to do. It was an epic but they still failed me for it. I got no marks for it at all.

Anna Scher had let the beast of creativity out of its cage: that was the problem. By then I was doing what I wanted to do and not much else. I was pretty disciplined within that framework, though. From the first time I went to Anna's and realized it was up to us whether we came back or not, I was really rigorous about keeping up with it.

Once I'm not forced into something, I'm much more likely to do it properly, and however much other stuff I had going on I'd always try and make it up there for her and Charles's classes. At the age of fourteen or fifteen I moved from the young actors' group on Tuesdays and Thursdays to the professional group on a Friday. And as we got a bit older we started going to the pub round the corner afterwards, which gave us even more of an incentive.

The funny thing about leaving school was, I never really formally did it. I'd sort of left to do an acting job and sort of hadn't. I turned up one day when I would have been in the sixth form and one of the teachers asked me what on earth I was doing there. I said, 'I think I'm still at school,' and he told me that, as far as I was concerned, school was over. So that was it: goodbye to Ballsache High.

I think I'd somehow got the idea that while I was still at school I couldn't get taxed on my earnings, but that I would be the minute I left. It was a good job that teacher broke the news to me, otherwise I'd have been turning up at Rutherford a couple of times a year till I was forty, in the misguided belief that as long as I carried on doing so, no one would ever tax me.

14: 'DAVID BAILEY –
WHO'S HE?'

Once we'd turned sixteen, Anna Scher relaxed her rules about us not being allowed to do adverts. This meant I was able to do the very first Olympus Trip TV ad with Alan Parker, which was quite a big money job. It was me and Bryan Pringle. He was a wedding photographer with a big old camera that kept going wrong. I had to say, ''Ere, why don't you try this Olympus Trip?' But he wasn't having any of it – 'Oh no, son, the old ways are best.' Then, to prove how much more clued up I was than him, I pointed out David Bailey and said, 'You know who that is? It's David Bailey,' and Bryan went, 'David Bailey – who's he?'

David Bailey only had a couple of lines but he had terrible trouble remembering them. He had to do it word by word in the end, like one of the contestants on *America's Next Top Model*. It was quite funny, that advert, though, looking back – because, although it seemed to be playing on the generation gap, it really showed a kind of continuity. And what with me and David Bailey in front of the cameras and Alan Parker – who grew up at the rougher end of Islington – behind them, you had three generations of working-class Londoners (kind of) made good.

It didn't always look like things were going to turn out that way in the weeks and months after I left school, though I sort of did my acting jobs and sat around on my arse in between. My mum and dad told me to go and get a proper job and I thought, 'Why not?' I liked to have a bit of money on a Friday night, and I'd always seen my dad work hard with his hands, so I had no objection to it from that angle.

First off, I worked in Woolworths for about a week before some geezer accused me of nicking a can of Coke that I'd actually bought from the shop over the road, so that was the end of that one. Next up I got a job at John Bell & Croydon, which is a famous chemist in Wigmore Street. I was goods inwards, basically – put on your brown coat and go and sweep up down in the basement. I didn't help myself to the drugs like they do in *Quadrophenia*, but for some reason I never expected to be there for long – I was always knew an acting job would come along at some point.

Not all the acting jobs we got offered were the kind you'd want to take, though. I remember there was this one guy who wanted to do a play 'about hugging'. He came along to one of our sessions and we all had to get up and hug each other for him. He said he wanted us to 'feel the ball of warmth growing, growing and growing', and a few of us got chosen to go to his house for an audition for the next stage of his play.

So we all went up this bloke's flat in Hampstead. It was me, Martin Phillips, John Blundell, Ray Burdis and one or three others who I've not remembered. I do know we made an uneven number, because he always got to have a go when we changed partners.

Some of us had already been in *Class Enemy* and most of us would soon be in *Scum* (Martin Phillips ended up playing the weak guy who slashes his wrists, but in real life he used to do kung-fu and was as tough as any of us), so we weren't really to be trifled with. Still, I remember we all felt a bit wary, hiding along the wall of the room when the bloke told us all to pick a partner, and quickly jumped in with each other so as not to get left with him. Martin Phillips got lumbered. When we'd all been hugging for a while, 'feeling that ball of warmth growing, growing, growing' (I don't think that was the only thing growing), you could see the sweat running down this bloke's head.

We all left and he wanted Martin to stay behind, but Martin (very sensibly) wouldn't. So we went back and told Anna and she gave the bloke his marching orders. People often see the world of the child actor as quite a vulnerable, sexualized one, and I'm sure sometimes it can be, but that was as close as we ever got to anything perverted.

I suppose it helped that we always seemed to be in a gang. I think the idea of groups of feral youths getting together is one society has always found troubling – from football hooligans to Victorian street-gangs – and in the atmosphere of social unease that prevailed in the mid to late seventies this was more true than ever. I presume that was one reason why dramatists were always writing for groups of us, but the gang also gives you a ready-made setting for conflict, as individual characters emerge and come into competition with each other.

When I was a bit younger – I think I'd just turned sixteen – I did a one-off TV drama based on a Graham Greene short story. *The Destructors*, it was called. This old man goes on holiday and me and this gang of kids dismantle his house completely while he's away. It was brilliant fun to do, 'cos they found an old house that was going to be demolished anyway and we just completely smashed it up. There are scenes of us taking all the floorboards apart and then fixing a chain to the back of a car to pull a wall down; when the guy comes back there's nothing left but rubble.

Michael Apted directed it. He's another one of those directors who were happy to employ me at the beginning of his career but looked elsewhere when the real money started to come in. I don't know if that says anything about me, but either way he seemed to lose my number when the time came to cast his Bond film.

Obviously the daddy of all films about gangs of violent kids is *Scum*. It was a bit of a funny one, though, because the version most people know is the one that came out in the cinema shortly after *Quadrophenia*. The original *Scum* was done as a BBC *Play for Today* a few years previously. It got banned at the time, so it wasn't allowed to be shown on TV till years afterwards, but the BBC came to their senses in the end, and you can get it on DVD now anyway.

I know this because I had to watch it again to do the DVD commentary. One of the reasons I think the TV version is better than the film is that we're all the right age for it, whereas three years later we've all bulked up a bit, and we look more like grown-up prisoners than kids in a borstal. We were all really young in the first one. I must've been sixteen or seventeen. I was cultivating a bit of a bumfluff moustache at the time, and the pre-punk long hair is superb. That was my normal look, I'm proud to say.

As I've said, the Anna Scher contingent in *Scum* was near enough the same mob who were in *Class Enemy* (and who would've been in the hugging play, had things turned out differently). Me, Ray Burdis, John Blundell, Martin Phillips, a guy called Herbert Norville – he's the one who goes, 'Cindy's dead.' ('Oh, your dog?' 'No, my wife.') Obviously it's quite dark, *Scum*, but there are some funny lines in it.

'Why am I so far away from my family?' ''Cause you murdered that kid.' That's another one. It's Perry Benson who says that – Peritos Bentitos, as I call him – he's a good mate of mine to this day.

The big difference in *Scum* was Ray Winstone, who had gone to proper stage-school but got kicked out. I think Ray had kind of knocked the acting on the head by the time *Scum* came along, though, and was working for a butcher or on a market stall or something. But the director, Alan Clarke, went and found him and talked him into doing it. Good job, too.

He was very hard-hitting, Clarkey, which definitely made him the right man for the job as far as *Scum* was concerned. He was from Liverpool originally, and was a bit of a scally himself, so he knew what he was talking about. Luckily he didn't pack the cast with Scousers (though Tarby would have made a great screw – he'd have looked good, with the old sideburns). I think he (Alan Clarke that is, not Tarby) tried to pull Anna Scher once (you couldn't blame him; she was quite nice) and there's all these famous stories of him hanging drunkenly off the balcony at the BBC club, and generally being the *enfant terrible* of BBC directors.

It was very rigorous on the set, though. He was very strict about you knowing your lines and always being on time. You didn't want to be turning up at Charing Cross late and missing your train to Redhill. It was horrible, the place we were filming in. I think it used to be an old people's home. I always remember we didn't have dressing rooms, so we had to get changed in these communal changing areas (I'm not sure what they'd have been there for – maybe they used to make the old people play competitive sports).

Looking back, it was a bit like spending the day at bloody borstal, really, except you got better dinners – just about – and you got paid for it. There was a lot of marching down corridors and a lot of drilling. We loved those borstal-shirts, though. We always used to nick those – I think I've still got one somewhere.

It's snowing in one of the shots, and we're all standing outside. It's a really odd old building – a right old shit-hole. I think it's still there. If you go on the train on the way to Redhill, you can see it on your right-hand side. It'd cost you a few million quid if you went on *Grand Designs* and tried to do that one up for a family of four. And you'd probably still end up with Kevin McCloud telling you it lacked integrity.

We love that programme at my house – especially when he joins in with the bricklaying or whatever, because he's so useless at DIY. He's the last person you'd want helping you.

He'd have got short shrift from Alan Clarke, that's for sure. You had to get it right for Clarkey. Over and over again. We all loved him, but he was one for a lot of takes. You'd do a good one first or second time out, then he'd gradually grind you down – by the time you were on take number twelve or thirteen you'd be getting a bit fed up, so you might do one really pissed off and angry. I think he did it deliberately.

Obviously the main difference between film and stage acting is that on film you just need one good take, so your mindset is different. Or at least it should be. But directors often want you to do a lot of takes – either to make sure they've got plenty of options, or (as I think it was with Alan) because they think doing more improves an actor's performance.

Now I don't mind that, and with Clarkey it was part of the deal that you were going to do a lot of takes and he was going to pick the bones out of them. But there's a real art in film-making where you can do a bit and then you don't have to go right back to the beginning to do the next bit; you just move on incrementally. But in *Scum* there was no way of doing that, even if Alan had been temperamentally inclined to, because there's so much hand-held camerawork.

With the hand-held cameras some poor geezer would be staggering round after you the whole time, with another one hanging on behind him, and this means you've always got to go back to the beginning of the scene to do a new take: because it shakes too much to mix and match different takes. It looks really good on the screen, but it's much easier now they've got Steadicam, which is smoother, so you don't have to do it all in one go the whole time. I'm sure David Bailey would agree with me on that one.

15: THE SCUM ALSO RISES

I've always got on really well with Ray Winstone, and we've been in a few things together over the years. But while we were making *Scum* Alan Clarke kept him and us Anna Scher boys as far apart as he could. He made sure we were all working well together, so we felt like we were running the show, but he kept Winstone at a distance from us so it would have more impact when he came in and took over.

He did that kind of thing a lot, Alan – he'd take you to one side and say, 'You're a good actor, don't let him do that to you.' It's a tricky old business, that sort of manipulation. A lot of directors do it, but you've got to judge it really well – and sometimes Clarkey took it a bit too far. I minded more by the time we made the second film, but first time round I didn't give a shit. I was happy to be there, and we enjoyed being given the freedom to smash things up – like at those schools where they let you do what you like, as part of your education.

It was all very sweaty and male already, and when these kids we didn't know came in for the murder-ball scene, the whole thing went up a notch. I think they were from some kind of youth club in Leytonstone. I don't know what Alan had said to them, but as the director he obviously wanted to make the film as best as he could – and the best way of doing that was to make the black versus white divide as clear as possible, and to have a real fight. So that was pretty much what happened.

We were left to fend for ourselves on that one. None of us complained, though, because we all fancied ourselves. It wasn't that bad
at first – just a few bruises and punches thrown, maybe – but the
second take got a lot more severe, and there was a bit of kung-fu
going on. There was a geezer on Ray Winstone's back, and I
remember him telling everybody afterwards, 'Phil helped me out.' I
always liked Ray for that, because it made me sound hard. Not as
hard as Ray Winstone, but I did help him out.

It was funny in those days, the way I always seemed to get cast as
the harder, more evil characters, even though I was a lot smaller than
most of the Anna Scher mob. My *Scum* character, Richards, had two
nicknames – 'Slasher' and 'Stripey' – that's how much of a bad boy
he was. He was always saying things like, 'When I get out of here I'm
gonna carve you two up, first chance I get.' That bit where he ran-
domly throws hot tea in some kid's face is just the sort of thing I'd
come up with on the spur of the moment. We'd do a lot of that sort
of stuff at Anna's (though not using actual scalding liquid, of course).

I'd see it at school – people trying to be tough – and then translate
it into improvisations. Watching *Scum* it's vital that you believe that
these are the kinds of people they are. Slasher was probably always
gonna be in jail. And of the rest of his little gang, Eckersley was the
manipulative type and Pongo was the big brute. The three of us
jump on Ray's bed and beat him up, then he gets us back one by one.

The scene everyone always remembers is where Ray gets me with
the snooker balls. In the second film I never come back after that –
I was damaged enough – but in the first film I do. The snooker balls
were actually ping-pong balls in papier-mâché, but they still left a
mark when Ray gave you a whack with them.

There's a switch in the scene that let us do it all in one take. After
Ray picked up the real snooker balls and put them in one sock, Little
Johnny Fowler was sitting there with another sock in his hand; and
as Ray walked past they swapped 'em over, using sleight of hand. Then
he smacked me with the lighter one. It's more Paul Daniels than Phil
Daniels, really.

The main difference in the casting between the first and second films is that in the original one it's David Threlfall who plays the clever, rebellious character that Mick Ford plays later on. He's a good guy, David, and very friendly. He's a good footballer, too. Shame he's a Man City fan. He's the dad in *Shameless* now, getting all the plaudits as a drunken old bum.

I was meant to be in another Poliakoff play with him around that time. *Shout Across the River*, it was called, for the RSC, but I was up for a big film part at the time – I think it must've been *Zulu Dawn* – and the deal was that if I got it, I'd do that instead. That was supposed to be the first time I worked with Mike Leigh as well, because he was meant to be doing another play for the RSC which would use roughly the same company.

That one never happened, though. You can imagine what theatre companies are like: everyone was always talking about what they were going to be doing – telling each other, 'I'm playing a postman,' or whatever – and no one's meant to know anything in the early stages of a Mike Leigh project, because it gets ruined if you tittle-tattle. He's very tough, Mike, but he's also very sensitive.

I think I upset him by saying on one of those *100 Best Films* programmes on Channel 4 that I still thought *Meantime* was his best work. After Phil Davis saw it he told me, 'You shouldn't have done that, he's very sensitive.' But it's only the same thing Mike said himself on the *Meantime* DVD.

The original *Play for Today* script for *Scum* was written by Roy Minton, and I think he and Alan Clarke maybe had a bit of a falling out during the filming, but they still worked on the second film together so it can't have been that bad. Obviously the second one probably wouldn't have got made without all the fuss that was caused by the banning of the first.

Looking back at the original *Scum* now, it's the racial stuff which feels the most shocking at first. In a way, that was probably already a bit outdated, and I've always thought that the play was maybe written with a slightly earlier period than the mid to late seventies in mind. The time it's set in is never really made explicit, and by then Ray would never have got away with telling Baldy to 'rub some coal dust on that', however hard he was, because the black kids would've already been running the borstals.

We used to have a laugh with Peter Francis, who played Baldy. I think he'd just won UK disco-dancer of the year, and there he was politely standing still while Ray smacked him over the head with a metal pipe. Talk about a change in career direction. I think he'd have been a bit quicker on his feet in real life.

Apart from that, I think Clarkey did a brilliant job. He got the right kind of actors, and by the end of the original *Scum* you really feel the same way we did – like you've been shut up somewhere you didn't want to be for a little bit too long.

That rape scene is really horrible. I'd forgotten it was in the first film – I thought it was just something they added to the second one to cause a bit of extra controversy. It's the screw looking on with that strange expression on his face – like he's enjoying it – that makes it feel so graphic. I suppose because it makes you ask yourself what you're doing sitting there watching something like that happening.

I would like to put it on the record now, for anyone who hasn't seen either version of *Scum*, or who has but would rather not remember the details, that I am not in the rape scene. There is no bumming from Slasher, Pongo or Eckersley. Although I think Ossie – the main protagonist, the Greek-looking one – is one of Anna's boys. But the Greeks invented that kind of thing, didn't they? They're famed for it. 'Anyone know how to bum? Fetch the Greek boy.'

Strangely, I don't think it was either the racism or the rape scene that really got *Scum* banned. There's a scene in it where a magistrate comes round and asks, 'Are they treating you well?' And all the boys say, 'Yes, they're treating us very well,' because they know what'll happen if they say anything else. I think the head of the BBC at the time was an ex-magistrate and that scene struck a bit of a nerve with him, because it reflected all he'd ever seen when he'd gone in to visit borstals. Obviously he'd never been shown the kind of harsh regimes that existed in real life, and so he didn't want the viewers at home seeing that either.

I think that was why they banned it. One of the arguments they used was that the series of events that unfolds in the film would be unlikely to happen in such a short period of time. But that's just what happens when you turn real life into drama – it gets telescoped. A film about World War II doesn't have to last six years, does it?

Besides, their other excuse for banning it was that *Scum* might be mistaken for a documentary (at the time the BBC were very down on any drama that people might 'think was real', though they changed their tune on that one pretty quickly when the docu-soap format came along). And I never really saw how you could hold those two positions at the same time without contradicting yourself.

Anyway, it was pretty disappointing for us when we found out that *Scum* wasn't going to be shown. I don't think anyone phoned us – we just saw it in the papers. I think everyone still got paid OK, though I can't remember how much. And there was a big press campaign about it afterwards. A lot of left-wing journalists kicked up a stink, and they probably had a chat about it on whatever the equivalent of *Newsnight* was, but that only made the BBC more determined not to give in. Another fourteen years passed before they finally showed it, by which time everyone had forgotten what all the fuss was about – which I suppose was exactly what the BBC would have wanted when they banned it in the first place.

Another film I made at around that time was *The Class of Miss MacMichael*, with Glenda Jackson and Oliver Reed. It wasn't banned, but it probably should've been. There were a few of us from Anna Scher's in that as well. We were all meant to be kids at a school for the educationally subnormal. Glenda Jackson was a conscientious teacher who wanted to do as much as she could for the kids in her care, and Oliver Reed was the cynical headmaster who did everything in his power to stop her.

The whole thing had obviously been set up as a vehicle for him and her to do their things, but it wasn't exactly *Women in Love* revisited. More like a knock-off version of *The Fenn Street Gang*. If ever you are unlucky enough to see *The Class of Miss MacMichael*, it's like watching two films at once. Glenda Jackson is doing it as kind of a crusade and being a very serious actress, but Oliver Reed is just doing it as an out-and-out Ealing comedy. Looking back, I think the latter approach was probably the more appropriate.

We made it in an old Victorian school in Old Ford, near Victoria Park in East London, so in that regard *The Class of Miss MacMichael* was pretty authentic, but in other respects it was a bit like those old *Top of the Pops* albums where the songs weren't sung by the real artists. The producer was this American guy called Judd, who brought lots of Americans into the cast and made us all go to watch this basketball match and have a bit of a riot.

The film's attitude to people with learning difficulties was not what you'd call enlightened (when it finally came out the poster read: '*The Class of Miss MacMichael*: they're Punks, Vandals, Thieves, Scrubbers, Loonies'). But in one way it was a bit too authentic.

As I've mentioned, Anna Scher used to take on people whom social services thought might benefit from her classes. There was one kid who was already a bit nutty, and he got a part playing a nutty kid, and it was all a bit much for him. It wasn't a very good idea to be encouraging him to be a lunatic when that was exactly what he was trying to stop being in real life; and when they told him to 'be professional' and stop when the scene was over, he didn't really get the message.

I liked Oliver Reed a lot, though. He was nutty as well, but in a good way. I remember turning up one day when the rest of the kids weren't in – I think I'd been chosen to show some visitors around the school or something. It was only about half past seven in the morning when I went into one of the classrooms, and Oliver Reed was sitting there with a big crate of beer beside him. He said, 'Let's take the edge off,' and we had a beer together. Happy days.

I had my eighteenth birthday on that shoot. And when Oliver

Reed found out he gave me £100 (which was a lot of money in 1976) for us all to go to some pub in Old Ford and get drunk.

There's a funny moment in the film where Glenda Jackson (who at the time of writing is still claiming her maximum London expenses supplement as Labour MP for Hampstead, having gone from being my onscreen teacher to my parliamentary representative) catches me and this nice red-haired girl up to a bit of mischief in the headmaster's office. Life imitated art a bit in that respect. There were a couple of nice girls in that film and a bit of canoodling happened on the set after hours, which was quite fun.

The only other good thing about *The Class of Miss MacMichael* is that Renoir got to do the theme tune. I had a song called 'Playing in Lifts', which I changed to 'Playing in Schools'. I realize that looks quite random written down, but it worked really well for the film. I put this line in it: 'It's all right till you're ten, then it's all ESN [educationally subnormal, as we used to call it]', which pretty much summed up what the whole thing was meant to be about.

There's a bit in the film where a guy is listening to a song coming out of his transistor radio, and by the time they'd added the soundtrack it was 'Anarchy in the KP' – Renoir's response to punk rock. We never got much credit for these musical contributions, though. I got hold of the film on video off eBay a while back to see if it was as bad as I remembered (it was) and the box says 'Music by the Manhattens'. I don't know who the Manhattens were when they were at home.

16: INSIDE BOB HOSKINS'
MUD HUT

I went to Austria with the school once, when I was fifteen or sixteen — skiing. Well, we never actually went skiing, because if you didn't know how to do it already, you had to go and learn. Fuck that. We just used to get our own sledges to mess about on in the daytime and then in the evenings we went on the piste. Other than that, by the time I was eighteen years old I'd hardly left England at all. Then I got this part in *Zulu Dawn*, and the next thing I knew I was off to South Africa for ten weeks.

The director was a guy called Douglas Hickox, who was very old school and had done a few things and now has a British Independent Film Award named after him. My part was the Boy Pullen, who was the bugler. I tried to learn but never quite got the hang of it, so I ended up just holding it to my lips while someone just out of shot played 'The Last Post'. In retrospect I like to think of him as a kind of stunt double in reverse. I still got to keep the bugle afterwards, though. I think my mum's got it now.

When I was young I never paid much attention to who anyone else was, or what they'd been in before — I was too busy doing my own thing. Normally I'd be in with a gang of people I knew from Anna Scher as well. But *Zulu Dawn* was one of the first times I'd gone off to do something without that kind of back-up. And it had people in it that even I'd heard of.

Peter O'Toole and Burt Lancaster, for a start, which quite impressed my mum and dad. Dai Bradley, who was Kes – he was the young soldier. And this was the first time I met Bob Hoskins, who I think had maybe done Dennis Potter's *Pennies from Heaven* by then, and was just really starting to get going in his career. Then there was Simon Ward. If you couldn't get Michael York in those days, you got Simon Ward (there was one actor at the time who was above even Michael York in the food chain, but I can't remember who that was).

Anyway, there were a lot of big stars in *Zulu Dawn*; and, if the original *Zulu* was anything to go by, it was going to be massive. I'd just done *The Class of Miss MacMichael* – jumping on school roofs in Old Ford – and now I was going to the other side of the world to be in a proper historical epic. Apartheid was still at its height at the time, so a few people said I shouldn't do it, but I was at an age where you feel you need to see things for yourself, so I sort of thought, 'Sod it, I'm going to go and see what's going on first hand.' Whatever the rights and wrongs of that decision, the trip was a political education in itself.

They flew us to Durban first, and put us up in a five-star hotel. I remember that the day I got there I was wearing a jacket I'd bought from Lord John. It was grey and had a picture of a cat on the lapel. It was a bit like a Harrington, but made out of hessian. When I turned up at the hotel this young black dude who worked there and had to carry my bag said, 'I like your jacket,' and I said, 'Well, if you can get me some dope, I'll give it to you.' He told me to give him my holdall, so I emptied it out and handed it over. Two hours later he came back with the bag full of Durban Poison.

I gave him the jacket and phoned up Hoskins and two other actors called Paul Copley and Nicholas Clay, who I'd also started to get a bit matey with. Nicholas was a few years older than me – he must have been twenty-six, twenty-seven, whereas I was eighteen or nineteen – but he was a really cool guy, and he kind of took me under his wing (we became good friends in the end – I went to his wedding and everything – but sadly he died really young). So there was him, Copley, Hoskins and me in Hoskins' room. They'd been talking about maybe getting a bit of puff, but when I opened up my holdall and said, 'All right then, have a look at this,' everybody basically shat themselves.

We had a bit of a smoke and sat around staring at each other for a while, then very quickly began to get paranoid that the Secret Service would be after us. This stuff was so strong – it was just like heads of the purest dope, basically – that you couldn't smoke much of it at once. Which was a good job, really, as the hotel was so lovely it would've been a shame to have been too stoned to enjoy it.

I'd never been anywhere as smart as this before. I had a giant room. I'd taken my guitar with me and I didn't have to do any work for about twelve days. So I pretty much just sat by the pool eating steak sandwich after steak sandwich after steak sandwich to get acclimatized. It was one of the best holidays I've ever had.

The first actual shooting we did was in a place called Newcastle, which was a bit of a dump. I went off there with Peter Vaughan (who was Wolfie's father-in-law in *Citizen Smith*, among many other things) for a couple of nights. He was playing the quartermaster, who was kind of meant to be my old sweat. (In the film I'm always looking up to him for advice and saying things like, 'Do we have weaknesses, quartermaster?') He looked after me in real life as well.

Where we were staying in Newcastle there were a lot of South African journalists hanging around, trying to find out why we were there and what we were doing. There was a lot of hostility towards us. It was very unusual to have any kind of major foreign film production going on at that point. The British weren't liked anyway, and the fact that the subject matter was the colonial period only added to the tension.

I think some of the journalists singled me out a bit, and were trying to get information out of me because they could see I was only a kid, and I remember Peter Vaughan walking up to one of them, taking the guy's glasses off, putting them on the ground and saying, 'I never hit a man with glasses on.' He's a big fella, Vaughny, and they backed off a bit after that.

The funny thing was, the whole story of the film was really anti-British anyway. It's the prequel to *Zulu*, which means the English get massacred because Lord Chelmsford is too busy having his breakfast to listen to everybody telling him the Zulus are coming (Peter O'Toole was perfect for the part of Chelmsford – he was really good at all the dismissive stuff). Then afterwards the victorious tribesmen go off to fight Michael Caine in *Zulu*. I suppose the implicit black-power message didn't go down too well with the South Africans either.

The second place we went to film was Pietermaritzberg, so we were staying in hotels there as well. All our drivers were black guys. We went out drinking with them one night – me, Bob, Copley and Nick Clay, always the same gang – and the police turned up and said, 'You can't do this.' They weren't going to do anything to us – it was the black guys who were going to get in trouble. Basically, it was divide and rule.

The bulk of the filming was done in the places where the battles had actually happened. We went to Isandlwana and Rorke's Drift, and it was fascinating because there were still rusty carriage wheels and bits of old bullet left over from the battle. No one had really been up there since, except the Zulus.

What they did was build a kind of garrison for us out of these Portakabins. Some of the better-known people had little houses. I remember Denholm Elliott had one. He was lovely to me – I remember him telling me he'd just discovered the music of Simon and Garfunkel. He certainly liked all the young boys – and the young girls; he didn't mind. Many a house guest left Denholm's with a cheeky grin.

The Portakabins they brought in for those of us in the lower orders were pretty plain, so I got these Zulu guys to paint mine all these stunning African colours. I got told off for doing it, but my hut was fucking brilliant. Hoskins went one further and had a proper mud hut built. Every night we'd go in Hoskins' mud hut and have a bit of a smoke. Mud huts are ideal for that because you're all sitting round the fire in the middle: if you want to join in the conversation, you simply lean in, but if you'd rather just lie on your back and feel a bit stoned, then that's OK too.

There was a strange feeling that we were allowed to do all these things, even though we were sort of being supervised as well. Everything was kind of on the edge. We had this black South African army guy (which was a strange one in itself at the time) who was posted with Bob to keep an eye on us. Once you were in Hoskins' mud hut, pretty much anything went, and the army guy would be in there smoking with us. But outside it was a very different matter. This copper nearly arrested me for smoking a roll-up once. The police would come in the bar at our billet and they'd want to nick you for everything – especially the Afrikaners; there was not a lot of love lost between them and the English.

Hoskins had a big beard, then, and looked a bit like Brian Blessed does now. He was quite hippiefied, but in a really strong way. His girlfriend at the time – this woman called Sue, who was as anarchic as he was – she was out there staying with him. They were a bit older and more politically astute than me, and helped open my eyes to some of the things that were going on. There were a lot of guard-dogs keeping black people out of places – even I could see that. And we got invited to a few parties that were in very securitized mansions.

Even though there was a lot of anti-British feeling, the white South African society still wanted to be recognized in the world outside. That's why things like films being made and rugby tours going over there were such a big deal for them. A friend of mine, John Taylor, who played rugby for Wales and the British Lions (he was in the famous team that beat the All Blacks in New Zealand in 1971), refused to go on the British Lions tour to South Africa in 1974, which was a big decision that I really respected him for making.

Going to South Africa was an amazing experience for me, though. I remember the first day we got out into Zululand. It's really beautiful and lush, with all these green hills around. I was sitting on top of this mountain, giving my guitar a bit of a twang, and

Burt Lancaster walked up to me and introduced himself: 'Hi, I'm Burt.'

'Hi, I'm Phil,' I replied. (It seemed best to keep things straight-forward.) After a few seconds of companionable silence, Burt said, 'It's beautiful here – I've never felt so good in all my life.' He got pneumonia the next day and had to be flown off the set for two weeks to recover. But I would always have my memories.

The physical traces on the old battlefields weren't the only strange echoes of the historical events *Zulu Dawn* was meant to be describ-ing. The Sakhali horsemen that Burt Lancaster was in command of – the ones who would have known how to fight the Zulus if only Peter O'Toole had listened to what Burt was telling him – they were played by real Sakhali horsemen. A handful of black British actors came out with us, but basically the Zulus were played by real Zulus. And, just to throw in that extra element of uncertainty, all the Redcoats apart from us were local prisoners who the producers had managed to get out of jail for a few days by means of striking some deal with the authorities. That was one reason for there being so many extra police and soldiers around – to keep an eye on the white criminal element.

It was quite a combustible mixture, as you can probably imagine. I'll never forget the big battle scene with all the Zulus running at us. They really went for it – it was like murder-ball all over again, only this time on an Imperial scale.

There'd been a lot of problems with recruiting the Zulus. If the pay was too high, too many of them turned up to do the work. When the wages were cut a bit, someone found out that there was a dog in the film who was getting paid more than the Zulus were. I think they had a sit-down protest about that, which you couldn't blame them for. And by the time they were charging at us it wasn't hard to get them motivated.

It was interesting how the same stark racial and social dividing lines that were the subject of the film kept recurring in the produc-tion itself. For example, Peter O'Toole was very enigmatic and was constantly being wined and dined and waited on in this hotel that we called the Babanango Hilton. Just like Lord Chelmsford would've been, had he been an actor. Whereas us lot, the Redcoats (well, Hoskins was a sergeant) we were just cannon fodder really. Or spear fodder, in this case.

There was something quite incongruous, though, about us lot being all laid-back and slightly stoned in the middle of this great spectacle of Victorian military discipline. One of the biggest scenes in the whole film was the crossing of Rorke's Drift. There were all these carriages and Redcoats and hundreds of Zulus involved. It took them all day to set it up, with different cameras everywhere, but then, when someone looked at the rushes of the day's main shots, they saw that Hoskins had a pair of sunglasses on, so they had to shoot the whole thing again. Minus Bob's shades this time, of course.

17: TONY SHER STICKS
HIS OAR IN

The funny thing about Bob Hoskins' mud hut was, it had a telephone in it. One morning I got a call on that phone, telling me that I had an audition lined up when I got home for some film called *Quadrophenia*. But this news hardly registered with me at the time, 'cos I was too busy making the most of the time I had left in South Africa.

I remember we went on one trip to Richard's Bay and swam in the water where you're not meant to – where the sharks are. Another time, me, Hoskins and Nick went off driving and ended up in some field in the middle of nowhere, and suddenly a young bloke appeared with a gun, shouting, 'What are you doing on my land?' Luckily, when we explained who we were he got a bit friendlier and invited us back to his homestead. Well, he said it was his, but just as we arrived at the house his mum and dad turned up – which was a bit embarrassing, although they were quite nice in the end and gave us a cup of tea. There were quite a few times like that, when situations that looked like they were about to get very edgy kind of turned out all right.

Basically we were like a load of hippies who'd been dropped into the middle of this very reactionary atmosphere. You could kind of already feel that apartheid was on borrowed time (it just turned out that there was quite a lot of that borrowed time left), and that made the people who were benefiting from it very jumpy.

Durban was lovely, mind. I've never been back since, but I'd be really interested to go some time and see how different the new South Africa feels. The World Cup might be the one – though I recently saw a TV programme on security men in Jo'burg that suggested watching it at home on the sofa might be the safer option.

Boy Pullen, the character I was playing in *Zulu Dawn*, was essentially a child soldier, but most of the white South Africans of my own age I met out there looked at me like I was some kind of weirdo because I hadn't been in the army. They were all a bit muscly and brainwashed because they'd had to do national service. But if I'd been born in Durban instead of London then that would have been my fate also.

It's easy to join in with anything if you're eighteen. If they tell you to join the army, you're probably going to do it, if only for an easy life. Even in terms of me accepting the part and agreeing to go to South Africa in the first place, you could see that tendency in operation. There wasn't a massive 'don't go' thing going on in Britain at the time, and I like to think that Anna Scher – who was really left wing – wouldn't have let me do it if it wasn't OK, but still, I only listened to the advice I wanted to hear.

By the time I got home I'd had my eyes opened a bit, politically. There was a lot of hypocrisy and self-righteousness about South Africa in Britain in those days. Especially given the historical role we'd played in making that country what it was. Even though I was still quite naïve, I could see that it was much easier to be critical of others if you didn't make the mental effort to imagine yourself in their position. 'Hey, man, what are you wearing for the race riots?' That's what they used to say to the liberals in South Africa, meaning: 'You're a liberal now; but when it all comes down to it, which side are you going to be on?'

While the battle lines weren't quite as clearly drawn back in the UK, the Britain I returned to in 1978 was certainly an increasingly polarized place. The Winter of Discontent was just around the corner, and, even though you'd have had to be psychic to know that at the time (Jim Callaghan's Labour government certainly didn't see it coming), the atmosphere in London was pretty tense. Even without punk rock overturning the tables and throwing bits of cake around, the Silver Jubilee street-party atmosphere was never going to last.

Before I came home, when I was writing my anti-apartheid protest song (I know it's a bit of a cliché, but it had to be done), I could see that whatever was wrong in South Africa, London was part of it. There was no point in pretending the two places weren't connected, and that trip had definitely broadened my political horizons. I must have been a bit homesick as well, because some of the first lines in the song were 'London, London, I miss you/Though my pen is black, my words are blue'.

Not long after coming back, I did another Stephen Poliakoff play – this time at the ICA. *American Days*, it was called, and it was all about these three kids trying to make it in the music industry. I was a sort of Billy Bragg figure (even though no one knew who Billy Bragg was yet – I suppose that was Poliakoff doing his crystal-ball thing again). I got to write and sing my own protest song about Northern Ireland on my acoustic guitar ('Northern Ireland/ Let's go to war/ Their accents are magic/The reason a bore').

I remember Anthony Sher was in that play as well, and one day he saw the old South African Airlines 'Fragile' sticker on my guitar case and told me to take it off. Given that he was gay, Jewish, and a liberal – three things that didn't go down too well in his South African homeland at the time – he had every right to have strong opinions on the issue, so I was happy to follow his guidance. But Tony Sher and I would have another heated ideological debate a few years later, and next time it would be me who was in the right.

The plot of *American Days* was basically that three kids were auditioning for one recording contract. The kids were played by me, Toyah and Caroline Embling. It'd probably look a bit dated in the *X-Factor* era, but it worked OK at the time.

I hated the fact that I didn't get the contract at the end, though (I can't remember which one of the other two did – Caroline couldn't really sing, but she might have got it for looking pretty). That said, in a few months' time we'd be doing *Quadrophenia*, in which I'd be spurning Toyah's advances and Caroline would be one of the two schoolgirls on the train who look at Jimmy and go, 'Ooohh!' – so it all evened itself out in the end.

When I'd gone off to South Africa, it had felt like the logical next step towards a new phase of being in major international films – 'Oh, I'm in the movies now.' But *Zulu Dawn* didn't quite work out the way everybody hoped. We had a theory that they were making this huge expensive film in South Africa as a way of spending money there which they could then recoup in Europe. (I don't think you were allowed to take South African currency out of the country at that time.)

On paper, this was quite a clever way of moving cash about, but in practice the scheme had one quite serious flaw. *Zulu Dawn* didn't make any money in Europe. They thought it was gonna be the last epic, but actually it was the film after the last epic. That whole time had kind of gone. They'd already done *Zulu*, which was massive – but in *Zulu* we won, and in this one we lost, and films where you lose ain't very good.

They had a few of us signed up to do another big film with the same director straight afterwards. It was going to be about terrorists at an airport. An actor called Barry Foster was going to be the copper and I was going to be the terrorist. I'd been on £250 a week for *Zulu Dawn* – two and a half grand altogether – which was already pretty good money for essentially being on holiday, and I was going to get four times as much for this new film.

Around the time *Zulu Dawn* came out Dougie Hickox asked me to come to his office. When I got there, he said, 'All right, what's the worst thing that could happen?' I said, 'We're not doing the film?' And he said, 'That's right.' I'd already spent the ten grand in my head, and I remember thinking, 'Why did you have to call me all the way in here just to tell me that?' I suppose by telling me in person he was just trying to do the right thing. He was a nice old boy, who had been really good to me.

These days when I go somewhere I might end up signing a few autographs because of *Quadrophenia* or *Meantime* or *EastEnders*, but it's rare that someone will come up as a *Zulu Dawn* fan, and if they do it's generally some old military historian. I think if you're one of those people you'd see it as a pretty sound representation of what happened – which is that Lord Chelmsford was a career lord, who went out there with his blinkers on and wouldn't listen to anybody.

Back home in Britain, the days of imperial hubris were seeming further off by the minute. The atmosphere around King's Cross was really changing at that point. The council moved everybody out of some of the local flats and houses, saying they were going to knock them all down and rebuild, then – bosh – all of a sudden anyone who wanted to could come in and live in this poor-quality short-let accommodation for £5 a week.

Although they were initially treated as freaks, these people quickly became a big part of the character of the area. The locals didn't like them because they tended to be more like soap-dodger types, but I was doing my own thing by then so I wasn't really bothered. They had a lot of parties, and there were some good people among them, but there were too many drugs around to really be seeing the best of everyone.

The sense of social breakdown that a lot of the plays and TV series I'd been in had been exploring – from *Four Idle Hands* to *Class Enemy* – was coming closer to home. And that seemed to feed back into the kinds of parts I was getting offered. A lot of writers in the mid to late seventies were trying to come to terms with what an openly divided country Britain was becoming. They could pour their words into me, and I could get 'em out and look genuine. And you could sort of feel 'em thinking, 'Thank God we've found some-one who can say this stuff.'

I did a thing called *Speech Day* by Barry Hines, who wrote *Kes* (I think it was with the cinematographer who'd done *Kes* as well). *Speech Day* was done for schools TV and meant putting a uniform on again, which I wasn't too keen on but at least I knew I could forget about wearing a blazer once the shooting was over. Then there was *Hanging Around*, which was like a slightly more hardcore version of *Four Idle Hands*. This was written by Barrie Keeffe, who later wrote *The Long Good Friday*.

It was just about these three geezers – Kip, Rod and Mull – who had nothing to do. They'd all left school and would just sit around on walls all day, and the whole thing was basically about how difficult it was going to be for them to carry on being mates. At a comprehensive everybody did get treated kind of equally, but once you got out into the wider world it was hard for the black kids and the white kids not to go their separate ways.

That was the first time I met Michael Elphick, who was in it as an old Teddy Boy (he couldn't believe it when he ended up playing my dad in *Quadrophenia*, though: he thought he was still too young for that – which in a way kind of worked for the character).

Barrie Keeffe was a proper East Londoner and a good writer. He'd done a play called *Gotcha* with Phil Davis. In terms of stage productions, Phil was more his actor, whereas I was more Nigel Williams' actor. But Barrie was different from Nigel, because he actually came from the territory he was writing about.

It was good to work with him once, but Nigel Williams had another good part up his sleeve for me. It was in a play called *Line 'Em*, about trade unions, which we'd end up doing at the National Theatre a year or so later. My part was this really militant young union guy who was on a picket line when the army turned up. I remember a lot of people saying that the army would never go and disrupt a strike like that – even Irving Wardle, who was one of the wiser theatre critics, said it was a bit far-fetched – but that was exactly what happened during the Miners' Strike just a few years later. OK, technically in that instance it was the police, not the army, but they were *acting* like the army.

A lot of the plays that were written at that time ended up being quite prophetic. In fact, you could say that in the 1980s Margaret Thatcher turned the dystopian nightmares of left-wing 1970s dramatists into government policy.

None of that was on my mind when I first got back from South Africa, though. All I cared about was that I'd got a strange virus out there, which meant I had no energy and my tongue went all yellow and split down the middle. I'd gone to see some South African doctor in the latter stages of the filming, but he'd done sweet FA. I remember going to Johannesburg at the end of the trip, and being ill, and buying my mum a diamond (I think someone knew someone who knew someone – there were a lot of rogues around).

Anyway, by the time I got home, I couldn't really do much other than lie down on the settee. I was still living with my mum and dad in King's Cross then, so I just went to my local doctor and he gave me some antibiotics that cleared it up in the end. But I was still quite sick when I went for my first *Quadrophenia* audition, and as a consequence didn't make a very good job of doing my reading. The fact that I'd chosen to wear a huge pair of pink flared trousers for the occasion and was swearing in Afrikaans a lot probably didn't help.

Even though I'd been away only ten weeks, I think I'd gone a bit native; and I couldn't blame the director, Franc Roddam, for ringing Anna and telling her he wasn't interested. But either she persuaded him or something else encouraged him to let me have another go, 'cos he called me back in the end – and this time I went along with a normal pair of jeans on, and was much more myself.

18: TAXI FOR MR
JOHN LYDON

There was a lot of fuss about who was going to play Jimmy in *Quadrophenia*. I think the *Sun* ran a competition or something, but that was more to drum up a bit of publicity for the film than anything else. In the end, the two other people who made it into the final three were Phil Davis – a really good actor and a great guy, who also taught me to play golf – and John Lydon; who I don't really know.

Lydon had barged into Miles Landesman's house once (before the Sex Pistols turned him into Johnny Rotten) and tried to take over a Renoir rehearsal with this big-bully mate of his who was a bouncer – Steve, I think his name was. But we weren't having any of that.

I didn't actually find out till a bit further down the line that he had done a screen test. Obviously I wouldn't have been too happy about him trying to muscle in on my part the same way he'd once tried to muscle in on my band. But apparently at that point the insurers said they wouldn't cover him, though maybe that was just something Franc Roddam came up with to save John's feelings. He's quite sensitive, apparently, beneath all the bluster.

In some ways, you could see the logic behind the idea of casting Lydon as Jimmy. He'd left the Sex Pistols by that time and was busy trying to sue Malcolm McLaren (I don't think Public Image Limited had really got going yet). So not only would it have been quite a coup in publicity terms, but also, given that the film was set in 1964, and they were making it just after punk – which was supposed to be all about everyone turning their backs on the past – the producers were probably worried that the whole thing was going to seem a bit out of date.

Lydon's involvement would certainly have helped them out in that area, but *Quadrophenia* wouldn't have been anything like the same film if Lydon had done it. It would have all been about him grandstanding the whole time.

My main basis for thinking that I was more right for the role than the other two candidates was how important the album already was to me. I'd always loved that record, and the pictures inside the gate-fold sleeve had already looped the imagery inside my head long before the film was even begun. Because my understanding of the story came through rock 'n' roll, which I'd grown up playing and singing in my own right anyway, I knew that this was a part that I could really do justice to.

When I went up for my final screen-test, I did that scene where Jimmy has just left home and he's pushing his scooter along and it's all about being a mod, and Steph says, 'You can't have a bit of the other without kicking your mate's head in.' The girl I auditioned with was an actress called Wendy Morgan, but obviously it was Leslie Ash who got the part.

Once they decided that I'd got the job, we all had to go and meet the Who at Wembley Studios. I was awestruck, because they were proper rock stars – always have been, haven't they? They've always held themselves a bit aloof. Whatever might have been going on in their lives, you wouldn't see them falling out of places drunk in the papers. Well, maybe Keith Moon would do that sometimes, but he'd always do it with a bit of style.

Later on, when the film was more or less done, I met up with Townshend again – and it was just me this time – for a photoshoot at a Shepherd's Bush pie-and-mash shop. There's a publicity shot that always turns up everywhere of him with his old army coat on and me sat next to him, gurning away.

Once all the roles were allocated, the next phase was to put the gang together and see how we all got on. I'd already done a couple of things with Toyah, and I'd met Phil Davis (who got another good part in the film, and never gave me any hassle about having wanted to be Jimmy) but the only one of them I really knew well was Trevor Laird, who started turning up in the latter stages of my time at Anna Scher's with his great big Afro. We're still great mates to this day, though he's not got quite as much hair now he's fifty-two.

There was a script when we first got there, but it wasn't the finished article. And we did a lot of improvisations before the production got properly under way; a writer called Martin Stellman watched these, then went away for a while and then a much better script turned up. I think I've still got my original script, which I could probably sell for a few quid if I ever needed to.

I remember Sting being quite good in the improvisations. I thought he'd be a bit shy, but he wasn't. He was playing it pretty cool, but that was what he needed to do for the part. And having him in the film definitely ticked some of the same boxes that having Lydon there would've done. The Police weren't yet that big, but they were about to be – and I think their manager, Miles Copeland, and the film's producer, Bill Curbishley (who was also manager of the Who), worked together to make sure the *Quadrophenia* connection worked to everyone's advantage.

You could tell they still had a way to go: during filming they did a gig at Camden Dingwalls which Sting asked me to come down to; I went along and it was not full at all – I remember buying a drink and being able to put it on the stage at half time. They were already doing 'Roxanne', 'Can't Stand Losing You' and all that stuff, though, and they were tight as arseholes; a really top band. I think their big break came a bit later on, when they did *The Old Grey Whistle Test* and Sting wore sunglasses because he'd got himself one in the eye when he was spraying peroxide in his hair.

I'm not sure how the *Quadrophenia* producers knew about them. I suppose Roddam might have seen them play an early gig or two up

North, because he's a Geordie. Well, he's from Stockton-on-Tees, anyway. They're hard up there. You're doing well not to get your head kicked in on a Friday night.

Although some of us had done quite a bit of work, we were all pretty much unknowns really. 'Phil Daniels out of *The Naked Civil Servant* and the Olympus Trip ads' wasn't going to be putting too many bums on seats. But the great thing about *Quadrophenia* was, they took a chance on us. That's very unusual in the film industry. The music business is generally much better at seeing the potential in youth than the movie business is – though maybe not so much back then, as I suppose punk was partly a reaction to the feeling that if you didn't know the right people, you'd never get a chance.

Some of us were really raw, however. Like Mark Wingett, who would take over the part of Iron in the revival of *Class Enemy* a few years later, and then ended up being DI Carver in *The Bill* for years. He was fresh out of the National Youth Theatre and as green as they come – when he improvised all hell broke loose. 'Farkin' 'ell, Jimmy!' – there was a lot of that going on. Ultimately it worked out really well for the film, but he was a bit wild. How else do you think he got the nickname 'Brain Damage'?

I once got told off by Roddam, who said I should look after Mark more and stop competing with him, 'cos I was more of a pro than he was. So I did that. He came and stayed with my mum and dad in King's Cross for a while during the shoot, and we're still good mates to this day.

Quadrophenia was Franc Roddam's first feature film, and he'd previously only done documentaries. I think the one that really made his name was called *Dummy*, about a deaf-and-dumb prostitute in Middlesbrough, so you could tell he wasn't into sugar-coating anything. It was really important to him that everything should feel gritty and authentic, so he put us through quite a lot of what I would later come to think of as Mike Leigh-isms.

For example, he made us go and see this old East London mod guy called Tommy Shelley. The plan was that we'd all sit around taking blues and get out of it to find out what it was like to be a pill'ead. It wasn't a great evening, as I remember it. I think Tommy was a bit worried (perhaps not without reason) that Franc was trying to steal his soul, and he started having a bit of a go at me because he thought I was a bit flash about the fact that I was going to play Jimmy. The more out of their heads everybody became, the worse it got. We ended up having to leave. He must have lived near the river somewhere, 'cos me and Trevor walked miles back along the Thames to get home that night. A proper little pair of Dexy's Midnight Runners we were.

The dancing school was much more fun. We had to learn the Watusi and the Mashed Potato and the Twist and all the other dances that the mods would've been doing to Booker T. and the MGs and the like.

Learning to ride the scooters was the best thing, though. In those days you could ride any bike up to a 125cc with just a provisional licence, so we all got Honda 125s hired for us and they sent us off riding them around London. I couldn't get mine up the stairs of Jessel House, so my dad locked it up for me in the garages round the back of our flats.

Before we were allowed out on the roads we had to go to the Hendon police training school to learn the basics. I remember us all going round in a circle, getting taught how to ride motorbikes by this huge fat copper. He'd clearly taken a bit of a shine to Leslie Ash, 'cos he always had her squeezed in behind on the back of his big Honda. She did have to learn how to ride on the back, obviously, but you could see how much he loved having young Leslie pressed up against him.

Obviously all this practical preparation was helpful, but it was the stuff you couldn't put your finger on that really made the difference. With certain parts you have to find the motivation from the outside world. Like later on, when I had to play a food critic called Gary Rickey in Tony Marchant's TV series *Holding On*: a lot of his life was kind of outside my experience, so I based him on Tony Parsons. But with Jimmy, it was all there inside me already.

Not just because I already had the music running round my head. But also because of all the tension that inevitably builds up inside you in your teenage years. All those times when I'd wanted to stay out all night with Renoir but my mum and dad wanted me back at eleven.

'You've got to play what's there' – that's what Anna Scher had taught me, so I just played what I was feeling at home. And because I was roughly the same age and going through similar things – acting and music were offering me the same kinds of excitement and opportunities that being a mod opened up for Jimmy – it all came really naturally.

At Anna's we were always encouraged to use our own experience and cultural surroundings as part of our acting. Not just for what this would bring to our work, but for what it would bring to our lives too. She definitely saw theatre as a kind of therapy, for want of a better word. She believed that acting out these situations helped people deal with them in real life. And it certainly worked that way for me.

But there was a political dimension to it as well. Anna was always preaching peace in one conflict zone or another. I remember at the height of the Troubles she took eight or nine of her actors out to do theatre workshops for mixed groups of Protestant and Catholic kids in the Falls Road. Very few other people would've had the bottle to do that at the time, and that kind of thing had a great influence on the development of my own political opinions.

I was a teenage leftie, I suppose, which used to cause more trouble at home. They were just the normal arguments that you'd expect kids to have with their parents. We'd all be sitting round watching the news. Richard Baker or Kenneth Kendall would announce that Margaret Thatcher was gonna give people twenty more years in prison for doing this or that, and I'd go, 'No, it should be fairer,' while my parents would go, 'Yes, it should be harder.'

Of course, what you don't realize at the time is that by the time you're your mum and dad's age you'll probably be more likely to see things their way. I still believe in the right to a fair trial and being innocent until proven guilty, but I've definitely got less militant as I've got older. I just think the way things have developed in this country makes it very difficult to think of yourself as a socialist now, because no one seems to know what that would mean any more.

The scene towards the end of *Quadrophenia* when Jimmy turns on Sting for being a bellboy is interpreted by some people as Jimmy acting out a kind of old-fashioned left-wing hostility towards popular culture. And if you want to look at it in that way, you can. But if you look at that situation through a seventeen-year-old's eyes, what Sting's doing is just a total cop-out. Jimmy's told his boss to stuff his job up his arse because of something this guy represented to him, then he's gone down to Brighton to see the Ace-Face, and there he is – not just still working, but carrying people's bags for 'em.

That betrayal is so bad it makes him think about killing himself; but then he realizes it's not worth it, even though it (almost) really is. That's why in the end it's not Jimmy who has to die, it's the scooter.

ACT II: AFTER

19: UP THE ALLEY,
WITH LESLIE ASH

If I had a pound for every time someone asked me if I'd really shagged Leslie Ash up that alley, I'd be a very rich man. The last time it happened was yesterday, when I was playing charity golf. I can see it coming a mile off – the way people build up to it. They think they're being subtle, and I'm thinking, 'Oh no, here we go again.'

Since no system of automatic remuneration exists for this routine conversational exchange, I would like to take this opportunity to say once and for all, 'No, I did not really shag Leslie Ash up that alley.' That scene looks good on the screen, but I remember it being quite awkward – she really didn't want to do it.

In terms of the final scenes on top of Beachy Head, it had been an advantage to shoot the end of the film first. But when it came to me and Leslie in the backstreets of Brighton a couple of days later, going as far as we were going to go was a bit more difficult.

The problem with Leslie and me – well, it wasn't a problem, because it worked really well in the film – was that I was very raw and young at that time, whereas she already had a boyfriend who was a lot older than her and drove a Porsche. I couldn't compete – even though obviously I wanted to, because she was very pretty. And while me having the sense that I was not in her league was good for *Quadrophenia*, it wasn't so good for me.

Especially as I'd seen the jealous bloody boyfriend hanging around the set a few times, not exactly giving me the evil eye, but almost. It wasn't my fault, was it? But you know what they're like, boyfriends: there's a bit of it in all of us, and especially in those who are going out with actresses.

It wasn't just the boyfriend issue. Those are the scenes you really dread, where you have to get your kit off and kiss people (or not get your kit off and kiss people, in this case). I haven't had to do that for a while, though there was a time when people always seemed to want me to be naked in the bath, or with a gun to my head (in a film called *Nasty Neighbours*), and I've had a bit of a roll around with Dawn French, which ended up being quite enjoyable.

In this case, though, Leslie really didn't want to do it. I think the whole scene was a big issue for her, and Franc had to tenderly coax her into it – 'Get in there for the old wallbanger . . .' The whole thing was just really awkward.

You wouldn't generally do too many rehearsals before a scene like that (and obviously I'd done my screen test with Wendy Morgan, rather than Leslie) so we were very new to each other. It was meant to be a closed set, but they always say it's a closed set, and there's always someone who shouldn't be there – a spark (electrician) or one of the crew with his face pressed up against the corrugated iron, trying to get a glimpse of tit.

I think I had a slightly insecure feeling of 'Is it me?' Could Leslie really not stand me? I had my new vented suit on, and my star was rising . . . I just hope that in subsequent years she's had as many women coming up to her as I've had men, saying, 'Bloody hell, you lucky cow, did you really shag Phil Daniels up that alley?'

Excepting the occasional set-builder with a wandering eye, Roddam was very good at keeping people at arm's length. He'd set us up in this kind of youthful, excited world, and he was determined to keep us there so we could just get on with doing what he wanted without outside interference. There were lots of people who wanted to get involved, but he really protected us. I never got Roger Daltrey coming up and telling me how to do it. Well, we did have a bit of a chat one day – sitting on a couple of deckchairs, down in Brighton – but that was fine by me.

Daltrey's most famous attempt to put his own mark on Roddam's vision was that because he wore white trousers in the mid-sixties, he insisted everyone else did too. When we were doing the crowd scenes in Brighton, they had to get a load of contemporary photos out and count the proportion of people who were wearing white trousers to prove to him that they'd got it right.

It wasn't just the fashion advice of rock legends that Roddam had to watch out for. I think he felt that quite a lot of the production team were maybe a bit more old school. There were a few old lags who'd done a bit with David Lean, lunched at Wheeler's every day, and felt they knew the game a bit too well to be bothered with a load of foul-mouthed kids in a low-budget film. Franc soon put them on their mettle.

Looking back at *Quadrophenia* now, it's a bit rough around the edges, and some of the dialogue is a bit end-of-the-pier, but on the whole I think Martin Stellman's script really stands the test of time.

Pete Townshend had written a rock opera that was poignant and interesting on several different levels. *Tommy* was interesting as a piece of music, but the film was a different thing altogether. Ken Russell took some of Townshend's more melodramatic conceptual ideas and ran with them, whereas with *Quadrophenia* Franc Roddam brought the whole thing back down to earth.

What Franc did was make a proper film, instead of just letting it be a film of an album. He built up the back story and brought forward the more realistic side of the plot, while getting rid of some of the more mystical elements – like all that stuff about *Quadrophenia* being a four-way split personality that supposedly added up to the single personality of the Who. You can see that on the original album sleeve, where the scooter's four mirrors each reflect the face of a different member of the band. All that kind of imagery was useful to me in the process of playing the part of Jimmy, but Franc wasn't giving it too much houseroom.

What he did was give the story back to the kind of young people it was supposed to be about, and then let us put bits of ourselves into it. Like, 'Don't touch the cloth, moth' – that was a saying I'd picked up off someone at school. And that whole scene where I lose it with the postman who's just crashed into me – that was totally improvised. The poor sod didn't know what had hit him, as he was only a stunt-man who was standing in for someone. I was there swearing at him and telling him he'd killed my scooter, and all of a sudden he was having to come up with responses as the camera was rolling: 'Forty years, I've been driving!' It's no wonder he looks so upset. (Top performance, Mr Stuntman.)

I don't like giving away too much about this kind of thing, in case it spoils people's enjoyment of the finished film, but quite a lot of that scene had to be post-synchronized, which is when you have to redo a bit of dialogue afterwards because of problems with the sound. There was quite a bit of post-syncing on *Quadrophenia*, as there was a lot of background noise.

It's a tricky business, post-syncing. You have to listen to the original dialogue on headphones while watching the film on the screen; a little squiggly line comes across and when it hits the point in the scene, you start speaking. There's a real skill to it, because you have to hit the mouth at exactly the right moment and let it all come out exactly the way it did before.

The whole process has got much easier now, because people can use computers to shift things and elongate words to make them fit. The worst bit about post-syncing these days is everyone trying to change what you originally said to water things down, so where you've said 'Fuck off' they want to have you saying 'Sod off' instead.

I was working on the BBC1 series *New Tricks* with Dennis Waterman recently, and he told me he'd called someone a wanker in it, and was then told, 'We can't really have that,' but Dennis was refusing to budge. I kept telling him, 'You could say, "You wangler",' but he wasn't having it, and good on him. I think he's been around long enough not to be messed around by some idiot in a suit . . .

That show will have been broadcast by the time this book's done, so anyone who watched it will know if the man from *The Sweeney* and *Minder* stood his ground or not.

Obviously Roddam would have had debates at the time about what certificate to go for with *Quadrophenia*. But I think the Who were the Who and – to their credit – they decided that they could make whatever film they fucking wanted. Even if an X-certificate was going to shave a bit off the box office.

Because Roddam was essentially a documentary-maker, he wanted the film to be almost like a documentary about these kids who got drunk and pilled up. So when we shot scenes like the party in that guy's house, where I give my cigarette to the statue to hold and then pick it up at the end of the scene, he definitely encouraged it to be more of a real party. I think actual penetration was achieved at one point – not by the star of the film, I hasten to add.

I owe him a lot, Franc. I've been in a lot of professional situations over the years where people haven't understood what I'm about, but he really did. He knew if he trusted me, I could deliver the goods.

Franc let you have your head, and I think when you're young and someone does that, you appreciate it. There're so many outside forces at that stage telling you that you're not good enough and trying to put you down – not even necessarily in the business, just in general – that someone having a bit of faith in you really gives you confidence.

When I see him now, I always feel like he thinks our careers sort of went the same way. That if things had gone differently, and Thatcher's actors hadn't taken over, we might have gone on to do a bit more together. It's almost as if we ended up being victims of *Quadrophenia*'s success, in a way. But I'm pretty happy with how things have worked out. There's no point regretting things you can't change, anyway – and Franc must have made a few quid out of inventing *Masterchef*.

20: THE BOYS IN BLACK

The night *Quadrophenia* had its première, I got picked up with my mum and dad in a stretch limo. When you see one of those now it generally means someone's out on their hen night, but they were a much bigger deal in 1979. The limo drove us the equivalent of four stops down the Piccadilly Line, from Jessel House to the cinema in Leicester Square. Obviously that was quite exciting, because it felt more like stardom than anything I'd been involved in before. And my mum and dad seemed to enjoy the occasion.

In those days I didn't generally give much consideration to what my parents thought about what I was doing. Only later in life did I start thinking, 'I'll do that 'cos my mum might like me in it' – that's one of the reasons I ended up in *EastEnders*. I think when I was growing up they probably saw my acting as a bit of a mixed blessing. On the good side they thought, 'He's getting a few quid.' On the bad side they probably worried that being a part of that whole film-and-theatrical world was going to turn me into some mad, gay drug-fiend, like Dean Martin (or was it Cary Grant?).

Because the things I was in at that time tended to be quite anti-establishment in political terms, and usually had a lot of swearing in them, there was often a slight sense of unease as to where all this was leading. But I knew they were proud of me, even though they didn't exactly go over the top when it came to telling me how wonderful I was.

Not congratulating someone too much can be a pretty good way of keeping them on the straight and narrow (there have certainly been a few England football teams over the years who might have done a bit better if they'd spent a bit less time being congratulated by everyone before they'd even stepped out on the pitch). And, because I was lucky enough not to need that kind of validation, the 'keep his feet on the ground' approach certainly worked out well for me.

The whole idea of me being in films and on TV was quite alien to my mum and dad, really. There was no showbiz tradition in the family. My sister Brenda had done tap-dancing and flamenco, but at an amateur level. Thank God they weren't those kind of pushy ambitious parents you'd see at other theatre schools (the ones that weren't Anna Scher's). Apart from anything else, knowing my contrary nature, I probably wouldn't have wanted to carry on acting if I'd had too much encouragement.

I've seen so many pushy parents over the years . . . It's still the same now – in fact probably worse. It can be really destructive when people try to fulfil their own dreams through their kids – not just in acting but on every level; in sport, or academically.

I had an embarrassing taste of that world a few years back, when they were making *Hideous Kinky* – the film of the Esther Freud book, which Kate Winslet was in. Unbeknown to me, they'd gone to my daughter's primary school to look for kids to play the two little girls who go to Morocco with their mum in the film, and she came back with a letter saying she'd been chosen for an audition, so I said all right and took her along.

Acting wasn't something she'd ever expressed much interest in, but it couldn't hurt to give it a try. I kept well out of the way, and she did really well and got through to the last four. So then we had to go to the casting director's house. Kate Winslet (who'd just done *Titanic* at the time) and the director and all the other main actors were there, so the kids could audition with the adult cast. And I ended up being stuck in this room with all these other hopeful parents. Obviously they see Phil Daniels and they all think it's an inside job – they were all asking suspiciously, 'Do you know this director?' I told them I didn't, but I'm not sure that they believed me.

Either way, Ella never got the part. She didn't seem too bothered about it, so I wasn't either. The only bad thing was that the casting people didn't let us know. That's the worst thing for an actor. If you go for a job and you don't get it, that's all right, it just means they thought someone else was right for the part. But you'd rather find out straight away. Sitting around for days on end waiting for the phone to ring is never very nice.

The release of *Quadrophenia* didn't mean my auditioning days were over. Quite the reverse. Because it's a film a lot of people have grown to love over the years, it's easy to overestimate its success when it first came out.

The comparison I always make is with *Trainspotting*. The contrasts in how those two films were originally received are interesting, because I think Danny Boyle had what Franc did with Pete Townshend's original material in mind when he came to adapt Irvine Welsh's novel. Why else would he have used the same cinematographer (an excellent director of photography called Brian Tufano, who's a very nice guy as well)?

By the time *Trainspotting* came out, sex, drugs, rock 'n' roll and swearing had become very fashionable in cinematic terms. Whereas when *Quadrophenia* came out it just really shocked everybody. It got some OK reviews, hung around in the cinemas for a few weeks, and then, as far as we were concerned, that was it.

Maybe the film was just a bit ahead of its time in terms of how uncompromising it was. No one in America would touch it – they said they'd have to re-dub everybody because no one would understand our accents. But they had no problem with a load of guttural Scottish junkies fifteen years later. Well, they might have given them subtitles, but that's much better than re-dubbing.

I wasn't recognized much in those days. I'm sure I would have enjoyed it if it had happened, but, even after *Quadrophenia* and the film version of *Scum* had come out, I could still get on buses without anyone noticing. The only articles anyone ever wanted to write about me in the papers came from the 'boy next door' angle, and I'd seen enough of those already.

I remember turning down the chance to do adverts for the army and the police as well, because the army had wasted so many people's lives and, coming from the sort of upbringing that I did, you always tend to think of the police as the enemy. (Though I'm a bit less knee-jerk about that kind of thing these days.)

In the years immediately after *Quadrophenia* came out, I had good reason to be a bit wary of the boys in blue, because I did have the odd run-in with the law during that period. I'd bought myself a trials bike around that time. I suppose riding that Honda 125 around London had given me a taste for it, and it was a bit like getting a tasty skate-board when you were younger – something to spend your money on. Anyway, I got nicked for drink-driving once, after pulling up outside this Chinese takeaway in King's Cross and nearly falling off my bike. On the face of it this was a fair cop, but there was one aspect of the situation that I had good cause to feel a bit aggrieved about.

Two hours earlier I'd been drinking with these two plain-clothes coppers from King's Cross in the Norfolk Arms in Thanet Street. When I got home, I felt a bit peckish and I thought (very wrongly, of course) I'd just hop on my bike and pop round the corner to get a Chinese. When I got there, one of the two coppers I'd just been in the pub with saw me wobbling along and fucking nicked me. I knew they were Old Bill, but I thought they were all right when they were off duty. But when I protested, they just said, 'Sorry, Phil, we've radioed it in, now.' Served me right for reaching out, I suppose.

One of them was on the fiddle anyway and got put back into uni-form from CID shortly afterwards, so he got his comeuppance. The whole thing became a total joke afterwards: obviously they leaked it to the paper, and in the *London Evening Standard* the next day it was said that not only was I done for drink-driving, but also I was appar-ently at the head of a gang of forty mods rampaging through King's Cross on our scooters. Given that I was actually arrested on a trials bike going to a Chinese takeaway, this was the first time I had to face up to the shocking realization that even the most reputable newspapers don't always tell the truth.

There was another incident at around the same time that in my memory always kind of mingles with this one, where I got done for being drunk and disorderly down by Trafalgar Square. This time I got really stitched up. Some young cadet copper told me I'd crossed the road at the wrong time and gave me a lecture. I said, 'Look, don't you fucking tell me what to do, mate, blah, blah, blah,' and that seemed to be the end of it. But then ten minutes later some geezer pushed me – really started on me. I went to fight back and, before I realized what was going on, four proper coppers arrived. I'd been set up, and the next thing I knew I was in handcuffs, nicked for threatening behaviour with intent to cause a breach of the peace.

The playwright Nigel Williams got me this really good showbiz lawyer called Bernie Simons. And when I finally went to court I saw that three or four of the coppers had turned up dressed up as mods. All these gangly twenty-two-year-olds were sitting there in their Sta-Prest and loafers with their ties on, getting the morning off for nicking me.

You forget that coppers are into their fashion as well (well, they try to be) – it wasn't just about *Quadrophenia*: that whole Paul Weller/Jam thing was happening at the time, too. But after I was found not guilty, one of them had the cheek to ask me for an autograph. So I told him that, while I was happy to have had my innocence confirmed, it was still going to cost me a hundred pounds to pay the lawyer, and on that basis I was unable to oblige him. Or words roughly to that effect.

I suppose in my own small way I'd become a bit of a poster-boy for disorderly youth, so it was only natural that I'd come under a bit of pressure from the local constabulary every now and again. Maybe I acted up to that idea a bit sometimes as well. But there was one time after that when I was more than happy to sign an autograph for a policeman.

One night, me and my mate Trevor Laird were going to a party, and one of us had got hold of a set of those dodgy one-size-fits-all car keys. We weren't real villains; we were only messing about. It was up by that reservoir alongside Pentonville Road in Islington. We tried a couple of car doors, and at first nothing happened. But then one of them opened. We sat in this thing trying to get it going, and – to our complete shock – it started. Just as that happened, this little Italian bloke came running out of the flats with a machete. We jumped out of the car and legged it, luckily thinking to chuck the keys away as we made our escape.

We managed to get away from the mad Italian, but as we were in the process of doing so a Black Maria came along, saw us legging it and nicked us. The police van took us back to the station, where fortunately we got thrown in cells next to each other. We decided to say that we'd seen someone acting suspiciously in the back of the car and were worried they were hurting someone, so we were just about to intervene when this bloke came running after us with his chopper out.

Even I knew this didn't sound entirely convincing, but luckily this Greek copper who was head of CID at Holloway said, 'You were in the film *Quadrophenia*?' After we'd both said a unanimous yes, he explained that there was a rare blood disease afflicting the Greek community, a bit like sickle-cell anaemia; he said that if we could get Sting's autograph for him to auction as a way of raising funds, then that would be the end of the matter.

I said, 'Yes, I certainly can,' and he let us go. As we were being released from the station, the bloke from the flats who'd been chasing us was in there making a complaint. He was going, 'What are you doing? Why are you releasing them?' but the sergeant said, 'They've done nothing wrong; I believe their story.' After that, I went straight home and got out my copy of the Police's first album, *Outlandos D'Amour*. I signed it myself – 'Best wishes, from Sting' – and then dropped it off at Holloway police station. Under the circumstances, it was the least I could do.

That certainly felt like a bit of a coup, but the film version of *Scum* didn't work out quite so favourably. I remember Alan Clarke saying that everyone was doing it for pork pies, and I think we were all on £150 a week. The deal was we were all meant to be on points if the film made any money, but it's amazing how often apparently successful films fail to turn a profit in those circumstances.

Making *Scum* for the second time wasn't nearly such a satisfying experience as making the first version had been. It's never as much fun trying to replicate something you've already done. With a play – if it's a good enough play – you can repeat it again and again over a long period of time and learn something new almost every time. But making a film is different, especially when it's gone from being a gritty and politically challenging *Play for Today* to being something that's being made for the commercial cinema, where they're looking for more violence and more sensationalism.

How I differentiate between the two experiences in my mind is that to do the first one, we all had to meet up and get the train from Charing Cross, whereas to do the second one, we met up at the same place but then got a special bus. The location was the old mental home at Friern Barnet. To get the go-ahead the producers had shown the local authorities a spurious script called *The Boys in Black*. In that one, matron was tucking us up in bed every night and we were all reformed characters. I was never sure if this had actually happened, but it was a good story either way.

One incident that definitely did take place while filming up in Friern Barnet was that a group of us nicked the bus. It was the usual gang: me, Ray Winstone, Johnny Fowler, Perry Benson, Ray Burdis, John Blundell. We jumped in the bus and drove it around Friern Barnet picking up some of the inmates. It's all flats there now, but it was still a working mental hospital then, and the patients were still wandering round in their pyjamas. They seemed to enjoy the joyride, though – it was like a scene from *One Flew Over the Cuckoo's Nest.*

I remember my mum wasn't too happy when *Quadrophenia* and

Scum came out in quick succession. She was always saying, 'Why can't you play a good boy in all these films you do?' *Scum* was certainly not a ladies' film. Though I suppose you do get to see Winstone in the bath again – just like in *Quadrophenia*!

21: A POOR MAN'S RODGERS & HAMMERSTEIN

My friend Cosmo Landesman was the only person who warned me about the effect being in *Quadrophenia* might have on my musical career. He thought that if I was serious about rock 'n' roll I should just stick with that. I remember him telling me that if I played Jimmy, no one would ever let me forget I'd done it. Which was quite profound of him, really, as it turned out that was exactly what did happen.

Cosmo obviously saw the bigger picture – that me doing something with the Who would take me away from doing my own music. In his book, he said that I was a good songwriter. And he used to tell me I was a bit like Jim Morrison (though I was less prone to removing my trousers in public), so he probably felt that Renoir would've had a real chance of making it if *Quadrophenia* hadn't come along.

There's no point regretting these things, though. And besides, we weren't really on the brink of anything at the time. I remember there was a band around then called AFT – Automatic Fine-Tuning, it stood for. They had a couple of John Birch guitars and they were a bit like us. Their music wasn't so good as ours, but they could really play. Whereas I think with Renoir, the whole thing wasn't going to progress unless we became much more accomplished musicians.

It was still all about getting stoned and listening to ourselves afterwards, and that's not really the way to get better. I remember we used to go down to a place called Sheepwash in Devon. The playwright Laurence Dobie had a cottage there and he lent it to me a couple of times. The Renoir boys moved in for a few days and it all got quite lively.

Apparently Ted Hughes lived on a farm nearby. A few years later, I did a version of *Oedipus* that he'd translated, but I didn't see him out and about looking after his animals, and he certainly never came round to tell us to turn the noise down.

The trouble with our band was, because of Peter having such complex musical ideas, it got to the point with some of his compositions where we were stretching ourselves to a technical level that we couldn't quite reach, and that caused a lot of frustration. We were quite a loud band – really noisy, in fact – but, while we used to do a lot of very fast tracks, we weren't punks. So when punk came along we got left behind. Punk rock beat us up, basically.

I could have been a punk at the drop of a hat, but I didn't like the style. It wasn't that I was a hippie. OK, I smoked a few joints and was therefore considered a bit weird by some people who didn't (we used to call them 'straights'). But in terms of the clothes I was wearing at the time, it would still have been Levi's Sta-Prest or the occasional combat trouser – khaki, not camouflage – maybe with a cheesecloth shirt, or something from Lord John.

Then I'd finish the ensemble off with monkey boots or – more likely – a nice pair of DM's. I had plenty of them, but always black, not the bright-red ones. As an overall look, it was free-thinker with a subtle undercurrent of boot-boy.

I don't know why, but I couldn't stand the way punks looked. Somehow it never excited me as a fashion – girls with great big holes in their stockings, and blokes wearing tartan trousers with straps all over the place. It just seemed really contrived (obviously all fashion is slightly contrived – that's kind of the point – but there are limits). And I felt the same way about a lot of the bands. They said something for a short space of time, and then it got harder and harder to get away from how manufactured the whole thing felt.

Loathe it or love it, there was no denying that punk was a big kick up the arse for the music business. It certainly did for Renoir. I remember Barrie Keeffe coming to see us at the Old Red Lion in Islington some time in 1978 and saying, 'No, your music's wrong.' I've got a very rough live recording Perry Benson made of us at the time, and it is quite funny listening to it now. Someone who heard it recently said it reminded them of Blur.

Those two songs for the *The Class of Miss MacMichael* ended up being the only proper bit of recording Renoir ever did. Stanley Myers was the producer – he did John Williams' version of 'Cavatina' as well, so there's one for all you buskers out there – and we did it in the studio where my old mate Keith Bradshaw from guitar lessons at Rurtherford school worked (who'd also been a notional member of Borax Flux alongside me and Gary Callard). I think we got £200 for letting those songs be used on the soundtrack.

As film themes go, 'Playing in Schools' was never going to be the big Bryan Adams number from *Robin Hood: Prince of Thieves*. 'Anarchy in the KP' was more of an instrumental jam – 'Hey, boys, we can *play*.' So the nutty kid in the film ended up listening to my satirical response to punk rock on his transistor radio. And that was the only time our music ever went out over the airwaves – in a bloody awful film about the educationally subnormal. Please don't tell me it's a fitting epitaph.

Another musical legacy that can't be pinned on me is the stylistic evolution of Gary Kemp. Not long after *Quadrophenia* came out, I remember Gary coming to see Renoir and telling me, 'Look, this music is good, but it ain't going nowhere. If you want to get a record deal, maybe you should reinvent yourselves as a mod band.'

The mod revival was in full flow by then. Gary's band at the time were called the Makers – they hadn't yet become Spandau Ballet – and I remember them playing on a Friday at the Old Red Lion, all dressed as mods. They obviously had a manager who knew the score (I think it was Steve Dagger, even then), and what they would do was jump on any image that came along until the right one eventually turned up (which it did, in the end). Whereas Renoir didn't really have an image. We were a bit stuck in our own way of doing things, and a few changes definitely needed to be made. What happened next just speeded them up a bit.

Gered Murphy, who produced Gerry Rafferty's old band Stealers Wheel – they did that song 'Stuck in the Middle with You', which was used as the soundtrack for the ear-cutting scene in *Reservoir Dogs* – he'd come and seen Renoir once, and told me I should go off on my own. I didn't want to do that at the time, but later on down the line, when these two blokes called Alan Blaikley and Ken Howard came along and took a bit of a shine to me – and wanted to help me get on – I was ready to listen to what they had to say.

They'd written hits for Elvis and Dave Dee, Dozy, Beaky, Mick & Tich, among others, and they'd gone on to discover Peter Frampton. First they turned up at Anna's and stood in the back while I played them a few songs. Then I went up to see them at their house in Hampstead. They had a big grand piano in their front room, and they played me this song they'd written that they wanted me to do as a single. 'I'm Your Meantime Man', it was called. 'Who'll come around at the drop of a hat? I can': that was one line from it.

The whole thing was very old-fashioned, and Blaikley and Howard were a bit like a poor man's Rodgers and Hammerstein. But the whole idea didn't seem like too much of a stretch. I think they were thinking initially about me being in a musical, but then it turned into more of a David Essex thing. He'd been in a film and then had some hits, so why shouldn't I?

When I first got it together and signed a deal with them, it was very exciting. The difficult part of it was deciding what I was going to do with Renoir. I knew I wanted to carry on working with Peter, 'cos we were a writing team. The bass player, Barry Neil, was really good as well, so there were no problems with him.

Mickey Dolan was (and, apparently, still is) a great high-energy drummer. He was the only one of us who Barrie Keeffe thought was any good. With hindsight, I might have been wrong to lose him, but I wanted to go for a more clinical approach.

Miles Landesman was the most heartbreaking decision. From his book, it's clear that his brother Cosmo thinks that when I left Renoir and formed the other band, I was being a bit of a cunt. But I suppose sometimes you have to be if you're trying to get a new band together.

He always had his own rhythm, Miles, and, although I loved him, I felt the whole Renoir thing had gone as far as it was gonna go. To cut a long story short, somewhere between *Quadrophenia* and *Broken Glass*, Renoir went out the window and Phil Daniels & the Cross came in.

I didn't see him for years afterwards, but we've picked things up again a bit now, and he's still one of the nicest people I've ever met. He's been in loads of other bands over the years, and had some success. You never know with Miles – maybe the best is yet to come.

22: 'VIOLA!'

You've got to have someone who'll give you a bit of backing in the music business, whether they want you to be the new David Essex or not. Blaikley and Howard had signed me up because they liked what I did; so, after a bit of to-ing and fro-ing, I was finally able to convince them to allow me to do mainly my own and Peter-Hugo's songs on the album.

It was quite a complicated arrangement, in business terms. I had a deal with Blaikley and Howard, and then they got me a deal with RCA. So we were in a bit of a Carlos Tévez situation. Anna was still acting as my agent at that stage, so her partner Charles Verrall negotiated the whole thing for me. I think it was a bit of a stretch for him, as he had no more experience of drawing up record deals than I did.

I remember that when I saw the final contract big chunks of it were painted out. I was allowed to see my part, but not the arrangement between the record company and Blaikley and Howard. I nearly didn't sign it, because I felt from the word go that there was a bit of uncertainty as to whether it was my deal or theirs. As it turned out, the record we ended up making wasn't successful enough for it to really make that much difference.

The album was produced by Zak Lawrence, who was a friend of Blaikley and Howard's. I remember him telling me, 'I know what's wrong with your lyrics: they're the wrong way round!' That shows you the level of understanding there was between us.

We didn't have a great sound worked out for the album. Not in the way that, say, Graham Coxon had a sound worked out for Blur. We just got on and did it.

They're a funny mixture, looking back at them, the songs on *Phil Daniels & the Cross*. There's one called 'Shout Across the River', which was the title of the Poliakoff play I ended up not doing 'cos I got the part in *Zulu Dawn* instead. I thought it was a good title for a song, so I recycled it. Then there was 'News at Ten', which was my South African protest song.

Music was the one thing you thought you could change the world with, which I know is a naïve concept, but that's how you think when you're young. Rock 'n' roll wasn't just about making the world a better place, it was the ultimate way of exploding – the ultimate high. And the more normal and everyday the raw materials you could fashion that excitement out of, the better. 'Cromer Aroma', which I've mentioned before, that was about King's Cross. 'Wet Day in London' was about my dad, and his technique for reviving tropical fish.

Sometimes one of his angelfish would be at death's door, and he'd put a bit of whisky on his hand and put the fish in it. The fish would get a sniff of the whisky, and the alcohol would give it a new lease of life. I suppose it was like smelling salts, or a Saint Bernard bringing you a tot of rum in an Alpine rescue. I'm not sure where my dad got the idea from, but maybe it's the origin of the phrase 'drinks like a fish'. It's certainly how I learnt.

The songs I was singing were just a mixture of all the things that were happening in my life – there was no reason to leave anything out. 'Free You' was about signing that fucking contract for the album. 'Ballsache High' was taken from *Class Enemy*. People have said it's a bit Arctic Monkeys at times. Feel free to download the album illegally (mine, not theirs) and hear for yourself if you don't believe me (there's no way I'd make any money out of any formal sales at this stage, even if someone did reissue it on CD).

From the first time I heard the Arctic Monkeys, I thought their singer had the same kind of voice and the same attitude as I had – all that stuff about the prossies on the corner just seemed very natural coming from him. Obviously their records have done a bit better than mine, though. *Phil Daniels & the Cross* got caught in the exhaust fumes of punk. It was totally carbon-monoxided out.

I still think it was quite a good album, but people were really dead set against me doing both things. As far as everyone else was concerned, it seemed that after *Quadrophenia* I was no longer allowed to be an actor and a musician at the same time. This seemed a bit unfair, because a lot of other people got away with it.

Being in that film didn't seem to do Sting or Toyah's pop careers any harm. OK, maybe it made some purists think of them as actors playing at being musicians, but if I was going to criticize them – which I wouldn't – it would be more likely to be from the opposite perspective.

I've seen the crossover between the two worlds of music and acting from a lot of different angles over the years. Not only from being in bands and then in plays, but also because I've played so many roles where I've been either a musician, or a manager, or someone hanging around the fringes of the music industry in some capacity or other.

Glitter; that was one I forgot to mention. It was something else I was in with Toyah – in fact, I think it was her first professional job. It was about two kids who broke into the *Top of the Pops* studios, and Noel Edmonds had a cameo role in it. I remember he was so amazed by how little money he was getting that he donated his fee to the Actors' Benevolent Fund.

It's not just the kind of impact you make on the audience that changes when you switch between acting and singing – the two activities give you very different feelings as a performer. Having been lucky enough to do both, I can honestly say that doing a play in front of ten people is much scarier than going on stage with a band in front of a crowd of tens of thousands.

I did a couple of plays around that time at the Soho Poly Theatre, which was a tiny underground garage that couldn't hold more than forty people. In fact our average audience barely climbed out of single figures, but that was still much more nerve-wracking than going on stage with Blur at Glastonbury in front of 150,000 people. Hiding behind a load of electric noise and having the audience stretch away for miles in front of you is much easier than being right up close to people when it's just you and them.

By the time my album came out, however, the feedback between these two different channels of my career was starting to cause real problems. *Breaking Glass* was the peak of that, really. My character in the film – Danny – is a music-industry bottom feeder who becomes Hazel O'Connor's manager. Even though he's a bit dodgy round the edges, he's a right little hustler and, in his own way, quite principled. The irony was that, away from the cameras, this was exactly the kind of person I needed to sort things out for me.

As far as life and art getting mixed up went (I know some people might question whether the film *Breaking Glass* should really fall into the latter category, but please bear with me), this was only the beginning. Looking back at it now, some of the things that went on around that film were so ridiculous that no scriptwriter would have dared to make them up.

I think Hazel O'Connor had already got her part, but I had to audition for mine. They gave me a bit of the script to read. She was in the room with the director, and I had to burst in and say this one word to introduce myself. I looked at the bit of paper and said, 'All right.' Then I walked in, pointed at the wall and said, 'Viola!' – pretending there was one up there. Of course everybody was in stitches, 'cos what I was meant to say was 'Voila!' I hadn't even done it deliberately, and I think it was probably that fact which got me the part there and then.

The director was a guy called Brian Gibson, who'd just worked on a really good TV show called *Private Schultz,* in which Michael Elphick (my dad in *Quadrophenia*) played a German soldier. We tried to get Elphick into *Breaking Glass* as well, but it didn't quite work out for some reason I've forgotten down the years. I think he was going out with Helen Mirren for a while at that time, so things weren't going too badly for him.

My former mentor Jonathan Pryce did get a part in it, though – as the deaf saxophone player who was also a junkie. This was a bit of a strange one, because obviously I wasn't a kid any more, so the balance of power between us had shifted slightly. He gave me a great bit of advice though. He passed me a note (an actor's term for a bit of constructive criticism) to be a bit more still and calm when acting on film, which to this day is something I remind myself to do.

I did have a certain amount to be agitated about at that time. My album came out around the time the film started shooting, and nothing much was happening with it, so I was a bit resentful of the fact that Hazel O'Connor's music was getting all the attention. Everybody was singing her praises and not mine, and there I was playing the manager.

Don't get me wrong. I enjoyed doing the film, and it was a very good part, but at that point it felt quite strange for me to be working in a fictional setting where I was surrounded by the music industry, when all I wanted to be was a performer. As it turned out, this tension would resolve itself in a quite unexpected and very happy way, but we'll get to that in the next chapter.

For the moment, the *NME* was telling me my album was no good. They thought I was jumping on a bandwagon – yet another actor trying to moonlight as a singer – and *Phil Daniels & the Cross* kind of got dismissed.

We'd have liked to have had a proper go, but the whole thing just petered out. The amount of advertising for the album was pathetic, and we didn't even do a proper tour. I think we played Camden Dingwalls – same as the Police had – and the Bridge House, Canning Town (which would soon give the world the Cockney Rejects), and that was about it. The record company lost interest, and not long afterwards so did Blaikley and Howard.

It was the first real setback I'd had in my career, and I was quite disillusioned by it, to the extent that I effectively gave up song-writing. People were forever telling me to stick to the acting; I remember Brian Gibson being particularly eloquent on this point – and from then onwards, Brian got his wish.

23: '. . .OR WILL YOU JUST, POLITELY, SAY GOODNIGHT?'

Whether all this stuff going on behind the scenes added an extra emotional charge to my performance in *Breaking Glass* is not for me to say, but it definitely gave me a sharp pain. And the passing years have added a further poignant lustre to some of the details of that film's making.

For a start, its executive producer was a certain Dodi Fayed. He was one of those sons of very rich men who try a lot of different things without settling on one particular career path. Essentially, he was the money. I remember meeting him once or twice at various functions, and him being perfectly civil to me. Charles and Diana weren't yet even married yet, so the foundations for his subsequent significance were not yet laid. He's dead as a Dodi now, though, God rest his soul.

The identity of its executive producer was not the end of the film's historical ramifications, either. In terms of the music industry – with all the chart-hyping my character was doing, and the jokes about multicoloured vinyl – I think it gives quite an accurate reflection of an era that now seems very distant. It's a bit like *Zulu Dawn* in that way. And people who've seen *Breaking Glass* more recently than I have say that, when you watch it now, you can see the seventies turning into the eighties before your very eyes. The way the clothes the audiences are wearing at the live shows change, it's almost like moving from black-and-white into colour.

The film was originally going to be based on the successful TV series *Rock Follies*, but when Brian Gibson came across Hazel O'Connor he decided to make it more of a vehicle for her. The other leading actor was Jon Finch, who was quite famous at the time for having done a Bertolucci film. He still pops up occasionally, being very ethereal in some big arty Euro-pudding or other. And in *Breaking Glass* he played a kind of producer/svengali character who took over Hazel O'Connor's career and basically destroyed her life. (There were no historical parallels here with what Blaikley and Howard did for me – at least he got her a few hits before it all went pear-shaped.)

Jon was meant to be some kind of martial-arts expert in the film as well, because he does me in a fight at one point. I throw a bottle at him and he kung-fus it. Obviously the bottle was made of sugar-glass. The character Jon was playing did draw inspiration from real life, though.

Tony Visconti (Mary Hopkin's husband, who'd produced David Bowie, as well as some of those T-Rex records I'd loved as a kid) was working on the music. Hazel O'Connor was recording the sound-track with him at the same time as we were filming. She did a good job of bringing all that together, really. That lyric everyone loves in 'Will You' – 'You drink your coffee, and I sip my tea' – was actually a bit of improvised dialogue that she wrote a song around.

Visconti was into his martial arts as well. And in his autobiography he said that a lot of Jon's character's most ludicrous utterances were things he'd actually said himself – like when he gets played one of Hazel's songs and exclaims, 'I hear strings.' I'm not sure I'd have been quite so ready to admit that, had I been in his position. But Brian Gibson was certainly very good at recycling reality in cinema.

Hazel O'Connor's manager was a young gentleman called Alan Edwards. He also co-managed the Stranglers with a guy called Ian Grant, and I ended up playing in a football team with him a few years later. He's a well-known publicist now – sort of like a classier Max Clifford – and I think he used to do PR for the Spice Girls, but currently has Bowie, Amy Winehouse and P. Diddy on his books.

I'd met Alan early on in the filming process, when we did a few rehearsals up at the director Brian Gibson's house. Brian used to go out and leave me and Hazel together, so she could try and seduce me . . . I think she half managed it once, but let's not go into that. This isn't that kind of book.

Anyway, I remember Brian saying to me, 'Look, Alan's a young manager, why not use his style a bit?' He used to dress pretty smartly, in long black coats and suits, so I started doing that as well, which turned out to be a really good way of getting into the character. All the parts I play are loosely based on someone. As long as you know there's at least one person out there in this world who would behave in roughly the same way your character does, you've got all you need to make it real.

Mike Leigh is probably the biggest exponent of that view. Whenever you play a role in one of his films, you absolutely have to base it on someone specific. But it's not just a question of copying them. For instance, when I did *Meantime* I based the character on three different people and mingled them together. But that was still a couple of years away, yet.

For the moment, anyone keeping an eye on the bottom end of the *Breaking Glass* cast list would've seen a lot of unfamiliar names there that would soon become a great deal better known. A trio of actors make early appearances in *Breaking Glass* who later went on to be big TV and film stars.

Michael Kitchen is in one scene. I think he's meant to be Pink Floyd's manager, and I'm talking to him in a stairwell. I remember Brian made us do that poxy take about thirty-five times. Richard Griffiths is the recording engineer in the studio – showing his little belly off while we mess about with his master-tape. And Jim Broadbent is t'guard on't train, who lets us get onboard after a gig even though there's meant to be a strike.

All sorts of other people turn up in *Breaking Glass*. Rat Scabies of the Damned does an audition for Hazel's band, with his ginger hair. Boy George is in the film as well. I think it's in the scene in that pub in Ladbroke Grove, where the curtains get ripped down by NF skin-heads. Ken Campbell plays the landlord, and I think Marilyn's in there somewhere too – those two were never far apart in those days (that's Marilyn and Boy George, not Marilyn and Ken Campbell).

It's like a time capsule, that film. It really captures the atmosphere at the turn of that decade, when punk had given everyone the notion that everything was starting afresh, and every few weeks there seemed to be a new idea flying around of what the next big thing was gonna be.

I remember going to a few clubs with Boy George and his crowd at that time. In theory, you wouldn't have thought it was my sort of thing, but in practice it was good fun for a night out. Heaven – under the Arches in Charing Cross – that was one of the big hang-outs for the New Romantics, or the Futurists, or whatever they were calling themselves that week. And there was another place at the Holborn end of Covent Garden. I think that might've been Steve Strange's 'Club for Heroes'.

I bumped into the DJ Rusty Egan (who ended up in Steve's group, Visage) for the first time in years on the tube a few months ago. He said, 'Fucking hell, me and Steve have got back together,' and a few weeks later I saw them on one of those programmes on *Living TV* where old bands get back together, get new teeth, lose a bit of weight, try to forget why they split up in the first place, and do a gig at the end in front of all their old muckers.

I knew a few of the leading lights in London's rapidly evolving club-land, but as far as being a New Romantic went I didn't make any fashion concessions. We always take the mickey out of Jan's brother Rob, because he wore his hair floppy for a while. I think I was still wearing my DM's in those days, so that was OK. But I should proba-bly take this opportunity to confess that at one stage, when I was with Renoir, I wore a little rust-coloured suede jacket – which looked quite good – only with blue crushed-velvet drainpipe trousers and a pair of red Kickers. Those were different times and we all make mistakes, but red Kickers? I'm still trying to live that one down.

David Bowie, who was the godfather of that whole New Romantic scene, is supposed to have come on the set of *Breaking Glass* once, because he was working with Tony Visconti at the time, but I never saw him. Apparently Hazel O'Connor gave him a haircut – which was only fair, as she'd taken quite a lot of her act from *Ziggy Stardust* and *Aladdin Sane*.

We were friendly enough, me and Hazel, but our off-screen relationship never touched the same heights of passion as our not-so-festive coupling in that British Rail sleeper-carriage. *Breaking Glass* did end up being the start of a love story for me, though. If I'd started to feel I'd got a bit of a raw deal from the British music industry after *Phil Daniels & the Cross* came out (which I had), a beautiful payback was just around the corner.

Jan – my missus – worked with Alan Edwards. I met her a few times, and we just got on from the start. Our paths had nearly crossed before, because she'd started out at Track Records, the Who's record label. I suppose this was a bit like my mum and dad living round the corner from each other in London for years before they finally met in Leeds, just on a much shorter timescale.

Readers might have noticed that I have not dwelt at length on matters of the heart. Or, indeed, the groin. I'm more of the old school who don't like going too public with that kind of thing. 'Puppy Love' with Dawn Jerraud, a bit of a fumble on *Anoop and the Elephant*, some after-school activities with *The Class of Miss MacMichael*, the youth leader who didn't get away, and the occasional Camden girl floating about with Renoir. Surely that's enough for any book of titillation? I'm not Russell Brand, after all.

Falling in love with Jan was the start of my first big relationship, and I'm really glad to say we've stayed together ever since.

Jan had a flat in Hertford Street in Mayfair at the time. It was an ex-chapel, fully serviced, and it cost only £12 a week, so it was a real find. She'd got it through the rock 'n' roll grapevine. The producer Daniel Secunda had it first, and then Johnny Thunders of Johnny Thunders and the Heartbreakers, who'd been on the Sex Pistols tour and I think were signed to Track Records. It'd been Johnny's flat, and when no one was in there after he went back to America, Jan took it over.

I think maybe she had liaised with Mr Thunders for a while – I definitely had the sense that something might've gone on there, but it wasn't my place to ask. By the time I came on the scene, she was sharing the flat with a mate of hers. But then I kept staying over, and I think the other girl's nose was put a bit out of joint so she moved out. Then all of a sudden I'd left home, and me and Jan were living together.

Her landlady was a German woman called Miss Schpicter, who used to come round on a Friday to collect the rent. She had a lovely moustache, but we fell out with Miss Schpicter in the end because she used to turn up whenever she liked – and one time she just walked in when I was watching the telly in my underpants. She made this shocked sort of 'ooh' noise (I don't blame her for that, obviously, as I'm sure it was an impressive sight), and I gave her a bit of an earful: 'That'll teach you to walk into people's houses without knocking,' or words to that effect. I think there was a bit of trouble at t'mill after that, but not bad enough so that we had to leave.

Hertford Street was just round the back of the Hilton. And in the final stages of filming *Breaking Glass* I used to walk round to the front of the hotel in the morning and get my car to pick me up there. My twenty-first birthday came around at that time, and people on the production got me a cake made with 'Happy Birthday . . . from the Hilton Laundry' written on it.

My mate Johnny Moyce used to be my driver, and he doubled up as my stand-in when they were setting up the lighting. He had a big old Jag, which really looked the business, and he'd done the same job for me on *Quadrophenia* for a while. At that point – before I met Jan – there were a couple of girls I was seeing, and he used to drop me off at their flats and then pick me up from the same address first thing in the morning. He was really good to me, Johnny.

Hazel O'Connor was big in the tabloids for a while after *Breaking*

Glass came out. She became one half of a kind of bargain-basement New Romantic Posh 'n' Becks with Ultravox's Midge Ure, or Urge Minge, as I called him. It's not an exact anagram, but I like to pretend it is. She was a bit of a novice in acting terms, Hazel, but the chemistry of her band worked really well on the screen. It was Tibbsy – Gary Tibbs – on bass, Brain Damage Wingett on guitar, Peter-Hugo on drums and Jonathan Pryce on sax. It wasn't Jonathan playing on 'Will You', though – it was Wesley Magoogan from the Beat who did that famous sax solo.

The last time I saw Hazel O'Connor was at Brian Gibson's funeral a few years back. He was a really good director, and he died really young – of cancer – so it was a very sad occasion. She sang 'Will You' really beautifully. The line 'Or will you just, politely, say goodnight?' was a real tear-jerker, in that context.

She lives in Ireland now, and I think she's one of the Orange People (the religion, not the mobile phones). She definitely had a picture of the Bhagwan round her neck – he looked like a Labrador, that geezer. She's still a lovely person, even if she is in a sect. A lot of people doubted her at the time, but she'd had a band and been out there doing it for years on a small-time basis before *Breaking Glass* ever came along. And she's still out there now, as far as I know, doing what she loves.

For all my envying how much attention she got, I don't think Hazel made much money out of all the hit singles that came off the soundtrack, because the rights went to the people who produced the film (Davina Belling and Clive Parsons – it was them who produced the film version of *Scum* as well, which I assume was how I got the part in the first place). Hazel had a second album later on, which Tony Visconti also produced, but I don't think so many people got to hear that one.

24: CHINA IN OUR HANDS

You could tell Jan's flat was in a posh neighbourhood, because a high-class prostitute lived upstairs. And if you looked out of the window to the back, you could see the mews house where the racing driver Stirling Moss lived.

It wasn't just the prossies who were lowering the tone of the area. I used to get a bit rowdy when I went out in those days, and I ended up being banned from most of the local pubs in Shepherds Market. King's Cross could stand my behaviour, but it was too much for Mayfair. Me and this guy called Tony London – who was in Nigel Williams' play *Line 'Em* with me – used to go out, get drunk and upset the landlords. He was a lovely bloke, Tony. He was in a film called *Party Party* a few years later, which was like the British *Porkies*.

It was good to be back working with Nigel Williams again. I'd had a few cinematic adventures, but if you're an actor you've got to keep going back and treading the boards. If you learnt your trade on the floor, without a load of cameras pointing at you, you need to make sure you go back to it every now and again.

It's a great medium, the theatre, in its own way, especially if you're interested in doing political stuff, which at that point I was. *Line 'Em* was about the Trade Union Movement and modern Britain clashing, which was about as topical as you could get in 1979–80. The year after the Winter of Discontent, with Margaret Thatcher newly in power, secondary picketing was very much a hot topic.

There was definitely an us-versus-them mood in the air, and in the great confrontations that were coming, the social group I would think of as 'us' was definitely going to come off worst. For the moment, though, the forces of militant trade unionism were still perceived as quite formidable, and they were the subject of *Line 'Em*.

The first half of the play is set around a brazier on a picket line, and it's an ideological battle between a young radical and a more moderate old sweat (guess which one I played). In the second half the army turn up, and I have a very foul-mouthed verbal duel with a posh captain. It ends with a Scottish squaddie pointing a gun at my head, and me ranting at him. Then there's a blackout.

Line 'Em was one of the longest parts I'd ever had to learn. That was a really exciting time for me. I was twenty-one years old, living with my girlfriend for the first time in the most expensive stop on the Monopoly board, getting massive parts with tons of lines and pulling them off, whether or not the critics understood what I was doing. They did *quite* like me, but they still felt that there was a certain art to acting that wasn't really being observed.

I think some people thought that because us Anna Scher boys and girls were a bit oikish, we'd have trouble learning really long parts, and I loved proving them wrong. When I played Alex in *A Clockwork Orange*, a few years later, I effectively had to learn most of the book. Plays are the easiest things to pick up, if you put the work in. Once you get the rhythm, they're more like songs, whereas TV scripts are very, very bitty.

Around this time we had a bit of real-life drama. One night, when my mum and dad were away on holiday, me and Jan stayed over in King's Cross – I suppose the long journey home to Mayfair must have seemed like too much hassle. I was woken in the night by a smell of burning, so I got up and had a look out of the window, only to see that the curry house downstairs had gone up in flames.

It was very fragrant smoke, but, given that the flat in Jessel House was only on the first floor, the fire was definitely heading our way. We got out of there sharpish, and we were standing down on Judd

Street – by the Salvation Army – watching the curry house burn, when the fire brigade turned up and started trying to break into our gaff to get me out. I was shouting, 'I'm here! I'm here!' Luckily, the fire hadn't had time to get up to our floor, so there wasn't too much mess to clear up afterwards.

Something dramatic often seemed to happen when my mum and dad went on holiday. My sister Brenda went out with – and eventually married – a Columbian called Julio. Another time my parents were away, Brenda, Julio and I had a few drinks one night. I went out to get some fags out of a machine at about two or three in the morning (I was still smoking like a chimney at that stage). I realized pretty quickly that some geezer was following me, so I started walking quicker and quicker, and next thing I knew there were two more of 'em after me.

I was jumping over fences, sprinting round the back of the flats, the lot. In the end, these three blokes caught up with me. It turned out – and under the circumstances, this was something of a relief – that they were Old Bill. Apparently there'd been an arsonist about (maybe it was him who set fire to the curry house), and they'd decided I was acting suspiciously.

I explained that I lived locally, and I'd just popped out to get some fags. I got a big lecture for running away (which was in itself a bit rich – what are you supposed to do if you're walking through King's Cross in the middle of the night and you realize someone is following you?) and then they insisted on accompanying me back home to check my story. They knocked on the door and took me inside, and obviously my sister got a shock, but for some reason Julio was nowhere to be seen.

It turned out he didn't have a passport, and he was hiding under the bed in fear of the immigration department. A few months later, Julio emerged from under the bed, and Brenda went off to live with him in Los Angeles. It didn't work out too well in the end, and eventually my mum and dad went over and brought Brenda back.

Now she's married to a really nice, easy-going Reading bus driver called Paul, and has two lovely kids called Bryant and Jenny. My other sister Barbara got married quite young to a guy she met at Raines Foundation school in Poplar. His name's Tony Rush (which is the same surname as Brenda's husband, strangely, so they're the Rush sisters now), and those two are happily married to this day, with two grown-up kids called Claire and Adam (who are lovely as well – I'd better be fair here or there'll be trouble at Christmas).

Although they both moved away when they were quite young, I think both my sisters would still say they've got a deep affection for King's Cross. But they didn't feel its lure as strongly as I did. After Jan and I had lived together in Hertford Street for about six months, the fair-rent rule suddenly went out of the window and living in Mayfair got as expensive as it was always meant to be. So I used the money I'd made from *Quadrophenia* and *Breaking Glass* to put down a deposit and buy a flat in Sandwich House. Nineteen grand, it cost, which doesn't look like bad value now for a one-bedroom flat within walking distance of the West End.

I knew it was King's Cross, but the estate agents (and most of the other people who lived there) liked to pretend it was Bloomsbury. My mum secured the purchase, and my dad was my caretaker, so I was really keeping things in the family.

My dad re-did the kitchen for us and made a little breakfast bar, which was really nice of him. I remember that at one point – thinking he'd done enough for us – I got a friend of mine called Les King in to do a bit of tiling. When my dad came round and saw it he said, 'That'll devalue the property.'

Even though I'd moved back to the place I grew up in, living in Sandwich House still felt like the start of a fresh chapter. Apart from anything else, Jan and I were meeting lots of new people – sometimes through her work, sometimes through mine. She'd gone on from working with Alan Edwards to become a press officer at Virgin Records. Les was a working-class guy from Birmingham whose girlfriend Pepi became Jan's best mate. They'd moved into one of the hard-to-let flats round the corner, and later on he ended up being

Big Country's tour manager, so we'd all go out drinking with them whenever they came down to London. Luckily they were very open-minded in terms of not making us all wear the checked shirts.

The writer and actor Ken Campbell – who'd played the stroppy barman in *Breaking Glass* – he moved in next door to us. This probably wasn't the best idea, as we'd never really got on. He was always doing very sixties-influenced one-man shows about the Illuminati. He had his own way of doing things, which wasn't really the same as mine. And we had a few heated debates, which made life interesting.

The most significant new presence in our lives had four legs, not two. Jan had a friend called Ouida, who was the singer in a group Alan Edwards managed called the Numbers. Ouida had bought her husband this dog, but then she had a baby so they couldn't really keep it (the dog, not the baby). I'd always wanted a canine companion, so we said we'd look after it for a while.

When we went to get it, this dog turned out to be the biggest fucking thing you've ever seen in your life – a giant Weimaraner called China. After a while China went back to Ouida's, but then he ran away. I think we had to go to Battersea Dogs Home to pick him up, and at that point I said, 'Right, we're keeping him.' We fell out with Ouida over it, because she didn't want to give us China's pedigree papers.

She said they were of sentimental value, because she'd bought him as a gift for her husband. I said, 'Why are you keeping the fucking papers when you don't want the dog?' Then it all went off. She was furious. Perry Benson jumped to my defence and I had to stop them having a fight. I love Perry Benson – I've known him nearly all my life. He was in that Shane Meadows film *Somers Town* recently. I still don't know why I never got the call for that one.

Anyway, all of a sudden, we've got this tiny flat and this giant dog. It was a bit cramped, but the three of us were really happy. In some ways it was a very domesticated set-up – we'd see my parents quite a bit, and me and my dad both drank in the Skinners Arms – but in others it was quite wild. China was a hilarious beast, and I got on famously with him 'cos he was as mad as I was.

I used to take him running up the Regent's Canal, all the way round Regent's Park then back to King's Cross. We'd get indoors and I'd sit down to have a cup of tea, then two minutes later China would be over by the door, asking to go out again. Not only was it good exercise, but he'd let me do anything I wanted: dress him up in football kit, all sorts of different fancy dress. That photographer who used to muck about with his Weimaraner all the time and take pictures of it – William Wegman – he had nothing on us two.

25: 'WHAT WAS THIS THING FROM OUTER SPACE?'

It was only after *Breaking Glass* that I finally came to terms with the profession that had chosen me, and stopped pretending that all my other options were still open. My mate Trevor Laird had a word with me. He said, 'When someone asks you what you do, just tell 'em you're an actor, instead of beating round the bush and being coy about it.' I suppose the whole enigmatic 'don't try to pigeonhole me' thing had become a bit of an act itself. Trevor could see it was a load of old bollocks, and he was right. I was better off being honest.

I'd always had it in the back of my mind that if I wasn't doing what I was doing, if the whole acting thing fell through, I'd maybe like to become a social worker. At one point in my very early twenties, when I was at a bit of a loose end for a few weeks, I went back to my old youth club, the Mary Ward. There was a guy who'd run the place for years – 'Ug' we used to call him. I popped in to see him and mentioned that maybe I'd like to come and help out.

'No, you wouldn't,' he told me. 'You'd do it for a little while, then you'd jack it in.' He sort of poured scorn on the whole scheme, but I don't think it was mean of him at all. He was probably right to think that I'd got my rose-tinted glasses on. Because I'd come from that area and got on a bit, I thought I could put something back by helping local kids – which was a nice idea in theory, but I'm not sure if I really had the right temperament to follow it through. I think it takes a special kind of character to be a youth leader – so Ug and Jay (who also worked at the Mary Ward), I take my hat off to you.

The best way for me to express my idealistic impulses was through my acting. And I got the chance to put my principles to the test when I was offered the lead role in a sitcom. I'd be playing a punk with green hair who had this sort of unlikely friendship with Brian Glover, and I'd be paid £800 a week. I'd never seen that much money before, but at the same time another offer came in that gave me a very clear choice.

I could either take the blood money for playing someone with green hair in a not-very-good mainstream TV comedy, or go to the Northcote Theatre in Exeter to play the Fool in *King Lear* for a pittance. I was much more righteous when I was younger, and didn't really care about the money, so of course I chose to take the serious actor's route and play the Fool.

Whether or not this decision worked out for the best in the long run, I can't really say; but it was definitely the right thing to do at the time. Under the circumstances, having a go at some Shakespeare was a much punkier thing to do than dyeing my hair green. And there were other compensations: at the Northcote I got to wear a codpiece.

The Northcote was basically the university theatre in Exeter, and I stayed in digs down there with the Swedish costume lady and her husband, who went out to work picking mushrooms every day in a tunnel. David Markham – Kika Markham's dad – was cast as King Lear. He was kind of acting royalty, like Gielgud or one of those people, only he'd never got quite that big. He was seventy-odd and quite frail, and now he was going to play Lear, so it was meant to be (literally, I suppose) the crowning moment of his career.

His daughter was in it too, playing Cordelia, but unfortunately the director hadn't quite grasped the regal implications of the casting. On the first day of rehearsals, he jumped straight into it – 'Let's do the heath scene: "Blow, winds, and crack your cheeks!"' – and the minute poor old David Markham got up to do his bit, the director started shouting at him: 'Louder! Do it louder!'

The next thing we knew, David had walked off the production and everyone except me found their part had stepped up in size. I've got a picture of me in my britches with my codpiece and coxcomb there for all to marvel at. It'll be interesting to see whether the publishers have let me use it in this book. It might be considered a bit too disturbing for a family readership.

Either way, I learnt a lot doing *King Lear*. I'd never done provincial theatre before, and I'd never done any Shakespeare. And there was one experience I had when I was down in Devon which suggested that there are more things in heaven and earth than were dreamt of even in the Bard's philosophy.

I had a Honda 90 motorbike at the time, which I took down on the train to ride around in Exeter with me. There was an actress in the company called Patti Love – I think Hoskins had gone out with her for a while, as he'd started out at the Northcote Theatre. Anyway, Patti was staying in a caravan right out in the middle of nowhere. And during rehearsals she invited me and a few of the cast out to her place for dinner one evening, so off I went on my motorbike out into the fields and hills of Devon.

I was driving along this country lane when I saw a huge ball of fire in the sky. It was maybe sixty or eighty yards away, over the top of a hedge. It wasn't really moving. In fact it was dead still. But I drove off one way, and it followed me. So I turned round and went in the opposite direction, and it followed me that way too. I stopped again and stared at it. I was kind of excited but also shitting myself at the same time. At that point, the ball of fire went 'Whoosh!' and was gone.

When I eventually found my way to Patti's caravan, I told everyone what had happened. I didn't know what I'd seen – the only thing it could have been was ball-lightning, but it wasn't a stormy night, and the fact that it followed me was still pretty weird. Obviously no one believed me. I think someone said, 'Oh yeah, some Martian just climbed over the trees at the back,' – so I've never really told anyone since about my close-ish encounter with an Unidentified Flying Object. I hope you believe me, though.

At this point in my career, I'd decided to pursue a policy of educating myself through Shakespeare. He's a wonderful writer – and thank God I'd been too busy keeping those British Museum mummies company to do any of his plays at school, so the teachers hadn't had a chance to ruin them for me.

I remember helping my daughter out when she was doing *Othello* for her GCSEs some years later, and she hated everything about it, because it was all about footnotes and 'What did he feel there?' Whereas I thought it shouldn't be about dissecting it all and looking into the historical background – you've got to act it out to understand what the whole thing's about.

Generally, if you read a Shakespeare play, you'll get a couple of inches of the actual dialogue and the rest of the page will just be notes by some intellectual explaining their idea of what's going on. Of course you have to be helped at times – when the original text just seems like a load of old gobbledegook, it's good to find out exactly what was meant. But it's only on the page in the first place because it's meant to be acted. That's when it comes alive. Otherwise the whole experience is just too scholarly for my liking.

I got the chance to do my bit to help make learning Shakespeare less painful for schoolchildren not long after *King Lear*, when I was cast as Puck in a BBC production of *A Midsummer Night's Dream*, directed by Elijah Mohsinsky. This one came up out of the blue, but it's been on the school syllabus for years, and I still get people coming up to me and saying, 'I saw your Puck.' Which is better than, 'I saw your Bottom,' I suppose.

Helen Mirren played Titania and obviously – as Puck – it was my professional duty to crawl all over her. This was a dirty job, but someone had to do it. There was a funny picture on the front cover of the *Radio Times* the week *A Midsummer Night's Dream* went out, of Helen lying there in her pomp and me all over her like a rash.

I'd actually worked with her before, when I'd had a small part in a restoration drama of some kind that she was starring in. I remember she used to read the *NME* at that point. I don't know whether she still does.

She came down to the Old Red Lion with her (then) boyfriend Liam Neeson for a pint with me once, and there was a bit of an altercation. One of the regulars in the pub was trying to get away with playing pool and darts at the same time – hogging the table and the board. And when I pointed out that by any conventional measure this constituted a clear breach of tavern etiquette (or words roughly to that effect), he threw a punch at me.

A full-scale bar-room brawl erupted, with me, Liam Neeson, Trevor Laird and Helen Mirren on one side and the pool-cue-toting darts player and friends on the other. It didn't last long, but I think Helen acquitted herself quite well. I can't remember the overall outcome, except that I was barred from that pub for years.

Brian Glover was in that version of *A Midsummer Night's Dream* as well, which in a way felt appropriate. I'd turned down the green-hair job, and as a result our paths crossed in a slightly more illustrious context. He was a wrestler, Brian, as well as an actor: Leon Aris, he called himself. I think he pretended to be French and wore a mask, but I don't know if he ever fought that other part-time grappler, Jimmy Savile.

The thing about Shakespeare that a lot of people don't get is that it's not just high culture, it's high culture and low culture at the same time. That was why I played Puck as a West Ham fan. Because it's all in verse, there are times when it feels almost like rhyming slang. So not only is it really easy to learn, but also the kind of sarcastic, rabble-rousing wit you'd encounter in a football crowd is very appropriate to the character. I really enjoyed delivering lines like, 'I go, I go; look how I go/Swifter than arrow from the Tartar's bow,' and then sort of ambling away at a funereal pace.

Given that a lot of the pleasure of doing plays in the theatre is how the performance develops over time, you'd think doing Shakespeare for TV – where you need only the one good take – wouldn't be half as much fun. But actually it works really well, because they can go in close on the big speeches and let you talk directly to the audience, rather than having to stand up and belt it out like you would in the theatre.

I remember they did a TV version of *Richard III* as well at around the same time – with Ron Cook as the hunchback – and that was fantastic. Iago in *Othello* would be fantastic on TV as well, 'cos he can just whisper it. That's probably the part I haven't yet had a go at but would most like to do; hopefully in the not-too-distant future as well, 'cos I'm kind of the right age now.

I did a bit of TV Dickens around the same time as Puck, and that was another eye-opener. I'd never really read any Dickens before, either, and then all of a sudden I was doing *The Pickwick Papers* in an eight-part series for the BBC. Nigel Stock was Pickwick, Patrick Malahide was Mr Jingle, and I was Sam Weller. He's quite sub-servient, Sam Weller, but he's one of the nicest people you could imagine – he means werry vell. And, having often been described as a bit of an Artful Dodger character myself, it was really interesting to go back to the linguistic source and have a bit of a bumble around with the Pickwickians.

This was exactly what I thought the life of an actor was supposed to be – doing it all, learning new things, and taking my own experi-ence into different areas, where I'd be able to add a twist of my own to classic texts. Unfortunately, just as this bright professional future was opening up in front of me, the 1980s happened.

26: DANNY DANIELS TAKES
IT TO THE BRIDGE

Timing the precise point at which a new decade begins is not as exact a science as you might think. People often say that the seventies started at Altamont in 1969, or that the eighties kicked off ten years later, with Mrs Thatcher on the steps of 10 Downing Street making St Francis of Assisi turn in his grave by nicking his prayer off him. For me personally, though, the real starting point of the latter somewhat problematic decade was the 1979 *Evening Standard* Film Awards.

I was up for two films at the same time – *Scum* and *Quadrophenia*. But the person the judges decided was the Best British Newcomer of the previous year was Simon MacCorkindale, for his performance in Agatha Christie's *Death on the Nile*. It was on that night that I sort of realized, 'Oh fuck! So *that*'s what they think an award-winning actor should be.' When you get to the ceremony and see him sitting in the front row, then you have to walk all the way up to a seat high in the gods, you know you ain't won.

There's no denying I was a bit disappointed. Although I did come up with a nice little conspiracy theory: *Death on the Nile* had been partly financed with money invested by Lord Mountbatten; and, since he'd got blown up by the IRA that year, they decided to give Simon the award as a political gesture. This theory still seems just as plausible thirty years on.

A couple of years later, when *Chariots of Fire* won its Oscars, and Colin Welland made his famous 'The British are coming' speech, it was clear that in this context 'the British' meant that lot (i.e., the floppy-fringed denizens of costume-drama's corseted dream-world, or 'Thatcher's actors', as I fondly termed them) not us lot. But, as is so often the case with this kind of apparently clear-cut class divide, the boundaries were a bit more porous than they initially appeared.

Colin Welland might have written *Chariots of Fire*, but he was also in *Kes*. I worked with him at the RSC a few years later – in Howard Brenton's *The Churchill Play*. He was all right, Colin. For some not-very-good reason that I can't quite remember, we used to call him 'Bobby Bollocks' and pretend he was an old-school Northern comedian rejoicing in that name – sort of like an imaginary *Viz* character. 'Oh look,' we'd say jokingly, 'here comes Bobby Bollocks.' 'Oh, don't do that, lads,' Colin would reply (in exactly the kind of voice that a Northern club comic called Bobby Bollocks would use), 'it's not fair on me.'

They're the ones you've really got to watch, though – the working-class actors who've gone native. I knew people who were in *Chariots of Fire,* and there were things about that film that I liked – even while finding it a bit portentous. It was clever, and it was based on a true story, but it portrayed an image of England to America that was old school, public school, and had nothing to do with anything that I was doing – or wanted to do – as an actor. That was probably why the Americans liked it so much.

I don't think the whole thing was even that calculated on the part of the people who made it; they just got lucky. Like the cast of that film about male strippers – *The Full Monty*. I'd been in a sitcom a few years earlier with Mark Addy (who played the geezer with the little willy). He's a good mate of mine and a really good actor – and he told me later that all the leads in that film got offered either a one-off payment or a share of its box-office takings. There's no way of knowing, when you do a job like that, whether it's going to work or not, and no one expected *The Full Monty* to do much at the box office here, let alone in America, so you couldn't blame the people who took their money upfront. But the ones who chose a percent-age were laughing all the way to the bank. (I would have probably gone for the money upfront, myself.)

In the early eighties I had to make a big professional decision of my own. I'd been feeling for a while that I needed to leave Anna's. And not just because the whole deal with my album had got well Tévez-ed up. Anna's forte was teaching kids, not being the agent for a whole generation of adult actors.

The trouble was that there were too many of us of roughly the same ilk. And, because we'd all come up at the same time, we were all going for the same jobs. We couldn't carry on forever expecting people to write scripts that needed a gang of us; the time had come to go out into the grown-up world as individuals. What I needed was to be part of a stable where different people did different things.

It was hard to leave, though, because Anna and Charles had helped me so much in the early stages of my career. There was a time when all we were interested in was going to the pub together after those Friday sessions. But, once you're an adult, the whole acting game becomes a bit more of a business. And by the time I was nine-teen or twenty I just wanted to get out and work and show everyone what I could do.

Anna was quite ill for a while, so I stayed on for a bit longer than I intended to, but when she got better, I moved to Sally Hope's. Sally was Bob Hoskins' agent – he must have told me about her when we were having the odd dooberry together on *Zulu Dawn*. As well as Bob, she also had Jim Broadbent and Cherie Lunghi. So it was a dif-ferent kind of set-up, and much more grown up. Sally was a strong, forthright, no-nonsense agent. Her office was in Islington – which was local – and we all got on fine together for the next few years.

Things didn't go quite so well for Anna after I'd left, sadly. Her continuing illness meant more time off – and when she got back, her theatre had kind of been taken away from her. It had been made much more formal (it was the Anna Scher Young People's Theatre, now) and it had become a bit of a production line.

To understand how this came about, you'll need a bit of background on the high-pressure world of London theatre schools. Before Anna came along, there were two main options for kids who were serious about becoming actors but didn't already have a plum. You had the choice of either Italia Conti's – which was a proper day-school, and people like Dennis Waterman went there – or a bit of Barbara Speake.

When you come down off the Westway, heading out of London, and you get to that big crossroads in Acton, there used to be two big furniture shops on the corner, called Speake Brothers. I think Barbara was their sister, and her school had been running for years. It was the most old-fashioned of the lot, all teeth and smiles.

I think Phil Collins went to Barbara Speake's too, because his mum taught there. He's one of those pop people who'll always tell you he's been an actor for fifty-seven years, which gets on my nerves a bit. He gets the right hump, Phil Collins, doesn't he? I remember Noel Gallagher cracked a joke about him once, and so he went straight on that TV show *Room 101* and dumped Oasis in there as an act of vengeance.

The way Anna Scher changed the game was that – at least up until I left, although it's all different now – you never had to have your song-and-dance routine ready for auditions. All you had was your skill at improvisation. Whereas those other places would insist that you learn how to do the old soft-shoe shuffle as well, which is why Ray Winstone still carries his ballet shoes with him at all times: he's always hoping someone's going to ask him to demonstrate his dancing skills. Try it if you see him in the street and see what happens.

I like *movement*, but not so much formal dance – those experimental companies who do shows about commuters walking down the street; I really enjoy that kind of thing. But I don't suppose you bought this book to read about mine and Ray Winstone's differing approaches to modern dance . . .

What happened in the wake of Anna's success – and especially once *EastEnders* got going, in the mid-eighties – was that other people started applying some of her techniques, but in a much more explicitly commercial way. People moan a lot about the seventies, but at least there was still a bit of idealism around then. In the next decade, caring about anything other than money seemed to go right out of fashion.

These new schools were like manufacturing outlets, turning out people who could get into soaps and maybe do a bit of presenting. And unfortunately, when Anna recovered and tried to go back to work, she found that her own school had been slightly remade in that image. I suppose things move on. But for me, Anna stands at the pinnacle of theatre-in-education as an innovator, peace activist, and the best teacher I ever had.

People sometimes ask if I wish I'd had the kind of agent who would've encouraged me to have a go at Hollywood during this period. The opportunity would probably have been there for me from the moment I got the part in *Zulu Dawn* onwards; but at that time Renoir still loomed large in my mind, and there wasn't anything I was doing that I was ready to give up.

I just never really fancied going to LA, and it never really came to me. Anna didn't push me that way, and neither did Sally Hope. Maybe if instead of being old-fashioned and just having an agent I'd had a manager as well – one of those people who will really push to maximize their 25 per cent – they might have talked me into it, but you've got to really go out there and chase it to have any chance of making it in America, and somehow I was always too busy enjoying myself at home. Besides, I knew there were big money-spinners out there for me right on my own doorstep, like becoming a football correspondent for the *Morning Star*.

Just down the road from the Skinners Arms, where I used to drink, was the headquarters of the National Union of Students. There was a guy called Chris Natrat who I met in the pub who used to work for the NUS and also the communist newspaper the *Morning Star*. He was a proper leftie, and a really good sportswriter – one of the first real investigative journalists in that area. I think he went on to work for *The Times*, where he wrote a column called 'Inside Sport'. Anyway, I got quite matey with him, and one day he told me, 'If you fancy doing a bit of journalism, there's a press-ticket for Chelsea going.'

Of course I said, 'No problem,' and I ended up doing it for two or three seasons. All you had to do was write a little bit about Chelsea every couple of weeks, and you got in for nothing to every home game, with sandwiches and a cup of tea at half time. Danny Daniels – that was my journalistic nom-de-plume. I used to phone in my match report to the stenographer on a Saturday night. Sometimes she'd tell me off and say, 'That's not very good English,' and there'd be a bit of grammar I'd have to put right, but generally it all went smoothly enough.

I was kind of looked on as a bit of a novelty at Stamford Bridge – when they saw this young geezer who was also an actor hanging out with all the football writers, they didn't quite know what to make of me. John Neal was Chelsea's manager for most of my journalistic reign, and I'd always turn up at the press conference after the game and pop in a question or two. Whenever I couldn't go because I was off on an acting job, my mate Trevor Laird would fill in for me. He'd turn up wearing a big Russian hat, in honour of the fact that he was working for the *Morning Star*. And because he was from a West Indian background we called him the 'Black Russian'.

Obviously, Chelsea in the early eighties wasn't quite such a high-profile operation as it is now that a different type of Russian is running the show. We were a Second Division team in those days, and the nearest we got to getting anywhere on my watch was losing 3–2 at home to Tottenham in the quarter-final of the FA Cup. It was the time of Micky Droy, Phil Driver and Mickey Fillery, and, basically, we were a bit shit. Even though I loved Mickey Fillery. Still do, in fact.

I used to enjoy sitting with all the big sports dudes, though – Brian Woolnough, people like that – and writing up my report on the press desk afterwards. I didn't alienate anybody, but I think the chairman, Ken Bates, put a block on the *Morning Star* in the end – in his slightly right-wing way, he decided that it was not a national paper. There was an argument to be had about that, but I didn't make too much fuss. The whole thing was just a bit of a wheeze, really, but it was fun while it lasted.

Standing in for Hugh Cornwell of the Stranglers – that was another good gig. It would also end up being a bit of a dress rehearsal for my later role as the elder statesman of Britpop, though of course I didn't realize that at the time. The whole thing came about partly through Alan Edwards (who was then co-managing the band), and partly because I already knew Hugh. He was also one of Sally Hope's clients, and he'd had the odd chat with me about wanting to become an actor.

What happened was that Hugh Cornwell got put in jail for two months. He was banged up in Pentonville – just down the road from me – for having some heroin on him. I don't think he was really expected to get a custodial sentence, because it was only a little bit for personal use, but he was unlucky and the judge went garrity because he was a pop star. That kind of thing doesn't happen so much any more – otherwise Pete Doherty would be doing a thirty-year stretch.

The Stranglers had two gigs booked at the Rainbow in Finsbury Park (and the fact that this venue was still open shows how long ago it was – my internet research tells me that the 3rd and 4th of April 1980 were the historic dates) that they didn't want to cancel. So Robert Fripp, Wilko Johnson and Robert Smith of the Cure played Hugh's guitar parts, and I was one of a series of guest vocalists, alongside Toyah, Ian Dury and Hazel O'Connor.

I know this all sounds a bit unlikely, but there's a live CD out there somewhere to prove it really happened. The Stranglers songs I did were 'Dead Loss Angeles' and 'Toiler on the Sea'. To make the whole scenario even more improbable, Joy Division were the support act for the second show, which must have been one of their last gigs (apparently, they played at the Moonlight in Hampstead on the same

Me as Spurio and Julie Legrand as the Duchess in
The Revenger's Tragedy, RSC, 1987

Ithamore, *Jew of Malta*,
RSC, 1987

My mum, with her hairy Shakespearean son

Me and my hound china on the dog and bone, circa 1987

Backstage with Toyah at a Bowie gig in the eighties

Me, Ella and Jan on holiday

Me and the Blur boys, Glastonbury 1996, getting ready for 'Parklife'

Who's the daddy? Chelsea vs. Middlesbrough Coca-Cola Cup Final 1997

Me and Damon playing for England vs. Scotland. 1:0 to England. Scorer, Albarn

Trevor Laird and me
walking through
King's Cross at the end
of the century

Me and a
cheeky little
Ella, 1995

Left: Me and Dawn French in
Sex and Chocolate, 1997

Below: Me as bulimic
restaurant critic Gary Rickey
with David Morrissey in
Holding On, 1997

Dunbar, Defence Solicitor,
Outlaws, 2004

'Jack the Hat' in
The Long Firm,
2004

Getting ready for my stint in *EastEnders*

Me and the lovely
Barbara Windsor

Another sixty-foot putt
goes down the plughole

Training for the
London Marathon
2008

evening and Ian Curtis had a really bad epileptic fit because of the strobe lights). It was quite a strange experience, all in all, but I enjoyed singing at the Rainbow – especially given that my character in *Breaking Glass* got thrown out of an after-show party there.

27: 'BABY, I'M YOUR MEANTIME MAN'

It was much harder for Mike Leigh to get the finance to make a film back in the eighties than it would be now, because there was no script at the start of the process, so people never knew what they were going to end up with. But somehow he managed to get a deal together that got *Meantime* going out on prime-time ITV – and me and Tim Roth and Gary Oldman going head to head certainly made a nice change from *Brideshead Revisited*.

Meantime was a hard-hitting drama about a working-class family in the East End of London. They were worn down by lost opportunities, and had long given up any hope of living the good life, but there was something about the painfully direct way they spoke to each other that conveyed their humanity as well as their frustration.

I think we had about eight weeks of rehearsals and then six weeks of filming. When you first sign up to work with Mike Leigh, you know there's a chance you could end up as a major character; but that's not always the case, and you won't know for sure till you see the finished film.

The first thing that happens is Mike Leigh tells you to make a list of all the people you know who are roughly the same age as you. Then there are various one-to-one meetings where you talk about them, and whittle down the names to a shortlist of three or four. You know he'll be doing this with all the main actors, exploring different possibilities, but you've no idea of the extent to which he'll have got everything that's going to happen worked out beforehand.

I'm sure there were things about *Meantime* that Mike had decided on in advance. He definitely knew it would be set in the East End – but suburban East London as well as the inner city, because there's that whole Chigwell thing going on as well. And unemployment was clearly going to be a major theme. None of the main characters worked – in fact, we all signed on together – except for Alfred Molina, who was Auntie Barbara's husband, and wasn't in the finished film as much as we'd expected him to be.

Mass unemployment was certainly big news in the early eighties, but it was an interesting departure for Mike Leigh to make a film about something political that was actually going on at the time. His reputation at that stage was based more on painful social comedies like *Abigail's Party*, or *Nuts in May,* which was about a couple of earnest vegetarians on a camping holiday.

The first of the three names on my character shortlist (and I hope none of them will take this amiss, as I'm not sure they all know) was Les King: the guy who did my tiling, and who'd arrived with the wave of newcomers to the short-term housing in King's Cross. He's quite a tough cookie, Les – uncompromising, but fun, which was something I'd always admired about him. He'd had a difficult childhood, and had done a bit of bird.

Cliff Maynard was number two. He was a born-and-bred King's Cross guy who was a bit of a wheeler-dealer. I didn't even know him that well, but I'd noticed he had a way about him that was a bit aloof. And, last but not least, there was Studs. He was another mate from King's Cross, who was a bit of a blagger. He always had a camera with him, and he used to take pictures of tourists and say he'd send them to 'em for money. He was a smudger – that's what you call them: he used to take smudges. I think he had a monkey for a while, as well. Up until about twenty years ago, it wasn't that uncommon for smudgers down the West End to have monkeys for tourists to have their pictures taken with.

I talked to Mike Leigh for hours about these people. There's nothing disrespectful about this – it's not like you're taking the piss out of them. It's just a way of accumulating detail, and getting yourself used to the idea of trying to get into someone else's head. It's very interesting, as you really open up and have a good chat. I think it's an important part of the process for Mike as well – to find out what you feel, and where you're coming from with it all. You do that for ages, and then gradually start to build up momentum in a sequence of improvisations.

Mike will stand you in a corner and say, 'Be Clifford Maynard making a cup of tea.' You have to face the wall for a while, but then when you're ready to start the improvisation, he'll always make you wait a little bit longer than you really need to, just to give it that extra edge. Then, after you've been Cliff Maynard making a cup of tea for a while, he'll send you into another corner to be Les King, and then another one to be Studs. Finally, once you've got your starting points clear in your mind, he'll ask you to join all three of them up and become Mark Pollack.

One of the main things about Mark was he was a bit obstreperous – he would never do what anyone else wanted. This ended up being quite funny, because while the integrity of the character was obviously very important to Mike Leigh, there were certain things he needed Mark to do for the story. So we'd have quite a lot of 'Could you find a way to do that?' conversations.

He would have a chat with me about going to my uncle and auntie's with the family for dinner on a Sunday, and then he'd ask if my character would ever do that, and I'd say, 'Fucking hell, no.' Then we'd have another session a while later and he'd say, 'Could he possibly? I mean, is there any way?' I'd stand my ground and say I didn't think he would. Then Mike would get a bit exasperated – 'All right, your character's dead.' 'OK then, I'll go . . .'

The early stages of doing this are great, then you get to a certain level and it's not so much fun on your own: you want to interact with other people, and you're impatiently waiting for that to happen.

All the secret-squirrel stuff that Mike insists on – the actors not being allowed to discuss what they're doing, or to speculate about how all the different characters might fit together – is designed to maximize the impact of these first meetings.

One day, the four of us were called together – me, Tim Roth and the characters Mavis and Frank, the mum and dad – and Mike told us we were a family. Pam Ferris, who played Mavis, was totally unknown then, but became very famous later on as David Jason's bountiful missus Ma Larkin in *The Darling Buds of May* (she's also fantastic as Mrs Trunchbull, the evil headmistress in that kid's drama *Matilda*). Her character in *Meantime* is about as far away from Ma Larkin as you could possibly get, though. Mavis looks a bit like that woman who kid-napped her own daughter to try to get the reward money.

Jeff Robert, the guy who played Frank, seemed initially to be an odd choice. He'd done a lot of stuff in the theatre, but hadn't done a lot of telly. I think Jeff had gone to Oxford University, and he hadn't really had much to do with people who lived in tower-blocks before, so he had to act his socks off just to hold his own, where the rest of us could slide into it a little bit easier.

Mike Leigh really pushed him – it would be fair to say Mike wasn't Jeff's favourite person by the end of it all – and that only enhanced his put-upon air. In the end his resentment about the whole situation came out in a way that was really plausible. So when he said things that were slightly wrong – like, 'Who's he think he is, Ernie Wise?' – it made his character's frustration and sense of impotence all the more tangible.

I think Mike had got Frank and Mavis together first, and worked on how they might've met, and how things would've been between them when they first got married. Then I was brought in, as their first child. At this point we had to sit around and do these strange hand improvisations. I'd never heard of this technique before, but it's a very good way of working out where you stand with people.

Mike would say something like, 'You're really young – a baby, even – now reach out your hand to your mum, and ask for affection.'

Then the way that she took your hand told you how she felt about you. Mavis was pretty fucking cold, I can tell you. I'd be stretching my hand forward, wanting something, and she'd maybe give me a little bit, but then snatch her hand away. At the same time, she and Frank would have their own hand thing going, and I don't think there was much warmth going on there either. David Jason's cockles would've frozen on him.

It wasn't as much like a séance as it sounds – you don't turn the lights off or anything. But it really gave you a sense of the characters' shared history, so that when you moved forward in time to the point where you actually had to start acting, you knew exactly how much Mavis loved you, and how much she and Frank cared about each other.

By the time Tim Roth got thrown into the mix, our parents had set the tone by rejecting us, and we were vying for superiority. He'd be reaching out wanting to be my mate, and I'd be knocking him back a bit. Then we grew up, and suddenly he'd gone a bit funny. On the DVD extras, he probably says something really sensitive like, 'Colin had to run away, and there was nowhere for him to go but inside.' But as far as Mark is concerned, his brother's a Muppet.

There was something missing with me for a while when we were putting the family together, and eventually we realized what it was. I was the only one not wearing glasses. I never wore them in those days, although I do now (I'd been told to as a kid, but I'd just never bothered). As soon as I got a pair of bins on, though, I fitted in. The minute we were all specced up, the Pollacks were a family.

It's a very exciting moment when Mike sends you out into the streets in character for the first time. We used to rehearse in an old disused factory on the border of Hackney and Haggerston – at the other end of the Regent's Canal from where I used to run with China. One day, I was doing an improvisation with Mavis and she said, 'Mark, go and get me a loaf of bread,' and gave me the money, so off I went, leaving the rest of the family to carry on acting.

At times like that, there was no way of knowing if Mike was

going to stay where he was or follow you to check you were still in character. I was round the corner, buying the bread from this little Indian shop, and as I took the loaf off the shelf, there he was, standing in the corner, watching. It was obviously a good way for him to work out what might make an interesting external shot without having to set the whole thing up first.

By this time, the characters were all pretty much formed, and I remember one night me, Tim, Gary Oldman, Paul Daly and Herbert Norville (who'd been in *Scum* with me as well) had to go to this bar and play pool together in character. Each time you do that, you wonder whether this is the time the locals are gonna batter you for being oddballs.

Hoxton was properly rough in those days – it wasn't the coolhunters paradise it is now. Our only failsafe was that if it all went off, we knew we could shout, 'It's him!' and point at Mike Leigh, sitting in the corner nursing his half-pint glass. As it turned out, we were kind of accepted.

Being accepted caused problems of its own, though. I remember one day, when we were filming in the estate, the camera was shooting me coming out of the bookies from the top of a block of flats, and this bloke I knew from the old days comes up and goes, 'All right, how're you doing?' The scene was going really well, and I didn't want him to spoil the take, so I pretended I didn't know him. At first he took offence and thought I was being all high and mighty, but luckily he was OK about it once they'd cut and I could explain what was going on. Basically, the minute someone comes up and says, 'You're Phil Daniels, ain't ya?' you just have to bail out and go back to the beginning. You can't afford to get into an argument about it.

It's important to bear in mind that you are taking a bit of a liberty. What you're doing in a Mike Leigh film is definitely method acting: you're not just acting like someone else, you're trying to be that person. And when you're out and about in the community, it's a bit like being *The Secret Millionaire*. You're coming across people who are just being themselves, and essentially lying to them, without even sweetening the deal by giving them thirteen grand for a new kitchen at the end of the show.

You're working hard enough for your money, though, that's for sure. After each day's filming is finished, you have to go on and improvise what you're going to do the next day (another unusual thing about Mike Leigh's work is that it's generally shot consecutively). He'll start the improvisation off by giving you the basic situation, just like Anna Scher used to do – 'You've got to go to the dole office tomorrow, and you haven't got your bus fare' – and then he'll have this script supervisor write the whole thing down in shorthand. It's amazing the way she keeps up.

When you come in the next morning, there's a script waiting based on what you've just done. Sometimes there might be lines that aren't in it but should be. Then obviously you pipe up and say, 'Why ain't that bit there any more?' and Mike will either put it back in or give you a reason why it's gone. Even once the script is there, however, it's not absolutely set in stone. If the old light bulb goes off when you're filming, occasionally you still might get to go for some improvisation. That whole routine about the ants which Tim Roth did in *Meantime* was done that way.

In subsequent years, I became slightly frustrated with the process of making improvised films, because I wanted that kind of spontaneity to be permitted more often, and to be filmed. But on *Meantime* it was all new to me, and I found the whole experience really exciting.

Now I just want to do the improvisations and film them, but because there are so many other things that have to be organized – like the little matter of where the camera is going to be – you often end up re-hashing an edited version of something that worked better the first time around. It's a bit like redoing *Scum*.

Effectively, you end up just learning your lines and doing a script, the same as you would do normally. So improvisation is a big part of the process, but it's not actually an improvised film. Obviously that's how Mike Leigh earns his 'devised by . . .' credit, and I don't have any problem with that at all. It acknowledges the fact that the people who are in the film have helped come up with the dialogue. And I've never been one of those actors who think they should get loads of extra attention just because they've contributed the odd line to the script.

One of my best lines in *Meantime* is when Mavis says, 'I'm eating, Mark,' and Mark replies, 'I know, I can hear you.' I can still remember Mike Leigh coming up with that one, and whispering it into my ear after I'd done a couple of takes without it that hadn't been so good.

28: CLARKEY'S ANGELS

There's a big moment at the end of *Meantime* where Tim Roth's kept the hood of his parka up, because he's had his head shaved, and I pull it down and call him 'Kojak', and we sort of smile at each other. In some ways it's the emotional climax of the film, because it's one time when it definitely feels like I'm being brotherly and protective towards him.

There was a bit of a tussle in the run-up to that scene, because there was meant to be this big discovery that Tim's character, Colin, had gone and got himself a skinhead. Mike had sneaked him off to get his head shaved in secret, and now there he was with his hood up. The only problem was that my character wouldn't have given a shit about whether he had his hood up or not. So we started the improvisation in the morning and went all the way through to dinnertime without me saying anything about it. In the end we'd both gone to bed, and I still hadn't reacted.

By the time we'd been doing that for about seven hours, Mike Leigh was tearing his hair out. He was getting fed up with his own process. It was important for the film that Colin's hood got taken off, but in real life Mark wouldn't have given him the satisfaction of seeming like he was bothered. In the end I think Mike told me, 'Just take his fucking hood off,' and that was the end of it.

It's an interesting one, *Meantime*, because some people like my character, and some people really don't. Of course Mark thinks everything he's doing is for the best – whatever character you're playing, they've always got to *think* their motives are the right ones, even if they're a restaurant critic, or a murderer – but whether that's actually true is debatable. It's kind of difficult for Mark and Colin, because Mark doesn't know if he's mental or not, but at the same time he's a bit jealous when Auntie Barbara asks Colin to do a bit of decorating for her, because he secretly fancies her a little bit.

Mike Leigh should have encouraged me and Auntie Barbara to have a shag – that would've been great. She's lovely, Marion Bailey, who plays my aunt. But maybe all that excitement would have spoiled the sombre mood he was trying to create.

As well as a certain amount of sexual tension in the air, there's a kind of weird, messed-up left-wingness going on as well, like when Mark's in the dole office and the woman working there asks for her pen back, and he goes '*Our* pen.' He's an intelligent guy, and you feel that he could maybe have gone to college and done this and that, instead of just being stuck sharing a room with his brother in his mum and dad's flat. So when he stops Colin doing Auntie Barbara's decorating, it's a matter of principle in one way – but not in another.

Some people love that film, though. Blur certainly do. I think it's one of the main reasons they wanted me to do 'Parklife'. Graham Coxon knows pretty much the whole script off by heart, and he was (and in fact still is) always coming out with chunks of it. I've heard it suggested that maybe subliminally he sees some kind of parallel between the way Colin and Mark are with each other and the relationship between himself and Damon Albarn, but I can't see that myself.

I think Damon has more in common with Tim Roth. Neither of them is quite sure where they come from: that's one of the things that makes them both so interesting.

Mike Leigh's the same, in a way. But the thing about Mike is that on the face of it he seems to come from a very distinct Mancunian middle-class background – just like the other leading directors Les Blair (who I think Mike went to school with) and Nicholas Hytner, whose dad was a famous barrister. And yet he's lived in London pretty much his whole adult life, and sometimes seems to have an almost obsessive hatred of people he perceives as being middle class.

When that kind of character appears in one of his films, they don't always have a third dimension. You can see that in *Meantime*, where even the guy who comes round from Hackney council is some wanker from Oxbridge (Peter Wight, the actor's name is – he does a lot of good work; and when I was in *A Clockwork Orange* a few years later, he played the chaplain).

I don't think Alfred Molina – who played Auntie Barbara's husband – was too happy with his part. He wanted to be part of the film's urban jungle, and do something a bit more interesting than play this uptight, rugby-playing, *Telegraph*-reading bully who didn't want the family round.

It could've been worse, though. There are probably actors still working in sausage factories up North because Mike sent them up there to learn how to do it for a couple of weeks and then forgot all about them. Fred's done all right since – he's Spiderman's multi-limbed nemesis in Hollywood now.

Gary Oldman and Tim Roth had both sort of sauntered up the same garden path as me when we made *Meantime*, but I was a few steps further along than they were at that stage. I'd had a career by then, whereas they were just getting going. Gary had done quite a bit in the theatre, and Tim had just been a skinhead for Alan Clarke in *Made in Britain*.

It was interesting working with them, and they made some bold choices, but they were both a bit more self-conscious than I was about creating characters. Oldman was playing a strange, heightened skinhead. Tim's character was an Asperger's Syndrome mod with asthma and National Health specs.

Tim and I got on fine, but we haven't really bumped into each other much since. He's been too busy working. Apparently he says some really nice things on the *Meantime* DVD – about how he looked up to me, and his favourite scene in the whole film is where

I'm walking across Trafalgar Square – but I didn't get that feeling so much at the time. When we were actually making the film, it seemed like he was quite competitive with me.

There was this whole thing about him dressing up as a mod, for a start. It made sense for the time (what with *Quadrophenia* and all that) for Colin to be wearing a parka. And obviously it worked quite well in terms of the dynamic between the characters, too – because Colin wanted to hang about with Mark, but Mark didn't want to hang out with Colin. I wouldn't put it past Mike Leigh to have borne that in mind.

People sometimes expect me to feel bad about the fact that both Tim and Gary went on to crack America, whereas I didn't. But I've never begrudged them their success, because they're both talented actors who worked really hard for it in ways that I wasn't prepared to.

I did have an American agent for about three weeks, but when she said I'd have to go out there and hang around for a few months shaking everyone's hand, I just couldn't be arsed. I was still full of optimism at that time about what British film-makers could achieve. If anyone asked me, I'd say, 'Our industry's better; Hollywood's shit.' And that wasn't just blind patriotism talking: I really didn't feel there were any limits to what we could do.

When Barrie Keeffe wrote *The Long Good Friday* for Bob Hoskins, that was a perfect example of the sort of thing that was possible. Barrie's usual muse, Phil Davis, wasn't in it for some reason: that guy who doesn't look at people when he's acting was in it instead. He was later famous for being in *Casualty* – Derek Thompson, his name is – and he's still pioneering a new kind of acting where you try to have a whole conversation without ever actually meeting the eye of the person you're talking to. Me and Al Murray (a.k.a. the Pub Landlord) used to do that to each other for days on end when we were making his sitcom *Time Gentlemen Please* together. It's really good fun once you get into it.

You won't catch Tim Roth doing that in *Skellig*. He triumphed as

Kafka's beetle when he did *Metamorphosis* with Steven Berkoff, and in *Planet of the Apes* he excelled as a psychopathic primate. Above average as a beetle, excellent as a monkey – that will be posterity's verdict.

When Mark walks across Trafalgar Square in Tim's favourite scene in *Meantime*, I'd imagined the reason that Mark was there was that he knew a bloke who had a monkey that tourists could have their pictures taken with and Mark was off to work helping him. If Mark had brought the monkey back to the flat, Tim Roth could've played him.

Joking apart, he's a very strong actor, Tim – very powerful. And Gary Oldman's done some good stuff as well. The other thing all three of us have in common (apart from being in *Meantime*) was that we all got a lift on to the old ladder from Alan Clarke – me in *Scum*, Tim in *Made in Britain*, and Gary in *The Firm*, where he played an estate agent who was a semi-detached Thatcherite football hooligan. No one ever called us Clarkey's Angels, though.

There was a lot of truth in what *The Firm* had to say about football violence in the eighties. I had my own little brush with suburban hooliganism in that decade. And since it coincided with me being on a train, you'll already have guessed that an element of extreme jeopardy was involved.

Chelsea were in the Second Division at the time, and we were on the way back from playing Luton away. When the train home got as far as West Hampstead, I started to smell burning, and I looked up to see that someone had ripped some of the seats up and set fire to all the fluff in them. Suddenly clouds of black smoke were everywhere and the whole train seemed to be on fire. Someone must have pulled the emergency cord because the driver stopped the train. Everybody jumped out and there were hundreds of us – all along the tracks – singing, 'We're worse than Man United'.

We ran over to the walls at West Hampstead station, climbed up them and then looked down to see all these Old Bill there with police dogs yapping at us. Most of us hadn't done anything wrong, but at that point the game was to get out of there quick, or hang around being herded for the next four hours. So I bolted off the other way, over some fence, down along the bottom and off into the not-so-mean streets of West Hampstead. Luckily I knew my way around up there, so I was able to make a reasonably clean getaway.

There's something in me that lets me know when it's time to beat a hasty retreat. I'm not one of those people who'll count steps to the nearest fire exit if they're staying in a hotel with their family, but I'll always check to see where the doors are, and whether you could drop down out of the window. I suppose it's the inheritance of being a caretaker's son. I'm like that at home as well – I'm always the first to notice if there's a cat-flap that someone could get their hands through; and if there's a door I'm not quite sure about, I'll always leave bottles in front of it so I'd get a warning if someone tried to break in.

When it came to exit strategies for the eighties, however, I didn't really have one. The best thing you could do was just grit your teeth and get on with it. And I'm glad to have had the chance to work with the two people – Alan Clarke and Mike Leigh – who probably came as close as anyone to capturing the essence of that decade on film.

It was interesting to be able to compare their techniques at close quarters. Clarkey would be more openly provocative, whereas Mike is more after subtly breaking your will to get something he wants. He's the one who's more likely to still have you working at five minutes to midnight on New Year's Eve as well. A lot of people don't like that – they find it a bit relentless – but I never minded it: that's the way good work gets done, and when you look at Mike Leigh's track record, there's no denying he gets results.

In some ways, the next thing I did with Alan would be the ultimate eighties film project. It's hard to think of another decade when a Brechtian snooker-musical with a vampire twist would have seemed like a good idea.

29: SNOOKER LOOPY

The strange thing about *Billy the Kid and the Green Baize Vampire* was that it wasn't even the first snooker movie I'd been in. I also did a film called *Number One*, which Les Blair directed in 1984. It wasn't improvised like Les's later films, and that was definitely for the best, as Bob Geldof was meant to be the snooker player, and I was playing his manager (Alfred Molina and Ray Winstone were in it, too, and it's not at the top of their CVs either).

It was one of those engineered ideas, where someone had thought, 'Bob Geldof is famous for being a bit outrageous, so let's make him a Hurricane Higgins type, and then everyone else can act around him.' Bob's role was just to be Bob Geldof, really, but even that was a bit of a stretch for him. He's done a lot of good in the world, but he's not the greatest talent. Obviously 'Cinnamon Stick in Cider-head' is a good song, but that's about as far as it goes.

Billy the Kid and the Green Baize Vampire looked a lot more promising. Clarkey was directing it, and there were a lot of other good people involved. George Fenton – who was doing the music – is a wonderful songwriter and musician who ended up being a five-time Oscar nominee, and I'd be playing opposite Alun Armstrong, who's a really good actor. The idea was that he would be a bit like Ray Reardon, but also a vampire with a sinister Thatcherite undertow, whereas I was more like Jimmy White: the spirit of youthful recklessness and flamboyance.

It's not every day you get the chance to sing, play snooker and act at the same time, and Alun Armstrong and I took that opportunity with both hands (and some surprisingly impressive long potting: that time I cleared all the colours was one take, honest, ditto the trick shot with the black off four cushions). But astonishing as this may seem – given what a sure thing it looked on paper – *Billy the Kid . . .* started to go wrong from the very beginning.

The original plan was that it would be shot on location, but then some of the money disappeared and they had to do it in the studio instead. Alan Clarke wanted to get out into the streets and make it all urban and *Clockwork Orange*-y, but suddenly, to hide the fact that we couldn't afford to go on location, he was having to go all surreal and internal – which wasn't his home turf (or mine) by any stretch of the imagination.

The guy who wrote it, Trevor Preston, started to look very depressed when he came on the set. He was often too down in the dumps to even talk to anyone, and I think some arguments went on behind the scenes that Alun and I weren't party to. To make matters worse, there's a shot where I'm walking up and down a corridor with my manager, and there was a grip – whose job it was to push and pull the camera as we did the huge number of takes that Alan Clarke always demanded – who keeled over and had a heart attack on the set. It turned out he'd had angina for some time, but, as you can imagine, an incident like that put a real hole in the atmosphere.

I enjoyed the snooker, though, and it was fun working with Al. George Fenton had written a couple of good tunes, too – there's a great production number called 'Supersonic Sam's Cosmic Café' (featuring the charismatic Zoot Money), where everyone's playing really old-school video games – but his music was more Brechtian than pop, and that didn't really chime too well with the mood of the mid-eighties.

It might have worked better on stage, but as a film the whole mixture didn't quite hold together – even though the DVD gets lots of five-star reviews on Amazon now, from people trying to turn it into a cult classic. And maybe if you think of it in terms of something like *Jerry Springer: The Opera*, *Billy the Kid and the Green Baize Vampire* was a little bit ahead of its time. At least the snooker players liked it.

We took the film up to the Crucible in Sheffield for a private screening on a Sunday morning in the middle of the World Championships. I went along with Jimmy White, who loved it (but then, we'd had a joint together in his hotel room in the morning). I still see Jimmy on the golf circuit every now and again.

I got on the practice table at the Crucible and had a game with him. The thing with that is, it's a bit like going on stage with the Who (an experience which at this point was still a decade or so ahead of me): it sounds like a good job, but in the end all it really does is put you in your place. When you play a professional at snooker, you basically become a lackey – you have the odd shot, miss, then from that point on all you do is pick the black out of the pocket and put it back on the spot.

I don't remember saying no to anyone selling lucky heather on the way into the Crucible that Sunday morning, but *Billy the Kid and the Green Baize Vampire* did seem to be a bit cursed. We knew Alan Clarke was already ill when he made it, because he was on a funny diet and he didn't have a drink with us, which he would have done before. He actually died in 1990, around the time of the World Cup semi-final, when Gazza cried and West Germany knocked us out on penalties. As if that wasn't a depressing enough event in its own right, the memory of it is always bound up in my mind with Alan's death. He was a lovely bloke, and the work he did speaks for itself.

Billy the Kid . . . was the start of a period of bad luck in my own life as well. It began with my mum and dad getting kicked out of Jessel House. London Housing and Commercial Property didn't have a pension scheme, so what had always happened in days gone by was that if you worked for them till retirement age, you got the flat to live in for as long as you wanted it. But when my dad got to sixty-five they just said, 'Ta-ta.' Because it was the eighties, the company decided it would be a better idea for them just to ignore their customary obligations, take back the flat, sell it, and kick my mum and dad out on the street.

My mum knew one of the company's more old-fashioned bosses, so she wrote to him, saying, 'Bill has worked for you for thirty years – is it right that he should get nothing at the end of it?' I think they gave him £2,000 in the end, but my mum and dad still had to apply for a council flat.

At least that system was still working (there must've still been a few flats that hadn't been sold off yet), and they ended up with a place in Kentish Town, which actually turned out to be OK. It was in one of those big old houses a bit further down from the Town and Country Club (or the Forum, as it prefers to be known these days).

I went to help them move on their last day in Jessel House, and it was a bit of an unhappy end to our time in a place where we'd really belonged. Me and my dad were sat there in the old flat, and I was pretty angry about the whole situation. I said, 'I'll get us some cans of beer,' and I bought us a few Tennent's Extras.

I remember him going, 'Cor! This is good stuff, isn't it?' He was really enjoying us having a drink together, whereas I just wanted to vent my frustration. When this bloke from London Housing turned up to give him a watch, I thought my dad should tell him where to stick it, but he was too dignified for that. He just took the watch, said, 'Thank you very much,' and that was it.

Because he was from an earlier generation, he was a great believer in keeping his emotions under control. Looking back, I suppose he thought that if he'd let me know he was upset about the whole thing, I might have been encouraged to fly off the handle. As it was, I respected his way of doing things, and in the end he was right. There was no point in getting angry about it. They just got a new flat and moved on with their lives.

Kentish Town turned out to be a bit rough for them, so when they got offered an exchange on another council place, in Bracknell, near Reading, they went and had a look and thought, 'Let's take it easy up here.' We'll come to my mum and dad's shocking flirtation with the risqué Berkshire am-dram scene a bit later on, but it worked out really well for them in the end, that move – my sister Barbara already lived quite near, and, once Brenda relocated over that way as well, they were all within twenty minutes of each other.

Before all these things could happen, though, the rough-and-tumble world of showbiz football was going to bring about a slightly less happy kind of family reunion. I'd been round the houses over the years, playing for various teams. It was probably Phil Davis or Trevor Laird who got me involved first off, because they played for the Entertainers' Eleven. A lovely old bloke called Hugh Elton ran it. He was an extra. You'd be on set at the BBC with the director telling you what to do, and he'd walk right up and go, 'You all right for Sunday, son? Twelve-fifteen coach at the Bush.'

The other main outfit I played for was the Showbiz Eleven. That team was run by Jess Conrad. Still is, in fact, at the time of writing. I turned out for them just the other week. Jess did *Joseph* on tour from the age of seventeen to about sixty. I think he might've been in *The Great Rock 'n' Roll Swindle* as well. Either way, he's a total fucking enigma. There aren't many football managers around who wear make-up.

It was good fun, the old showbiz kick-around, especially in the seventies and eighties. You'd get good crowds, then – I suppose there wasn't such easy access to people who were considered to be celebrities. You'd play pick-up football friendlies against local sides in places like Thamesmead or Hayes, and sign a few autographs for any punters who wanted them.

The only problem with it was, no one would insure you. I played for the Arsenal Celebs for years as well, until a singer/presenter called Matt Mansfield broke his leg and that was the end of it. I think we all got together and gave him a grand or something – to tide him over – but you don't want to be doing that too often.

Something else you don't want to be doing too often is spending three weeks in Milton Keynes General Hospital. But that's where I ended up in the dog days of the mid-eighties, after an ex-Darlington centre-half crunched me (breaking my fibia and tibia) for scoring two goals in the first ten minutes when I was meant to be playing as a sweeper.

All I remember was going, 'Aargh!' Then seeing a fist flying past my face as a huge fight broke out. Ray Winstone was playing, and an actor called Glen Murphy who was in *London's Burning*, and of course Daniel Day-Lewis. They all piled in looking for vengeance on my behalf, which I appreciated. The guy who did it never came to see me in hospital afterwards, but he wrote me a letter apologizing and bought me loads of beers, so I forgave him.

Those initial three weeks in hospital in Milton Keynes turned out to be more fun than I might've expected. There were two boys in there who'd been in a car crash and broken their feet. It's incredibly painful breaking your feet, because there are about fifty bones in each one, and they told me, 'When the nurses come round in the evening with the trolley, say you're in real pain and they'll give you the injection that's much better.' I felt advice of that quality merited some kind of reciprocation, so I told them about all the beers the opposing team had bought me to say sorry, which the nurses were looking after for me, and we resolved to get our injections sorted and then have a bit of a party.

You wouldn't believe it if this happened now, but not only were the nurses quite happy to get the beers out for us, they also let us smoke. In our beds. On a public ward. It was like the Wild West in that place. We spent the evenings on booze, fags and morphine, while all these oldies wandered around looking a bit confused as to why people in hospital would be having such a good time. I don't know exactly what it was they were giving us, but it certainly stopped the pain.

It was only once I got out of hospital and the opiates wore off that the truly problematic nature of my situation became apparent to me. Before that fateful late tackle I'd been up for him with the sweaty hands in Dickens – Uriah Heep – but obviously my injury put paid to any chance of that happening. The seriousness of the break meant I had no option but to sit on my arse and do nothing for nine months while my leg healed.

To make matters worse, I'd just sold my flat in King's Cross to buy a place near Holloway Market, but then that fell through at the last minute, which meant that me, Jan and China the dog were now – to all intents and purposes – homeless. First of all, we moved in with my mum and dad in Kentish Town for a bit. It was really good of them to put us up, but things did get rather cramped.

Then we moved into a tiny room on the top floor of the Skinners Arms. Obviously this wasn't ideal. And not just because my leg was still in plaster and the stairs were really narrow. We had China with us living in the single room, which was bad enough in itself, but the landlords had their own dog at the pub, too, and those two animals hated each other. So I was always having to break up dog-fights, which wouldn't have been easy even if I'd been able to walk properly.

Living above a pub did have its compensations, though. I used to hobble out of that tiny room in the morning, stagger down the stairs to the pub, have a few pints and get carried back up at the end of the day. It was a bit like *Time Gentlemen Please*, only with a broken leg.

Luckily Jan was still working, otherwise we'd have been in a bit of bother, financially. But she was a press officer at Virgin Records by this time, and so, when a flat they used to put producers up in became free at short notice, we were able to have that for three months while we sorted out something more permanent. It was one of those nice old mansion blocks round the back of Paddington Station. You weren't meant to have a dog in there, but we managed.

All this time I had to keep going to hospital while they sorted my leg out. There were a few problems with the metal plate they'd put in initially, because they'd tried to fix it without pinning it. In the end I went to see a guy at St Mary's who'd worked on a lot of footballers' legs, and he told me that he could do the operation I needed. I'd have to wait ages to get it on the NHS, but if I went private blah, blah, blah. So I went ahead and did it – two grand or something, that cost, and I had to keep going back to have smaller and smaller casts put on. I've still got a nice scar, but by the time we finally managed to buy ourselves a proper house, I was just about up on my feet again.

Our new place was in Stoke Newington – or St Okeney Wington, as I prefer to call it – which was further east than I was used to. But it was also the location of Renoir's first rehearsals, so I had a bit of history there. And on the day we moved in, Prince Andrew married Fergie. Only time would tell us how good an omen that was.

30: TONY SHER STICKS
HIS OAR IN, AGAIN

The first proper work I did after my leg got better (well, I was still limping, but luckily that worked OK for the character) was a one-off TV drama called *Will You Love Me Tomorrow?* Joanne Whalley and my old Anna Scher and *Meantime* sparring partner Tilly Vosburgh were in it. The director was Adrian Sheergold, who'd been an early champion of mine – I'd done a play with him at the Soho Poly, which we took to the Edinburgh Festival. In that we were all adults playing seven-year-olds. I was a Catholic kid who bullied these two Protestants and ended up getting thrown on the bonfire as a guy.

The TV drama was based on a true story about Mary Bell, the famous murderer who'd killed another kid when she was little. When she's eighteen or nineteen, she breaks out of prison with her mate, and they meet these two guys who've got a van – me and Iain Glen. He's all mean and moody, and I'm a bit weird, but that doesn't stop the four of us having a nice dirty weekend in Rhyl together, before the police recapture the two bad girls.

I couldn't rely on that kind of glamorous part coming up all the time, though. The fact that my first job back involved a trip to Rhyl was symptomatic of a broader shift in the balance of cultural power. The residual fondness that the rest of the country had felt for working-class Londoners since the ordeals of the Blitz seemed to be fading a bit by the eighties. Maybe it was because we were perceived (unfairly not only in my case but also a lot of other people's) as having have 'done all right' out of the Thatcher years, while the miners and everyone else suffered. Harry Enfield's 'Loadsamoney' character probably had a lot to answer for in that respect.

At the same time, Thatcherite deregulation of the TV industry – which was designed to make things easier for Maggie's best mate Rupert Murdoch – had the unintended consequence of opening up more opportunities for regional production companies. In many ways this ended up being a good thing, but at that time it was bad news for my career. It's perfectly natural for new writers and directors coming through to want to bring on board their own people; and, even though I'd always wanted to help expand the parameters of what was considered interesting to write about, maybe I was perceived as being a bit old school.

Either way, all of a sudden, a lot more TV programmes were being made about the North, and I wasn't in them. When I was a kid, we'd always felt like Manchester and Leeds and Newcastle were a few months behind. There was that kind of carrier-pigeon mentality, where news seemed to take a little while to get up there, so they'd still be wearing flares six months after we were. But some time in the eighties, all that changed – I think it was the scally football casuals and then the Madchester music scene that did it. Now they were wearing flares six months *before* us.

The British film industry wasn't exactly setting the world alight at that point, either. It still hadn't really got over the shock of *Absolute Beginners*. My agent, Sally Hope, thought I needed to do something to change the industry's perception of me, and I agreed with her. My way of following Norman Tebbit's advice and getting on my bike to look for work was to go and join the Royal Shakespeare Company.

I've always been someone who, if I see a contract on the table, and there ain't nothing else going on, then bosh: let's do it. I don't want to just sit around on my arse. The idea of classical theatre was definitely something different. Stratford is the only place in the world where your whole life is dedicated to doing Shakespeare. And Bill

Alexander – who I'd done *Class Enemy* with all those years before – was in charge up there now. So when I got offered a deal to do four plays in a year, I jumped at the chance. I did enjoy the whole thing, but it wasn't all that I'd hoped it would be.

Obviously I'd been involved in mainstream theatre before. I'd done a thing called *Tibetan Inroads* at the Royal Court, where I played a Buddhist monk (I know, typecast again). And I'd done a bit of Shakespeare with Peter Gill, who was a big wheel in the theatrical world and had played the bugler in the original *Zulu* – so he'd been me (or I'd been him, as he never failed to remind me).

The Riverside Studios, Hammersmith, that was the church of Peter Gill, and I'd played the boy Lucius who entertains Brutus on the lyre in *Julius Caesar* (Lindsay Duncan was Brutus' missus in that one). Rocking it up on the lyre in the early eighties was all very well, but by the time I got to the RSC, in 1987, I was more interested in being a leading man. I would have liked to have maybe been considered as a Hamlet or a Macbeth, but I was new to the company and was ready to give anything a go.

The quartet of roles I'd signed up to do was very much a fool's package. Pompey in *Measure for Measure* – or Pompey Bum, as his friends know him – is kind of a pimp. The play is about the state being racist and wrong, and we did it in modern dress, but set in Berlin in the 1930s. Nicholas Hytner directed that one, and it was very well done. Then I was the bastard son of the duke in *The Revenger's Tragedy*. That was all right too. It was a bit like a Glasgow Citizens Theatre production – we were all there in our frills, but the court was in disarray, so we were all poxed up, with some very grisly make-up.

Ithamore in *The Jew of Malta* was definitely the pick of the four, though. That was a much better part – much freer – in a brilliantly written play by Christopher Marlowe. Alun Armstrong played the Jew and I was his slave – I did him as a Turkish minicab-driver. We were both really disgusting, and went around having a suitably evil time of it, raping unsuspecting nuns and strangling friars.

It's a sign of a good part when you get more out of it the longer it goes on. What tends to happen over, say, eighteen months – which is how long we did *The Jew of Malta* for – is that a play will stretch. Everybody works out the way to get loved more (which is what actors care about more than anything else), so you'll find people really milking all the bits where they can get laughs, until someone says, 'Come on, this is getting a bit self-indulgent,' and you do what's called a 'speed run'. It's always the same: everybody (and that includes me, obviously) thinks it ain't them, but when we did one for *The Jew of Malta* we still knocked eighteen minutes off it.

Lancelot Gobbo – the unfunny clown in *The Merchant of Venice* – was the opposite kind of experience. The longer it went on, the sooner I wanted it to end. Unless you've actually played Gobbo, you can't know what a shit part it is. By the time I'd done 165 performances, the whole thing had really started to grate, and it was a great relief that I didn't have to carry on with the part when it went to London and my understudy took over.

In theory, it should have been interesting to do these two plays about anti-Semitism in such close proximity, especially as Tony Sher was playing Shylock. But because Bill Alexander had done *Richard III* with him, and Tony had written a book about it – *The Year of the King* – which was very successful, and was a big thing for Stratford, the RSC at that point had to some extent become the Tony Sher Show. He was the leading man, so that's the way it went, but Tony's word being law didn't necessarily bring out the best in him.

Tensions came to a head over the ridiculous issue of Tony Sher's collecting buckets. There's a tradition with the RSC in Stratford that every year, all of the ambassadors are invited to a show. Given that the cultural boycott of South Africa was in full force at the time, there was a strong feeling that the South African ambassador should be excluded. But the RSC said he was a foreign dignitary, the same as all the others, so it wasn't up to them to turn him down.

The whole company had a meeting about what we should do next, and two main proposals were put forward: either to go on strike, or to go ahead as normal. I voted – with Tony Sher – to do the show, and at that point (and I can't think whose idea this was) it was proposed that Tony should get up and say something on the cast's behalf at the curtain call. Then various volunteers would go into the audience with buckets and collect for a charity called the Defence Aid Fund.

It's not a political charity, it's for South African orphans, and I'm sure it does very good work, but I don't like after-show collections as a matter of principle. I don't think people who have paid to see a show (and there were going to be paying punters in, as well as ambassadors) should have buckets shoved in front of them to salve the consciences of the actors. So I got up and said, 'That's fine if people want Tony to speak, but I vote we don't have fucking buckets: that's not the right way to do it.'

I won the vote – no buckets. So, on the night, we did the play and at the end of it Tony got up and did his bit of grandstanding, and that was fine. Then all of a sudden, there were all these actors and actresses coming around shaking buckets at people. I asked a few of them what the hell they were doing. And they said, 'Well, each person who's making this collection is doing it as a personal gesture.'

I said, 'I'll tell you what this stinks of to me, and that's white middle-class South African supremacy. Tony lost the vote, but he didn't like the result, so he went against a democratic decision and did what he wanted to do anyway.' He came up to me afterwards and said, 'I thought you were on our side,' to which I replied, 'I *am* on your side, but I don't agree what you've just done.'

After that, I felt like I was slightly sneered at by the people who wanted to keep in with Tony. It became a bit of an 'us and them' situation, and two of the only people who'd admit to agreeing with me were David Bradley, who's in some of the *Harry Potter* films now, as the weasely caretaker, and the shit-hot young Glaswegian actor David O'Hara (of *Braveheart* fame). And David O'Hara – as I'd find out for the second time, a few months later – is a good man to have on your side in a sticky situation.

I'm glad to say that there was more to my first year at the RSC than pitched ideological battles. I had digs in a nice flat on the waterside. We took turns with the dog – sometimes Jan would keep him down in London, and sometimes I'd have him up in Stratford. I'd let him off the leash and he'd go bombing up the towpath. It was good to have that release of taking China for a run, because the atmosphere up there can get quite hermetically sealed, with everyone being very intense about what they're doing with their parts.

Basically, you rehearse all day, do your shows, and if you get some time off, you get pissed. I'd always liked a pint, but my missus reckons Stratford was where I promoted myself to the drinkers' premiership. There was this pair of old boys in the company called Bill McGuirk and Dennis Clinton. They didn't have too much to do in acting terms, but they were very industrious when it came to getting their rounds in.

It was a bit of a *Last of the Summer Wine* scenario, with these two old gents and their young follower. I've often been a bit susceptible to those situations – I think it's because I'm always trying to recapture the atmosphere of going for my first pints with my dad when I was younger.

I've never directly lost a day's work because of alcohol, but I've done myself a fair bit of damage by getting pissed and speaking my mind to the wrong people at inappropriate moments. I can often be my own worst enemy when I've had a few. I'm never less clever than when I think I'm at my cleverest. And there have been plenty of times when I've been hungover and just about managed to hold it together. I can't do that any more, though – I call them 'school nights' now: if I've got to work the next day, I can't really have a drink.

I think drinking was a bit of a defence mechanism for me at the RSC. Maybe I had a bit of a chip on my shoulder about the fact that it wasn't quite a level playing field, and that the really big parts always seemed to go to the same kinds of people. I had nothing to complain about, really; I just felt Stratford was a little stuffy.

There's a certain atmosphere of reverence there – a deserved reverence, in a way, because Shakespeare's such a great writer, but in another way not deserved, because there's a kind of floating aspect to it, which is basically reverence for reverence's sake, and that gets in the way of what you're trying to do. They have this strange institute up there, where some professor gets paid a fortune for knowing more about Shakespeare than anyone else.

Now I'm not anti-scholar in any way, but some scholars get it right and some scholars get it wrong – the same as the rest of us. I got paid £60 to do a talk there once, and I don't think they liked what I had to say, which was basically that there are two ways of approaching Shakespeare. You can either work hard to find interesting and real ways of doing it, or you can be very self-conscious and actorly, and fall back on making it all about declaiming the poetry in a certain kind of accepted voice.

In so far as I had any heroes in acting, it was people like Richard Burton or Robert Mitchum – Oliver Reed, even. They were all hell-raisers, and I probably looked up to them as much for how they lived their lives as I did for their professional achievements. The camper, more theatrical side of the business never seemed so appealing to me. But it wasn't as if I'd kept myself totally apart from it. I was working at the Royal Court when I was fourteen, and I'd even done plays at (thespians' Mecca) the Hampstead Theatre.

The fact was that I'd joined the RSC because I liked the idea of seeing myself in that context. I'd got a bit conned by the headline – and it is a bit of a headline there sometimes, because the actual productions aren't always so good. Yet if someone asked, 'What are you up to at the moment?' I was pleased to tell them I was at the Royal Shakespeare Company. There's no harm in that, but if you go somewhere for its snob value, maybe you shouldn't be surprised if it turns out to be a bit snobby.

In my own way, perhaps I was being a bit snobbish as well. When I was up in Stratford, I used to go out and get drunk with the same kinds of people I'd always hung out with, while keeping myself at arm's length from the 'actors'. Some of the more theatrical set were very nice people; they just weren't what I was used to, and I found it difficult to mix with them, socially. Maybe I was a bit insecure in their company.

It was Alun Armstrong who set me straight a bit on that one. He told me, 'Not everyone is out to get you – people *like* you, and you should try to like them back a bit more.' He was right. And that was probably the main thing I got out of the RSC in the end: no great technical or intellectual breakthrough, just learning not to be so dismissive of people, simply because they perceived things differently to me.

31: CLOSE TO (THE) EDGE

When you first join the RSC, you sign on for two years, and in the second year you start wheeling and dealing. I ended up going up to my ancestral home in Newcastle and doing a new set of plays up there for three weeks, and then coming back down to the Barbican.

Howard Brenton's *The Churchill Play*, that was the best of them. It starts at the funeral of Churchill, with four servicemen standing by the coffin, then all of a sudden the lid comes up, out comes the man himself, and it turns out we're all inmates in some kind of internment camp, doing a play about Winston.

I think my old mentor Jonathan Pryce had originally done my part, and the main thing about the character was, he was a Glaswegian. I'd not done that accent since Stephen Poliakoff wanted me to be a spiky-haired bus conductor at the age of fourteen, so I thought it might be a good idea to go up there and brush up on my Scottish pronunciation.

David O'Hara – my new mate from the RSC – came from Pollock Shields, which is quite a tough part of Glasgow, so I told him that if he wanted to go back home for the weekend, I'd be happy to pay his air fare if I could come too. He said OK. It turned out that his dad had helped build this block of flats there, and now lived in a place on the top floor, so that was where we were going to stay.

The night we arrived, we went to a snooker club and had a couple of drinks. I think I was innocently having a piss up against a wall outside, when some bloke came up to me and said – and apologies for the lapse into phonetic spelling, but I'm trying to build a bit of atmosphere here – 'Yoor shewin yoor cock to ma burd.' Needless to say, I refuted his allegation in the strongest possible terms. Nonetheless, it soon became clear that he and his two mates were gonna jump me anyway, so I legged it.

After they'd chased me I struggled to find David, and I was hiding behind a hedgerow when I heard someone calling my name. I came out into the open, but there were these three geezers again. Luckily, just as I was diving past a flashing knife-blade, Dave pulled up in a car, dragged me in and whizzed me off to safety. When we got back to his dad's flat, he wanted to go out again. I couldn't fault his stamina, but I opted to bail out and have a bit of kip instead. At that point it seemed like discretion might be the better part of valour.

That impression was confirmed the next morning, when we were in a bar in Greenock – I think Rangers were playing Celtic that day, so there was a bit of an atmosphere – and this bloke kept looking at me. In the end he said, 'Are you Phil Daniels? You did that gig with the Stranglers, didn't you?' I tried to fob him off at first (in my traditional manner, i.e., by denying who I was), but he wouldn't leave me alone, so in the end I owned up. Then he said, 'No you're fucking not. Phil Daniels would'nae drink here, yer wee barm-pot!' Things got very nasty very quickly, and this time we had to beat a hasty retreat out of the toilet window.

We were all right in the end, but it was a bit hairy. I was glad to get on the aeroplane back to London in one piece. I've been to Glasgow several times since and nothing similar has happened. So maybe we were asking for trouble, going out drinking in snooker clubs at two o'clock in the morning. David had always been a bit of a hard-nut, but he might have lost his accent slightly from being down in London, hanging out with posh Southerners like me.

Alongside *The Churchill Play*, there was a little season called 'Not the RSC' where we could put on our own shows. I directed a version of *Fen* by Caryl Churchill, which is just about five women getting on with their lives. We did only one performance, and I really enjoyed it, but I remember Bill Alexander calling me into his office afterwards and telling me it was 'a play about a play', which I wasn't too happy about.

An actor called Donald Sumpter directed Ted Hughes' translation of *Oedipus* as well, in which I played his dad and his uncle (that play is all about keeping it in the family anyway, so the multiple roles seemed to make sense). That got put on at the Almeida in London and took the place by storm. It was great: we were Play of the Month and everything.

That was what going to the RSC could do for you – give you a certain extra confidence, and skill, and maybe even turn you into a classical actor in a big way (not that I think a 'classical' actor is really any different to an ordinary one) – but it didn't necessarily help your career in the long term. TV and film directors don't tend to go to the theatre very often (and similarly, theatre directors don't seem to watch much TV), so if you're expecting the reputation you've acquired in one sphere to transfer directly to another, you might be in for a bit of a shock. The only time that does really happen is when a writer or director you've done good stuff with early on makes a move and takes you with them.

My craving for leading-man status with the RSC did get satisfied about a year and a half after I left, though, when they called me back to play Alex in *A Clockwork Orange* at the Barbican. In a way, this was a bit of a 'Be careful what you wish for . . .' situation, because there were a hell of a lot of lines to learn and a fair number of bruises to be sustained, but it was also one of the most satisfying pieces of work I've ever done.

A lot of people found it difficult to understand why the RSC would want to take on such a provocative text, but it made perfect sense to me. If you were looking for contemporary echoes of the kind of linguistic grandeur you get in Shakespeare or Marlowe, surely *A Clockwork Orange* was exactly the place to find them? It was still a pretty controversial production, though, not least because of all the violent incidents there'd been when the film came out in the seventies, leading everyone to get so worried about life imitating art that Stanley Kubrick banned his own movie.

Even though I was fairly confident that no one was going to try any ultra-violence on me while I was on stage, it was clear from the very beginning that Anthony Burgess' most notorious work had not lost the power to shock. Even while we were workshopping it, an actor called Paddy Godfrey – who was playing the doctor who gives Alex the pills and makes him watch the viddies – pulled out 'on moral grounds'.

I couldn't work out why he did that, because as far as I'm concerned the message of *A Clockwork Orange* is very strongly *anti*-violence. To me it's a very challenging but powerful statement about government-instilled savagery. How the production worked was that we had an initial rehearsal period of about six weeks, and then the director, Ron Daniels (no relation – I didn't get this part through the nepotistic intervention of a previously unmentioned theatrical uncle, honest), went off and wrote a script, using the book as a model.

By the time they'd worked out how they were going to do everything, U2 were onboard. I got summoned to meet them. As will happen with rock stars, they were put in a room somewhere at the RSC, and a couple of quid had been spent on sandwiches and drinks. I went along to say hello and tell them that I was playing Alex, and Bono told me they'd been determined to get involved because *A Clockwork Orange* was one of their music's formative inspirations.

I can see a few readers out there with question marks over their heads at this point, and I've got to admit that the influence of *A Clockwork Orange* on the music of U2 doesn't seem all that readily detectable to me either. I assume they just wanted to jump out of the comfort zone of rock 'n' roll and try to do something different, the same way as Damon Albarn does now.

There was no doubting the sincerity of their commitment to the production. I think they definitely provided the state-of-the-art musical equipment, and it's possible everything was a bit free, even the music they'd recorded for us. I went to the studio while they were doing that, which was really good fun. Edge wrote the music. That's plain old Edge, remember, not *the* Edge: it's very important to get that right. They were lovely to me, though, U2. My daughter Ella was born in the middle of the production, and they gave me some beautiful flowers and a posh bottle of champagne to celebrate.

Their name certainly helped sell tickets. And they didn't even seem to mind that their music wasn't in the final show all that much, 'cos you've got to use the Beethoven – the 'glorious, glorious' Ninth Symphony, which is utterly fantastic. The only problem with the Beethoven was, I had to do a couple of wanking scenes to it, which was even more embarrassing than that rather sensitive bit of self-love I had to get up to in *Quadrophenia*.

When *A Clockwork Orange* finally opened at the Barbican, it was a really big hit. It was an amazing piece of theatre – we had all these fake cats that I used to boot out into the audience, and the whole thing was very physical. I got very fit doing it, and had to do lots of fighting and jumping out of windows with Britfer, Noj and Chain. Alex was a great part for me, and I played it well. In theory, I was a bit old – he should be seventeen, and I was thirty-two – but no one seemed to mind. I think it's a bit like *Hamlet*: unless you've got the experience to be able to hold an audience for that long, you can't really do it.

We did the proper ending as well. The way the book was published in America, the novel didn't have its last paragraph – it ends with him getting banged up, whereas in the proper version you see Alex in the street one day and these kids are going, 'How's the big droogy today?' They're getting ready to test him out, but he just doesn't want to know. He's not into violence any more – he's got a wife and a kid, and all he wants to do is settle down in the suburbs, and that's the end of the book.

It was funny that this should be considered the most shocking part of the whole story – Alex growing out of this amazing violence that he'd made into an art form. But the Americans just wouldn't have it. You've got to pay for your crimes: that's how they looked at it.

The thing I really loved about doing that play was that I could really make the lingo my own – all the *devotchkas* (women) and the *ptitsas* (that's a small bird, for those whose grasp of Nadsat is a bit shaky). I wish we could talk like that all the time. It wasn't John Terry's *Clockwork Orange*; it was mine.

People often asked me what I thought of Malcolm McDowell's performance in the film. I made a decision not to watch that till after our production had finished, so I could be sure that my version was all my own work. But when I did eventually see it, I thought he was good – really good, in fact. He looked right, but he played it quite Northern, whereas my Alex was more of a Londoner. The other main difference between doing it on film and doing it in the theatre is that there's so much less dialogue in the movie version, whereas on stage you're more or less doing the book.

One day, during rehearsals, the director told me that Anthony Burgess was going to come in, and asked if I wanted to go out for a drink with him. Obviously I jumped at the chance, and we went for a pint together, somewhere near the Barbican – needless to say, I knew a quiet little pub.

It was just the two of us, and he had a pint of bitter, which I was pleased to buy for him. He had a very studious air about him, sucking on his pipe and his hair swept over his head. I asked him why the book turned out the way it did, and he said that at the time he thought he was dying of cancer, so he wrote it out of the bottom of a whisky bottle, and then, by the time he found out he didn't actually have cancer, *A Clockwork Orange* was finished.

He also told me he wrote it partly as an introduction to the language of Serbo-Croat. I was thinking, 'Fucking hell, hold up, mate!' But apparently it is quite true to the Russian variant of that particular tongue. He'd gone to Russia in the fifties, and there were a lot of guys in suits hanging about smoking fags and a lot of violence in the air, and that was kind of what he wanted it to be about, but with a bit of extra social comment over the top.

He was in America when the film first came out, and when he went to go and see it at the cinema the guy on the door told him, 'You don't want to go in there.' He said, 'But I'm the writer,' and the guy said, 'Sorry, mate, you're too old.' I think it ended up being a bit of a monkey on his back. He felt that he'd written more important books, but that that's the one he'd always be known for.

A Clockwork Orange is much more accessible than a lot of his other stuff, though. I tried to read *A Dead Man in Deptford* (which was about Christopher Marlowe) afterwards, but I couldn't really get into it. The reason *A Clockwork Orange* is so fantastic is that it mixes everything up. It's so full of stuff that's modern and clever without being lofty. For example I love the fact that the pub is called the Duke of New York.

Anthony Burgess didn't have much to do with our actual production, but the Countess – this Italian woman who was his wife and also his agent – was very tough with Ron Daniels about what he could and couldn't do in the script. Burgess – who was a composer as well – had written a jazz score, which he was hoping they would use. I think there was quite a lot of back and forth with that; so when they'd eventually decided to go with U2, he hadn't been too happy about it.

'Who's "the Edge"?' he asked me. 'I've never heard of him.'

'It's just "Edge", without a "the", Anthony,' I corrected him, respectfully.

32: 'BLOW HIGH, BLOW LOW'

It's a funny old job to be having your first child in the middle of – playing the lead in *A Clockwork Orange*. It's a good thing for Alex to be in a heightened emotional state, but there are limits. It didn't trouble me, though. I think the fact that there were a lot of things going on in my life at the time made it a release for me to get up on stage and kick some dead cats into the audience.

Jan and I have never actually got around to formally getting hitched. I always thought we'd have children at some point, though; and when our daughter Ella came along, it was just one of those things that happen and are good.

She was beautiful and I cried at the birth – like men do. She was a good little kid who became a good bigger kid and now she's grown up lovely as well. I won't be saying too much more about Ella, because I think people's families should be allowed a bit of privacy – and besides, I've embarrassed her enough already.

Ella's full name is Ella Bella Mandela Daniels. She was born the day after Nelson Mandela was released from prison. We thought about it for a while, and then when we went to register her birth at Camden Town Hall I said, 'Come on, let's do it,' and Jan and I filled that in as her name. I think she quite likes it – she uses it when she wants to and not when she doesn't, and she's never tried to change it by deed poll.

Time Out magazine in London got wind of it at the time, and they said: 'Congratulations to Phil Daniels and his partner on the birth of their daughter Ella Bella Mandela Daniels, which puts Bob Geldof's Fifi Trixiebelle in second place in the "poor dear" stakes.' I suppose they had a point, but E. B. M. Daniels does have a distinguished ring to it.

What with *A Clockwork Orange* and Ella coming along (and let's not forget Nelson getting out), the new decade had certainly started with a bang. But if someone had told me then that before the end of the nineties I'd win two Brit Awards and do a week on stage at Madison Square Garden with the Who, I would probably still have thought they were being a bit optimistic.

Before those exciting things could start happening, there were a few hard times to get through. As an actor, you're not always working. That's part of the job. When you have a bit of a break between parts, you just try to relax and enjoy yourself; at least, that's what I've always done. It's good for an actor to be a bit short of money every now and again, as it stops you getting complacent (if I was absolutely stinking rich, I'd probably never do anything), but obviously it can get to a level where life starts to get tricky. And Jan and I reached that level in the years immediately after Ella's birth.

Jan gave up work when Ella arrived, so that was fine. But then my successful debut as a West End leading man (*A Clockwork Orange* transferred up West in the end, though to be honest it was never as good there as it was at the Barbican) ushered in the longest professional lean spell I'd ever had.

It was just one of those things. It happens from time to time to actors, unless you're one of those people who are out there selling themselves the whole time (and even then, it still happens). I'm a worker by nature: give me a job and I'll do it. But I won't go round driving people mad till I get one. Whether you think that's a fault or a strength depends on your point of view, but there was a bit of a recession going on at the time, so people from all walks of life were finding things tough.

Either way, just about the worst thing you can ever be is skint and a bit famous. It's really embarrassing when you're standing in line at the Stoke Newington dole office and someone asks for your autograph. Being unemployed is nothing to be ashamed of in itself, and obviously my *Meantime* training came in handy – 'Not your pen, *our* pen' – but it did get a bit difficult when dole officers started asking, 'Could you do this?' and 'Could you do that?' I felt like a bit of a chancer saying, 'No, not really: I'm an actor and I'm resting at the moment, darling.'

It's strange being in those kinds of everyday situations where your presence is a bit incongruous to people who vaguely recognize you. Like when I had to do jury service. The first time they asked me, I tried to get out of it on the grounds that I was famous, so one of the villains might've seen me on the telly and come after me for revenge. I got a letter back saying that even if I was Roger Moore, I'd still have to do it (which was quite witty of them, under the circumstances, although I didn't appreciate having to pay the fine).

When I got called a second time, I turned up at Newington Butts, down in Elephant and Castle, ready for my first case, only to find Ken Campbell (my former next-door neighbour, who I didn't always get on with) was there already – ''Ello, Phil.' It turned out we were on the jury together. And first up was the case of the pigmy vicar.

I know this sounds a bit unlikely, but it did happen. This tiny African vicar was in the dock: when they told him to stand up, he said, 'I already am.' He'd been done for nicking some crap jewellery from somewhere like Selfridges or D. H. Evans. The store detective said he'd caught him red-handed with this chain in his hand, but all these British vicars came along from the church to speak up for him. They said it was impossible for him to have done it because he didn't believe in earthly riches. I was pleased; he'd suffered enough.

Then I had another case – this time without Ken alongside me – where one of these two black youths had battered the other one for treading on his crocodile-skin shoes on the tube. He totally did it, so bomp: he was guilty.

I was at the bus stop on my way home afterwards, when three of the guys who'd been in the witness box turned up and one of them recognized me – 'Hey man, you was in *Scum*, innit?' I was a bit apprehensive for a moment, as the racial politics of *Scum* aren't exactly what you'd call enlightened, but it turned out they really liked the film, so that was all right. And it also proved my point that I was too well known to be on a jury. Unless there was a case involving a pigmy vicar, obviously.

When you're waiting for that dole cheque, it doesn't matter how many people recognize you, all you care about is cashing your £67. In the end we had to take out a second mortgage on the house in Stoke Newington to see ourselves through. I remember the guy at the building society (luckily for him, I can't remember his name), after years of asking for my autograph and patting me on the back willy-nilly, suddenly demanding to see a contract for some TV programme or other before he'd sign it off.

It was a worrying time. All of a sudden there were new kids on the block getting the parts that I would have been up for a few years previously. When I'd done *A Clockwork Orange*, I remember Robert Elms confirming my suspicions by saying he thought I was too old for the role (I like Robert, but he's lucky he's not too old for the radio).

It's never a seamless transition from juvenile lead to adult, and mine was less seamless than most. There's a gap in the middle where no one knows what they want you to be. One day you're wearing a leather jacket, and the next you've got two kids and you're wearing an overall. The whole thing just takes a while to settle. I think that's why my agent Sally Hope had sent me to the RSC – to be seen to grow up – but the kind of parts I'd got there didn't really help casting directors to see me in a new way. When it comes to playing the Shakespearian fool, you can be eighty or you can be seventeen and it doesn't really make any difference.

I could've been very philosophical about it, but instead I decided to do what actors have done from time immemorial: I blamed my

agent (not to mention the legions of copycat actors who were steal-
ing my birthright). So around that time I left Sally Hope's and went
to a slightly more corporate agency called Conway Van Gelder.
Shortly afterwards, the person I was working with there moved to
ICM and I went with her. They were good at the beginning, like
they always are – it's a bit like a football team getting a new manager:
they'll often win the first few games on the bounce. They didn't find
me the part that got me out of trouble, though. That just came to me
out of nowhere.

I've not generally had much luck with musicals. Partly because
when I go to auditions, I never sing what they expect me to: I
always like to pick a song with a slightly different musical agenda, to
see if they can appreciate someone with a fresh approach. I'll say, 'I'm
gonna sing "Sandy".' They'll go, 'What, from the musical *Grease*?'
and I'll say, 'No, the Bruce Springsteen song.'

I went up for *Snoopy: the Musical* once. (I've done some things
in my life – did I ever tell you about the silent Yugoslavian knife-
throwing play?) I sang 'How Much is that Doggie in the Window?'
and they didn't like that much. I auditioned for Alan Parker when he
was casting *Evita* as well, and he wouldn't even let me finish my
song. I was probably meant to sing some crappy ballad, but I decided
to do Bernard Cribbins' 'Digging a Hole' instead. (I've got a lot of
time for Bernard Cribbins – I did an interview once where I said that
doing 'Parklife' with Blur had turned me into the Bernard Cribbins
of my generation, and afterwards he sent me a really nice letter thanking me.)

There was none of this kind of caper with *Carousel* at the National
Theatre. Nick Hytner was directing. I'd done some good work for
him at the RSC, and we seemed to get on well together. I think
they'd already cast Billy Bigelow and a couple of the other main
parts, and they were having a meeting about who to get for Jigger, the
disreputable seaman, when someone said, 'We need someone like
Phil Daniels.' I think they assumed I'd be busy, but luckily they took
the trouble to check, found out I wasn't, and – bingo – I'd found

myself a job. They were looking for someone a bit like Phil Daniels, and they got someone exactly like him.

It was a real godsend, getting that part in *Carousel* – on professional as well as financial grounds. Rodgers and Hammerstein's use of fairground imagery certainly struck a chord with me at the time. The last couple of years had been (as *X Factor* contestants love to say) a bit of a rollercoaster, but what I had lost on the swings I was about to gain on the roundabouts.

We did all the early rehearsals with just a piano while we worked everything out. And by the time we came to try it out with the full orchestra, we knew all the songs backwards. That was the day of days – to see that forty-five-piece orchestra sitting there and then hear myself singing this amazing musical with them was an incredible feeling. It was a brilliant production that cost a hell of a lot of money, but luckily Cameron Mackintosh had got behind it, as he was sniffing a West End run.

Cameron Mackintosh has of course done many of Andrew Lloyd Webber's great triumphs, which have done so much for the British theatre, but *Carousel* is a class musical. Not like *Cats* or any of that shit.

My character was a seafaring baddie, which meant I could make him a bit like Popeye. 'Blow High, Blow Low' is his big number, which is all about the joy of whaling, so he gets a few black marks from an environmental perspective as well. You have to stay very true to what's written, though, as the Rodgers and Hammerstein estate are very picky. You can't really blame them for that – those guys knew what they were doing, and there's no reason for anyone to mess about with their stuff.

How it works at the National is you do seven or eight weeks of rehearsal, then a ten- or twelve-week run, then you go into the repertoire, which means you fit performances in with other plays – you might do four days on and three days off. What you get is a basic wage with performance money on top, so you're getting paid even if you ain't working, which is always a nice feeling. It's a full-time job if you're in two plays at once; but if you're only in one you can fit in the odd game of golf, which is one of the perks of the actor's life.

The thing with doing a musical is, you basically have to get it up to a certain level and then keep it there. Once it's right, it's right. You can't really sing a different note or play it slightly differently, because that's the nature of the beast – it's on tramlines, and you can't bend it. But once you've accepted that, it's fine. By the time we'd gone into the West End and had a bit of a hit with it there as well, I'd spent almost two years doing *Carousel*, and it'd all been thoroughly enjoyable.

I put my foot in it a bit with Nicholas Hytner a few years later, when I played Autolycus in a production of *The Winter's Tale* he directed, also at the National. He invited me to a party at his house, and I got very drunk and decided to get a few things off my chest. It wasn't really the time or the place, but I suppose that was probably why I did it. You can take the man out of King's Cross, but you can't take King's Cross out of the man.

There were a lot of serious directors there – Richard Eyre, Declan Donnellan – and I managed to insult pretty much all of them. I never got invited back, and Helen Mirren told me off afterwards for being rude. I hope she's forgiven me, even if the others haven't, because she'd sent me a lovely note after she saw the show (in which I had to play the guitar) saying that I was like Keith Richards in his prime.

Fortunately for me, I was about to enter a new social circle in which behaving like a drunken bum was virtually *de rigueur*. The latter stages of *Carousel*'s West End run coincided with the beginning of my entanglement with Blur, and I really enjoyed switching back and forth between singing an old-fashioned musical and narrating a new-fangled pop song. It felt like a good mix.

Alex James was living in Covent Garden, then. So I'd be trundling in to do my matinee performance at the Shaftesbury Theatre, and he'd say 'hi' to me as he headed out to the café with his mates, having only just got up. Ironically, his flat was just around the corner from the Oasis (the sports centre, not the band).

33: THE BERNARD CRIBBINS
OF MY GENERATION

Showbiz football taketh away, and showbiz football giveth. (Well, if you can call the *NME* team showbiz.) It took me almost three years after breaking my leg to get back on the pitch. They wouldn't let me play while my leg still had a metal plate in it – I thought that'd just be like having a ready-made shin-pad, but the people at the hospital saw it differently.

When I did finally start playing again, it was in a team a guy called Steve Sutherland was in charge of. He was the editor of *Melody Maker* at the time, but none of the other journalists were in the team, because they were all too skinny and intellectual to play football. Instead my old mate Alan Edwards used to turn out for us, and there were a few other PR guys, some A&R men and the odd photographer. Then Steve Sutherland moved to the *NME*, and it became the *NME* team, which was a bit strange, really, as you don't normally change the name of the team when the manager moves.

One day Steve told me there was some young band with a song they wanted to talk to me about. Steve put me in touch with Damon, so I had a chat with Mr Albarn, and he told me that he and Graham Coxon were fans of my work. They arranged for me to come down to the studio they were using at that time – which was in Chelsea, so that was a good omen – and put a vocal on this tune for 'em. When I turned up I was treated like royalty. I had long hair then, which I'd had to grow for *Carousel*. I think they thought I'd be a short-haired nineteen-year-old, wearing a parka.

Stephen Street was producing the album, and I think the original plan had been for me to be on a different song, but they were having a bit of trouble with 'Parklife' – I've got a tape with Damon singing it all somewhere, and it's all right, but not as good as the version I did, obviously – so they decided I should give that one a go.

The first time Damon showed me the words for it, I thought, 'I can do this.' I just imagined flowers and parks and not having too much to do. You never knew exactly what the song was about, and I still don't – which is part of the magic of it, really. What I do know is that as soon as it began to get played on the radio, dustmen started apologizing for waking me up in the morning.

When we'd first recorded it, there'd been no way of guessing anything like that was going to happen. It didn't seem as if 'Parklife' was gonna be that big a deal. Blur were a bit of a shambles at that time, and there were a lot of stories flying around about them nearly being dropped by their record label and always being drunk on stage. 'Parklife' wasn't meant to be a single, either. It only ended up being one because everything else on the album was such a raving hit they thought 'Why don't we get this out as well?' And then it went on to win Best Single and Best Video among the four awards Blur won at the Brits in 1995.

When we did the video, they originally wanted it to be with me as a cab driver talking to Damon in the back, but I said no, because I thought that was a bit of a cliché. So Damon and the director Pedro Romhanyi (who's another big Chelsea fan) thought again, and I ended up being a door-to-door double-glazing salesman, which was much better.

I was never given any kind of political briefing about the whole thing. And there was no sense that my being involved was part of some kind of overall vision, although a certain amount of forethought had obviously gone into it. I don't know what it was that Damon picked up on – whether the whole Britpop thing unfolded exactly according to his cunning plan, or whether it was just luck, or (most likely) a combination of the two. But either way, there was a lot of energy around, and when it all kicked off, you knew something was happening.

Britpop was very much of its time, but there was also a strong nostalgic side to it – when you went to see Blur play live, they'd always have the DJ playing 'We are the Self-Preservation Society' from *The Italian Job* before they went on. And I think that was probably where I came in. Not only were *Meantime* and *Quadrophenia* films that Damon and Graham felt nostalgic about, but also *Quadrophenia* was doubly nostalgic in itself – in that it captured some of the energy of the late seventies through a story about the mid-sixties.

Obviously the other aspect of my involvement was the class element. Damon was born in the East End of London, and his grandma used to live in Whitechapel, but he was brought up in Stanway, near Colchester in Essex. Sometimes it's coming at these subjects from slightly outside that gives you a unique perspective, though. Had Brian Wilson actually gone surfing, the Beach Boys would probably have been just another band.

I know a few people thought that I was being used to give Blur some kind of stamp of working-class authenticity, but I never had a problem with the whole thing from that point of view. The *NME* had a cartoon for a while where I was Damon's man-servant, teaching him how to talk Cockney. I was always drunk, and I'd tell him: 'You've got to say, "Leave it out, squire."' It was a bit like *My Fair Lady* in reverse.

The funny part of all this was that I was probably living a much more middle-class life than Blur were in those days. After we all palled up and started hanging around together, I'd get up and do my bit on stage, then I'd be off home for a nice glass of wine with Jan, and maybe a game of golf the next day with one of my mates from the Stage Golfing Society. I was playing the odd round with Scott Gorham of Thin Lizzy at the time (he's still got that long hair, but it's gone grey now). Chris Morrison, the guy who was then managing

Blur, used to look after Thin Lizzy, so that gave Scott his own distinct perspective on the whole situation, and I enjoyed talking about it all with him.

After all those years of being in a band, and then playing so many managers, it was perfect for me to be a part-time pop star. I was quite happy in an elder statesman role: I was ten years older than Blur, after all, so I could only keep up with the pace for about three days before I'd have to go home and go to bed for a week.

Obviously there was a tiny part of me that felt it was a shame not to be up on stage doing my own thing. But the great thing about being a part-time pop star is, you can have all the fun and then go home, rather than having to live a pop star's actual life, which is all about getting on a plane at seven o'clock the next morning to go to Japan, before rushing straight off to Mexico. None of that stuff was anything to do with me – I was living too much of a Parklife to be bothered with any of that.

It was quite nerve-wracking, in a way, doing that song live, because it's very wordy. But generally it was all over before I knew it, and sometimes it felt like I was coming on stage and thanking my warm-up band – the crowd were so ready for it that they'd just see me and go mental. When Blur played in Moscow, Damon had asked me if I wanted to come along and I'd been delighted to do so. The crowd didn't know who the hell I was, but I translated 'We've Got a File on You' into Russian, and the band performed it, which was a good *craic*. I'm sure Anthony Burgess would've enjoyed it.

In terms of Britpop's own cold war – Blur versus Oasis – all I'd really like to say about that is it made both parties a lot of money. I was having a piss at some do once and Liam and Noel came into the toilets and Liam said (with apologies again for the phonetic spelling, but where the Gallaghers are concerned it would be patronizing *not* to use it), 'Fookin' 'ell, man, we really like *Quadrophenia*, what're yer doin' with those wankers?' I said, 'Well, you know, Blur are all right,' and they were fine with me after that.

I still see Liam every now and again when I go for a run on

Hampstead Heath, and he's a lovely guy. I think the rest of Blur were a bit scared of Oasis, and they were probably right to be. In those days there was a fair amount of falling over going on with both bands – and even though it was fun, it could get a bit hairy.

It wasn't till a few years later (13 May 1998, to be precise), but I think the time we went to the Cup-Winners' Cup final in Stockholm is probably as good an example as any of the kind of thing that went on. Trevor Laird didn't come with us, but otherwise it was the whole little gang of us who had got used to going to the football together – me, Damon, a guy called Ceri Levy, and another mate of ours called Wimpy.

We flew out there from Stansted early in the morning, had a little snooze, then went for lunch and had a few beers. Then had a few more beers and went to the game.

We won 1-0, which was one of the highlights of the Vialli era. And after the match, some record-company people of Damon's who were kind of looking after us took us out to some club. By the time we got there, we were all pretty pissed, and I had words with this big Swedish geezer in the toilets. His mate came in – who was a bit of a Viking as well – and it was obvious I was going to get battered.

Luckily for me, at that moment the Chelsea fan and rugby player Brian Moore (who used to be hooker for England) walked in (had it been the elderly football commentator of the same name, it probably wouldn't have been so helpful). Brian instantly sized up the situation. 'Oi! Phil, out!' he barked. 'You two – if you want to fucking have a go, have a go with me.' He had this great big lock-forward trailing in his wake, and the two Swedish guys just peeled away. I certainly owe him one for that.

We ended up going all over town together that night, and the next morning everyone was very hungover. Nonetheless Ceri Levy (who's an art dealer, among other things) insisted we all go to the Swedish Museum of Art. Unfortunately, we'd started drinking again by the time we went, and there was a bit of a furore about someone touching the exhibits. Obviously that ain't allowed, and by the time we got

out of the gallery we were a bit late for our flight. One of the differences between Britain and Scandinavia is that here they don't want
drunk people flying, whereas in Stockholm they're so desperate to get
you out of there, they just lob you on the first plane they can find.

I've got a vague memory of seeing Damon being carried bodily
through customs, and the next thing we knew, we were on this
plane that was so full of Chelsea, people were standing up in the
aisles drinking as it took off. It was total mayhem, and it wasn't long
before another incident was under way. This meaty-looking bloke
started picking on Damon. He was the kind of guy who it's safest
not to answer back to, and Damon is the kind of guy you can rely on
not to let something like that affect his behaviour in any way, so I
had to sober up quite quickly before things got really nasty. Luckily
I remembered the right angle to come from, and we just about got
off the plane in one piece. You get a good story to tell afterwards in
those situations, but you don't want things to get completely out of
hand. The problem with violence is, it hurts.

For me the great boon of the whole Britpop thing was that it kind
of gave me a new set of people who thought I was cool. And when
Patrick Marber's poker play *Dealer's Choice* came along at the
National Theatre right in the middle of it all, that was perfect timing.
Ray Winstone got me that job. I think Marber had sacked someone
and Ray said, 'You should get Phil to play this part,' so he did.

The battle-lines had been well and truly drawn by the time I
came on board, so the atmosphere got a bit edgy – not quite as bad
as on that plane back from Stockholm, but not far off. Though I
suppose, given that one of the themes of the play was that kind of
jousting and competitiveness that goes on within groups of men, the
tension probably contributed to the atmosphere of the finished piece.

Patrick did well to direct us. I think he'd done some comedy
before, but never anything in the theatre. I must admit that because
so much of the dialogue was improvised, there was a bit of feeling –
certainly more so than with Mike Leigh – of 'I wrote that bit'. I
remember Nigel Linsday (who played the lead role, Muggsy) saying

that quite a lot, and there were a few times when Ray and I improvised something new on stage, then Patrick would call a meeting
afterwards to ask if we could 'go back to the script'. We'd be saying,
'But it ain't your script – we made it up.'

He knew his stuff when it came to the poker, though. I wasn't
very good at it – I gave too much away, that was the trouble. Ray
Winstone was just as bad. We'd get cleaned out in about ten minutes.
But Ross Boatman, the guy who played my part after I left, he's a
professional poker player now. He's part of the Hendon Mob, who
make lots of money and are on telly the whole time.

Patrick Marber is a bit more restrained as a person than I am, but
we got on all right. We had our ups and downs, but he's one of those
people you can do that with and still be mates. One thing about our
relationship that I do slightly regret, though, is the day I told him I
was Jewish.

Don't ask me why I did that, but I suppose I've always looked a bit
Jewish, and obviously my name's Daniels – which has a nice Jewish
ring to it – so I thought it was worth a try. But as soon as the words
had left my mouth I knew it was the wrong thing to do. And by the
time we were looking for press and he said he was going to get the
Jewish Chronicle to come and interview me, it had all gone a bit too
far. I had to say, 'No, I ain't into religion any more; I've left it behind
and I'm an atheist now.' Looking back, I wonder if maybe he'd rum-
bled me at that point, and was having a bit of a wind-up of his own.

That was the thing about Patrick – you never quite knew where
you were with him. He gave me another good part a couple of
years later, when he rewrote this Strindberg thing, so he must've
liked me on some level. He's a funny bugger, though. I remember
that when we were doing *After Miss Julie*, he told me not to get talking to any of the crew. I suppose that was his way of getting me to
concentrate, but I was just a friendly person who was up for a bit of
equality. I've learnt my lesson now of course. Bollocks to 'em . . .
Where's my driver?

34: GOODBYE SHEPHERD'S BUSH, HELLO MADISON SQUARE GARDEN

It was fun turning up at the 1995 Brit Awards after acting in *Dealer's Choice* the same night. There was another time – once the play had moved to the West End – when I was meant to be getting one of those taxi-bikes to take me to Shepherd's Bush Empire in time to do the encore with Blur, but it never turned up, so I had to get the tube instead. I met two of Pulp on the train, and it turned out they were on their way to watch the same gig. The Britpop stars were certainly in alignment that night.

You couldn't really imagine bumping into the Who on the tube. But, just to give the whole situation an extra cross-generational perspective, it was around this time that I ended up doing *Quadrophenia* live at Hyde Park. I remember Roger Daltrey getting hold of me at a rehearsal and asking, 'What's it like playing with a fucking proper band?' 'Oh, lovely,' I replied. I was in band wars. I'd got Blur and the Who fighting over me, and Oasis were after me in the toilets. Luckily, my formative experiences with the Stranglers stood me in good stead.

I like to describe narrating *Quadrophenia* on stage as being one of the worst jobs I've ever had. Obviously this is a bit of an exaggeration, and from one point of view it was a dream come true, but as the person whose job it was to interrupt the thing the crowd did want to hear (the Who) with stuff that they didn't (me talking), I was on a bit of a hiding to nothing.

It started out as a small-scale endeavour. I got a phone call from Pete Townshend saying he wanted to play a few local club and pub gigs, with him doing some numbers from *Quadrophenia* on his acoustic guitar, and me doing some bits of narration in between. I thought that sounded like fun, but then the trail went quiet for a while. About two months later I got a call from Bill Curbishley, the manager of the Who, informing me that this little *Quadrophenia* mini-tour of the old blues pubs of Richmond and Barnes had turned into a full-blown Prince's Trust extravaganza in Hyde Park.

Pete had sort of repossessed all the dreamy imagery that Franc Roddam had taken out, and turned the theatricality dial up to eleven. They'd made this little film with some camp blond guy on a scooter, and Jerry Hall was going to come out of the sea as the 'Goddess'. The Who would play a song and, just as it finished, I'd have to come in and say, 'Yeah, and that was in 1964 . . .' and do a big spiel from the autocue.

Obviously the crowd didn't want to hear me; they wanted to hear the songs. It wasn't so bad at Hyde Park, but then I was asked if I'd do six dates at Madison Square Garden. Of course you can't really say no to that, but I was already thinking, 'Hmmm.' By that time, we'd got Gary Glitter doing 'The Punk and the Godfather' and Billy Idol doing 'Bell Boy'. I'm not joking, they really were in it. Gary Glitter had to have an oxygen tank on the side of the stage 'cos he didn't quite have the puff to do it.

The whole vision was nearly fantastic, except that there I was sat on a chair in front of a packed Madison Square Garden. This time, as the band finished '5.15' and it was my time to speak, all I got from the American fans was, 'Shut up, you limey fag,' or less respectful words to that effect. Don't get me wrong, it was great to do it. I sat next to Entwistle's bass stack, and he was brilliant, and we had a party every night up in his hotel room. Pete and Roger would always wander off on their own after a show (which is probably why they're still alive and John, sadly, isn't), but Entwistle was a bit of a legend. Whatever rock 'n' roll antics he'd been up to, he'd always go on stage and somehow be perfect. I suppose that was why they called him the Ox.

Obviously everything was a bit political between Pete and Roger – just as it always had been – and I really enjoyed watching how Bill Curbishley negotiated the various issues between them. I remember sitting in a bar with Bill once, and he told me, 'Fucking hell, Roger's been going on at me for five years to get the Who back together. We finally get on tour, and now he wants to go home.'

Another time he said, 'Do you know what I should fucking do? I should have special golf balls made with a picture of Pete Townshend on one side and a picture of Roger Daltrey on the other, then which ever one of them was getting on my tits, I could smash their face up the fucking fairway.' He's a lovely feller, Bill, but you wouldn't want to get on the wrong side of him.

It was interesting that his younger brother, Alan, ended up as boss of West Ham, because it shows you how the two worlds of sport and showbiz cross over. Way back when we did the film version of *Quadrophenia*, Alan was actually playing for the Hammers, which everyone was very excited about. He's in the riot scene in Brighton as a mod, throwing a table through a café window.

I think the temperaments needed to manage a football team and manage a band are slightly different, though. You're both leaders, but rock 'n' roll requires you to be a bit more of a Mafioso. That's one of the things I really admire about Damon Albarn – he somehow combines trying his hardest to make the world a better place with running that band and his own career with an absolute iron fist.

He can be a tyrant when he needs to be, but sometimes that's the only way to keep things together. You're in your mid-twenties and suddenly you've got to run a multimillion-pound business. Everyone and their lawyer wants a piece of it, but you've got to keep them all at bay while making sure there's a little bit of space left in the middle to try to be creative in. In that situation, you just can't afford to take any prisoners.

It's never been in my nature to be in charge – I'm happy keeping my part of the bargain, but I don't want to be having to confront everyone around the edges. That's why I've had the odd thought about directing, but never really taken it any further. Maybe I'll give it a go at some point in the future.

There's a real art to being able to run things properly, though – whether you're working in film or music or any other field. The other day I was looking at that album Robert Plant did with Alison Krauss, which sold millions and won loads of Grammies, and there was a thank you on it to Bill Curbishley, 'for his great management over the years'. I thought, 'Wow, Bill's cracked on again.'

I've always been fascinated by the glamour of that old-school rock 'n' roll world – people living off borrowed money in big houses in South Kensington. I enjoyed the fact that Jan was on the fringes of that for a while. She used to co-manage a band called Girl, who were hair-metal before hair-metal happened (I think one of them ended up in Iron Maiden, somehow). She did that with Danny Secunda, who was Tony Secunda's cousin. He knew all those old showbiz hardmen like Sharon Osbourne's dad, Don Arden, and he certainly used to tell us some stories.

I'd added a few anecdotes to my own stockpile by the time I'd finished my week at Madison Square Garden. The Who were just heading off to Brazil for a bit of a world tour when one of the main roles in Tony Marchant's BBC series *Holding On* came through for me. In one way it was a shame to get off the *Quadrophenia* bandwagon just as it was heading for Rio, but in another I was quite glad to get out of it.

My destiny as an actor has never been easy. I've not tended to have nine jobs laid out in front of me so I can plan things and go, 'OK, first I'll be a hippie, then I'll be a working-class guy.' Generally I've just had to make the best of what's there and say no to things that are really shit if I can afford to.

The great parts that have come along for me have always tended to be where someone like the screenwriter Tony Marchant has seen something in me that no one else had seen before. I wouldn't necessarily be the first person you'd think of getting to play a restaurant critic in a BBC1 drama in 1997, but that kind of imaginative casting enabled me to bring something new to the table (if you'll pardon the pun).

Gary Rickey's real name was actually Billy – Billy Rickey (this was his mum and dad's joke, because they came from Billericay in Essex). But either way, Mr Rickey was a wonderful role for me, 'cos not only did he live in a different world to the one I normally found myself in on the small screen, but also he was allowed to talk directly to the camera. I'd have to eat my tasty morsel of foie gras with a slice of lemon, and then do a bitchy piece about it straight into the lens.

The fact that Gary was bulimic only made that sense of him vomiting up all his inhumanity straight into the viewer's face even more intense. There's a hilarious bit where he's talking to some other journalist and he takes a bite of something and then just throws up. The lady thinks it's terrible, but Gary's going, 'What's your problem?' Because for him it's the most normal thing in the world. He's always rushing off to the toilets to stuff himself with crisps and Mars bars and then make himself ill. I also love the scene when some Italian restaurateur he's slagged off waits for him outside his flat in Islington and stuffs his review down his throat. He's such a coward, Gary Rickey, he's going, 'I'm sorry, I didn't mean it – I only say these things to entertain the readers.'

Obviously he's quite a grotesque character, but I watch lots of those foodie programmes on TV – I'm a bit of a cook myself, on the quiet – and you can see with those restaurant critics the contestants have to cook a meal for near the end of *Masterchef* that they're always just on the verge of pulling someone to pieces. It's fun to watch them struggling to keep themselves in check, especially that big bloke from the *Evening Standard*.

I based some aspects of the character (not the bulimia and the cowardliness, obviously, just that kind of slightly self-satisfied aggression of the working-class guy made good) on Tony Parsons. I read a quote somewhere where he said, 'Gary Rickey is nothing like me.'

But he would say that, wouldn't he? I've got nothing against Tony. He and my old mate Cosmo Landesman have both been married to Julie Burchill at one point in their lives, and that's certainly a badge of honour. The funny thing about *Holding On* was that Cosmo's colleague at *The Sunday Times*, A. A. Gill, apparently thought he was the inspiration for it. He probably thinks that Carly Simon song is about him as well.

People sometimes ask if Gary Rickey was a way of getting my revenge on critics who'd slagged me off. There was certainly some bile in that part, but it was more the poetry of the bile that I was into. In that sense Tony Marchant had written something that I could really – ahem – get my mouth around.

I've not done too badly at the hands of the critics over the years, but everyone gets slaughtered occasionally. The first few times hurt the most, but sometimes when you get a bad review it's actually a sign that you've done something right.

A few years after *Holding On*, when I played Autolycus in *The Winter's Tale* in 2001, Charles Spencer of the *Daily Telegraph* really went for me. It was a very modern production, and in the second half there's a kind of festival. We made it a bit like Glastonbury, and I took a liberty and said, 'Hello, Olivier,' to the Olivier Theatre. Fair enough, Charles Spencer didn't like that, but for the layman in the street turning up to watch their first bit of Shakespeare, seeing Autolycus coming on like Bob Dylan and Bob Marley rolled into one might have been the highlight of their evening. And in that context, maybe me pissing Charles Spencer off was actually a good thing. Helen Mirren described my performance as 'sexy', so it can't have been all bad.

There's still a lot of snobbery in this country when it comes to opening up new cultural experiences to people. But the best guidance doesn't always come through official channels. When I was a kid, I really had only one book that I liked, and that was Enid Blyton's *Tales Before Supper* (which for some reason I always used to think was called *Tales Before Super*). I like reading now, though.

When I went on holiday, I used to just be diving into the waves all the time. But now I'm a bit older, I'm just as likely to sit under a tree with my head stuck in a book. And it wasn't any of the high-flown scripts I've been involved with that got me started, it was my mate Ceri Levy, who had cancer in the nineties and was reading a lot to pass the time during his convalescence. I asked him if he'd read anything interesting lately, and he pointed me in the direction of *The Wind-Up Bird Chronicle*, by Haruki Murakami. That kick-started my renaissance with books. Bulgakov's *The Master and Margarita* was another big book for me – I started reading all his stuff after that. And Hanif Kureishi has always been a favourite of mine.

It's not my individual literary preferences that are the issue here – it's the fact that when you're a bit older you can quite unexpectedly come to things that can really enrich your life. My mum and dad's involvement with amateur dramatics was a bit like that. Now, for a professional actor, there's nothing worse on this planet than am-dram – they're the biggest luvvies of them all (I've done it now – 'Daniels Slams Am-Dram'). But my mum and dad got into it after they'd moved to Bracknell.

They'd joined this over-sixties club that used to go on coach trips and group holidays. I think my dad's handyman skills helped integrate them into the community, and he and my mum ended up effectively stage-managing these shows they used to put on. The lady thespians would dress up as Roman goddesses and have a real laugh. My mum and dad would get up on stage themselves, too, and I remember being slightly embarrassed and shocked when they told me about this distinctly blue routine they used to do: 'If I was a little Boy Scout and you were a Brownie, I'd grab your toggle and pull it off.' My mum's got a picture of them in the gear.

He was able to enjoy a good twelve or thirteen years of retirement, my dad, before the cancer got him. I still find his death too distressing to think about, even ten years on.

We lost the dog at around the same time. China got older and greyer and his back legs went. He'd been to the vet a few times, and I knew I was keeping him alive. When he was younger, he was a very powerful dog. I remember there was this workmen's ladder once – as long as the room I'm sitting in now – that China decided he was going to pick up. He got it in his mouth at one end but obviously couldn't balance it, so he worked his way gradually along to the middle, until he could finally carry it, then he managed to take about eight steps forward, before the weight of it got too much for him.

That huge Weimaraner coming towards you with a giant ladder in its mouth was certainly a sight to remember. Our house in Stoke Newington had three little steps leading up to the kitchen, and one day he just couldn't get up them, so I picked him up, put him in the back of the car, took him to the vet's up at Highbury Barn, and that was it. China was eleven, and he'd done a lot of mileage – he'd definitely been around the clock a few times. But if it's always sad with dogs, how much sadder is it with people?

My dad was his own man, and he'd always know where to get stuff. I suppose that's what being a caretaker is all about, but if you stop and think about his superficially unglamorous job title, its meaning is a lot more romantic than it initially seems. And that's how I feel about my dad, too, really. In his own unassuming way, he was an inspirational figure who taught me everything I needed to know about the kind of person I wanted to be.

35: NEXT STOP, ALBERT SQUARE

In Al Murray's sitcom *Time Gentlemen Please*, I played a bloke called Terry who was in the pub all the time and was basically in a bit of a state. I based him on this geezer I knew from Stoke Newington who was a minicab controller. He worked all night and finished at about eleven in the morning. Then he'd go to the pub and drink till about quarter past four, have something to eat, go to bed for a few hours, then get up and go to work all night again, before going back to the pub.

This was quite a grim vision of someone who didn't do much except drink, but I thought the show as a whole was very funny. The characters had a bit of depth to them, and, even though the humour was very broad, it was intellectually quite superior. It had a little bit of that same mood of melancholy running through it that made *Steptoe and Son* so special.

There were thirty-six episodes made altogether – in three sets of twelve – and I did thirty-five of them. It was unusual for Sky to be making an original comedy, and the production was almost up to the levels of intensity you get with a soap. It was like one of those American sitcom factories, except with just two writers instead of a whole team.

The scripts were always pretty much there, even though Al was writing them with his mate Richard Herring as we rehearsed, with Stewart Lee acting as script editor (which as far as I could see meant hanging around in the background looking a bit ominous). We'd build up each show through the week, have a camera rehearsal on the Thursday, then shoot the whole thing as live that evening. We'd come in the next morning, work on the new show till about one, then go to the pub for the rest of the day. Just like my mate who worked on the minicabs. It was practically method acting.

The old boy who was in *Only Fools and Horses* – Roy Heather – he was my main boozing buddy. He's a lovely fella. Obviously I was more on the lookout for someone who reminded me of my dad to have a drink with than ever at that point. It wasn't all about going to the pub, either. I was remembering the other day what a big home-brewer my dad was. He'd make beer from kits, and then gooseberry and rice wine. I never knew where he got all the gooseberries from, but he used to pick up the other raw materials from the wine-making shop up by Exmouth Market. We used to fortify the rice wine a bit, which made it really delicious – like sake.

Even despite all the drinking, *Time Gentlemen Please* was a very professional operation. We'd have to do the odd scene twice, but we did our best not to bore the live audience with too much stopping and starting. If anything went wrong, Al would stand up and do his Pub Landlord routine – which the show was basically a vehicle for anyway. The audience probably preferred that, judging by the way the character's taken off since, with his own chat show and sold-out live shows at the O2.

Al's been lovely to me, and he was good as gold on that show – full of respect for everyone he worked with. It's like he's made the pub landlord this huge ego and the rest of him's all right. I think he'd been somewhere near the bottom of the pile for a while – he was the drummer in Harry Hill's band, and all those other Avalon people he'd known when he was at college (the Lee and Herring's of this world) were all seen as a bit higher up the ladder than him – so when he finally made it big, he managed not to let it go to his head.

Doing that show is really bound up in my mind with my memories of living in St Okeney Wington, even though we left halfway through it. When I first moved there, my mates Peter-Hugo Daly and Trevor Laird were sharing a council flat just up the road (they were like the odd couple, those two, though sadly they've had a bit of a falling out now) so that really helped me settle in. Tony London and Mark Wingett were in that flat too, for a while, so you had to feel a bit sorry for the neighbours at that point.

Mine and Jan and Ella's place was down at the Newington Green end, so we got used to the good olives and all that Turkish stuff, and we were very happy there (especially once the *Carousel* dividend had helped us pay off the second mortgage). But, as the turn of the decade approached, Jan decided it was time for a move.

These things are never really down to me. She's the one who makes all the deals. I'll live anywhere, except south of the river. (Looking at that written down, I feel I should probably make it clear that I am joking . . . Although I wouldn't actually live there.) We ended up in NW3 (you might call it Hampstead, but never Highgate, though I suppose it's more Gospel Oak, really), which had a nice kind of circularity to it, as a destination, since it was just round the corner from where my mum and dad had lived – wholly unaware of each other's existence – when they first came to London.

It's funny how, as you get a bit older, you start to see events in your life forming these kinds of patterns. Like when I got to be a rat in *Chicken Run* – that was down to Patsy Pollock, the same casting director who'd picked me out for *Quadrophenia* all those years before. She calls me and Ray Winstone the 'oiks'. (She's an oik too, so she means it nicely.) And this time she teamed me up with Tim Spall (who'd made his film debut as the projectionist I played cards with at the advertising agency in *Quadrophenia*, just to complete the squaring of the circle).

You might think I'd be worried about rodent typecasting after Hazel O'Connor said I looked like one in *Breaking Glass*, but playing a rat called Fetcher is definitely better than playing a geranium. I was in a sitcom some years ago with Cliff Parisi, where we had to sit behind a set while these two geraniums talked to each other. It never took off, for some reason. But *Chicken Run* was never going to be anything other than a huge success.

What happens first with an Aardman Animations blockbuster is the two top guys, Nick Park and Peter Lord, film you a bit, just being yourself, so they've got something to base the animations on. That's why, when you look at the rat with its gabardine sock, it looks a bit like me. Once they've got that in the can, there's a day where the whole cast (well, everyone except Mel Gibson) sits round in a studio with the script and reads it all the way through a couple of times. That's probably the best bit of the whole process as far as the actors are concerned.

After that, they split you up into groups. Tim and I did a long session together where we had to do each scene from every different angle and with every possible emphasis. That got a bit boring, to be honest, but that's kind of the point, in some ways. The methodology is so meticulous and painstaking, but then you come out the other end with this thing that everyone gets incredibly excited by.

Once they've done a bit, so they know roughly the way it's going, you head down to Bristol and do another day there, and that's kind of it. Their studios are amazing – more like a factory than studios, really. And they seem more like boffins than film-makers. When you see how complicated the whole process is, it's amazing how much spontaneity they manage to keep in, though (for example, all that stuff at the end where we go on about Mel Gibson and the chicken and the egg was just me and Tim freewheeling). And despite spending all their time with Plasticine characters, they're really lovely, down-to-earth people, and not plastic at all.

I met up with all the Aardman crowd again recently, when I had to make a speech presenting them with a Special Award at the Baftas. They've got Oscars galore, and they must be what Ray Winstone calls 'cake-o, bake-o' – i.e., very rich (I don't know where he picked that one up from, but it works for me). But they still hire a minibus together to come up to London in, and prefer to get home to Bristol the same night if at all possible, rather than staying over in a hotel.

The great thing about them is that they've managed to make modesty and unpretentiousness a virtue in an industry where those attributes tend to count against you. I realize that might sound a bit cynical, but I've learnt some harsh lessons in that area over the last few years. One painful experience in particular led me to completely reassess how I approached my career.

In 2004 I did this series called *Outlaws*, in which I played a defence solicitor who'd go round the police stations every week, looking for someone to represent. A guy called Steve Combes wrote it, and it was really good. As well as being a bold exposé of an aspect of the legal system that wasn't really working, there were some really strong characters in it. It was on BBC3 originally, but then because something got pulled they stuck it on BBC2 very quickly afterwards.

With no advertising campaign or advance publicity, it got brilliant reviews and was put straight up for a BAFTA for Best Programme. Yet for some reason it didn't get re-commissioned. It was said that it didn't get good enough viewing figures, but they never really gave it a fair crack of the whip. The BBC had this other series called *Blackpool* at the time, which they'd decided to really go for because David Tennant was in it and he was coming through; and even though it shouldn't have been one series against the other, I felt that was kind of how it ended up, and *Outlaws* lost out. There were scripts written for a second series – all the ideas were there – but we never did it again, and it really upset me, big time.

I've generally managed to stay pretty philosophical about things that have and haven't happened over the course of my career, so I'm not sure what it was about this situation that got to me so much. I suppose I felt guilty, because I was probably the best-known actor in *Outlaws*, and it seemed like I was responsible for the fact that everyone who'd worked so hard on it wasn't going to get the chance to make a second series. If I could do some of the best acting of my entire career in a really good programme, yet my name wouldn't draw enough viewers to get it re-commissioned, maybe I just wasn't well known enough.

At that point, I realized that I needed to get my face out there in front of a few more people. It looked like the way the business was going was towards being all about celebrity – obviously it's always been about that to a certain extent, but there used to be another superstructure of actual talent that underpinned how famous everyone was or wasn't. In the first few years of the twenty-first century, that more creative framework seemed to be rusting away.

Alongside an awareness that I needed to up my profile in order to make sure things I wanted to do actually get commissioned, there was also – if I'm honest – a certain amount of anger and selfishness: 'Fuck this, I'm gonna earn myself some money.' Either way, it was next stop, Albert Square.

A woman called Kate Harwood, who'd been script editor of *Holding On*, had become a really big cheese and was now executive producer of *EastEnders*. She told me that they wanted to get some actors in who were known for other stuff, and Tony Jordan – who had created the whole show in the first place – was gonna come back and write some scripts for me. I um-ed and ah-ed for a while, but people advised me that it'd be OK for me to do it – because I'd got a long enough history to be able to go in there for a while and come out still known as someone who'd done a few different things, and not just as 'Phil Daniels off *EastEnders*'. So I did.

So now I'm in *EastEnders*. Tony Jordan writes one episode and it's funny. My character's quite light-hearted. My son, Dino – Matt D'Angelo – has come in and told everybody I'd died. Then I turn up to find him but I've got nowhere to stay so Pat puts me up and – bomp, bomp, bomp – we're in as a family. My daughter comes along. She's going out with this Greek bloke and there's a big punch-up between my family and his family. It is hilarious and I'm enjoying it, but unfortunately, as is *EastEnders*' wont, things will eventually take a turn for the worse. The problem with that programme is, it can't sustain anything but misery.

They said at the beginning, 'You've got a son and daughter, plus you had another son, Jimbo, who died of cystic fibrosis when he was young. You had to look after him but your wife wouldn't help.' So there was always this hanging over me, and I was waiting for it to rear its ugly head.

People say it's hard graft, doing *EastEnders*, but I really enjoyed the actual experience of it. There was nobody in the cast I didn't get on with. With a show as big as that there are going to be a few egos about, but if you listen to all the gossip you'll never get anywhere – you've got to take people as you find them, and everyone was all right with me. I'm a bit of an early bird, so I never minded driving myself up there first thing in the morning. You have to be over seventy to get a chauffeur-driven car on *EastEnders* and the dressing rooms are in Portakabins. Obviously it's the BBC's flagship programme, but you wouldn't know it judging by some of the conditions that cast and crew work in.

I didn't mind that, though. I *liked* the fact that no one's bigger than the show (they could have done with a bit of that spirit at the RSC) and for the first few months my storylines were working out really well. Obviously Tony Jordan never wrote me another episode, but after a while they got me into a relationship with Diane Parish (who'd been in *Holding On* too, although she was in a different strand of the plot to mine), and I was thinking, 'I'm in *EastEnders* with a multi-racial family: this is really quite good.' And it was good. Apart from anything else, it's given me pin-up status with Britain's Afro-Caribbean ladies: 'OK, Kevin, how's Denise?' That's the usual greeting. Followed by: 'You like black women, don't you?'

Unfortunately, Kevin's first wife (brilliantly played by Linda Henry) had to turn up and spoil everything. From that point, the ugliness of the story with the son started to take over, and my character steadily became more and more miserable until it was unbearable to act, let alone watch.

It's a good programme in many ways, *EastEnders*, but its biggest fault is that it believes it's a kind of window on the world through which the British public can see things like how a family copes with cystic fibrosis. It thinks it's doing everybody a favour, but it's not, really, because what they don't ever do is follow through with anything.

They'll have a story like the one where Billy and his wife Honey were trying to bring up a Down's syndrome baby, but it'll only go so far; and then they'll be thinking, 'What's gonna happen? Is the baby gonna grow up?' No, they can't do that, because people might get bored of watching it, so poor old Honey has to leave the Square. Because they've brought the issue to everyone's attention, they think they've ticked the box, so they pat themselves on the back and move on to the next storyline, but they've not really dealt with anything properly: the issues are just cannon fodder for the ratings, in my opinion.

I'm not saying that the producers don't mean well on some level. I think a lot of them genuinely have the best of intentions. But the worthwhile things they'd like to be doing can't actually be reconciled with the fundamental goal of the show, which is to maintain its viewing figures. And when you're watching the pattern repeat itself from the inside – issue raised in blare of publicity, issue toyed with, issue dropped – it's hard not to get a bit sceptical about it.

36: WE AIN'T FOOTLIGHTS,
WE'S ANNA SCHER

The criticisms I have of *EastEnders* don't relate to the actors, who are sterling and do great work under an enormous amount of pressure — it's four episodes a week, so you don't half churn 'em out. I think the show's real weakness is the quantity of material that the writers have to come up with, and the power that is afforded them because of this. It's the story that's important, not the characters, so the tail is always wagging the dog.

I'm not in principle against writers having power. But the men and women behind *EastEnders* aren't the sort of people you'd imagine. It's not so much cutting-edge individuals living in Bethnal Green and writing about what they know — it's more of an Agatha Christie scenario, where an old dear knocks the whole thing up to a formula from her back shed in Brixham.

There were some top writers, like Simon Ashdown, James Payne and Sarah Phelps, who all did some excellent stuff for me. Sarah used to turn up at the studios, so you could have a chat about things with her as the story unfolded. But the top brass often get a bit uneasy about the better writers, because they tend to make life more complicated (both in dramatic and practical terms). There was a fantastic left-wing playwright called Doug Lucie, but he was a bit too hardcore for 'em, so he never got called back.

With some of the others, you'd often find yourself doing things your character just wouldn't do, in order to lay the foundations for some unfeasible future plot development. Some of the actors protest a bit when that happens, but they're often too busy worrying about future contracts to rock the boat too much.

I don't blame them for that. As a character you don't wanna do too many big stories. Now and again you want one. But basically you're happy popping into the Vic for a pint and blending into the background. As long as you're in the episode, you still get your fee, whether you say two words or 500. Obviously they have financial people keeping an eye on that sort of thing, but every now and again they miss one, and you get your money just for saying, 'All right, Peggy?'

A lot of people think all the main actors are the same as their characters. In some cases there's probably a bit of truth in that, but sometimes how difficult it is to see the join is just a testament to very good naturalistic acting. It was interesting going into *EastEnders* such a long time after starting out with Anna Scher: in one way it was like coming home, and in another way it wasn't.

Anna's techniques have obviously been very influential on the development of the show. Not only because a lot of the best-known cast members – people like Susan Tully, Gillian Taylforth and Jake Wood, to name but a few – started out at Anna's. But also because the structure of the work you do tends to be very similar – it's mostly short, sketch-type scenes, where you're just trying to be as real as you can.

EastEnders is very much the mass-market version, though. There are a lot of telephone exchanges – 'OK then, I'll be round in a minute' – to help you get from A to B as quickly as possible. And, even though your scenes do often have a beginning, a middle and an end, they'll be crammed into such a short space of time that they're almost more like scene-ettes. That's why the rhythm of the show often goes a bit haywire when they try to do something that lasts a bit longer. Like when I had my 'special'. It was fun to do – wandering around Dungeness and looking at Derek Jarman's house with

Burn Gorman, who ended up in *Oliver!* afterwards – and they were trying to get somewhere interesting, but we just didn't quite make it.

I did 158 episodes in the first year and about 90 in the second – you do a lot at first, and then it calms down. I think I could've probably signed for another year if I'd wanted to, but I'm glad I got out when I did. Once I get a bit of a habit going, it's hard for me to get out of it, and I could definitely feel myself starting to get institutionalized.

It had all gone a bit downhill for me, character-wise, and there wasn't really anywhere else left for Kevin to go. Plus a new executive producer had come in by that point, and all of a sudden he was bringing in people like Bobby Davro. No disrespect to Bobby, but if that's who they got to replace me, it was time for me to make my exit. I suppose Anthony Sher must have been busy.

Because *EastEnders* has become the repository of a certain kind of working class-ness on TV, a few people asked if I felt like I was being exploited. But to be honest, I was using the show every bit as much as it was using me. Going on it was part of a deliberate strategy to make a bit of money and get myself a slightly bigger profile.

It certainly achieved the first of those goals – if I did all four episodes and got my repeat fee for the omnibus, I could earn very good money. And the fact that even now Kevin's been dead for three years I still can't go to the supermarket without someone asking me if I'm still in it suggests that *EastEnders* has at least made me a bit more recognizable.

There was another, more general reason for doing it as well, though. I was a bit fed up with being good old Phil Daniels. All that 'salt of the earth' stuff had started to get a bit patronizing, and I felt like it was holding me back. So doing something a bit more mainstream was definitely a reaction against that. It was a bit like when the bloke out of the White Stripes deliberately upset everyone by doing that Coke advert. Or when Jimmy drove Sting's scooter off the cliff and went back to London to get a job, come to that.

Sometimes you've got to do something people don't expect, just to stop them taking you for granted. I had to broaden my scope if I wanted to survive. That was definitely where *Strictly Come Dancing* came in. If I had my time over, I'd definitely do *EastEnders* again, but I'm not so sure about *Strictly* . . . The second stage of my commercial-outreach strategy involved a few more sacrifices than the first, even though it was over a lot quicker.

I like to say that I was the real winner of the 2008 series, because I got the same money as everyone else for doing the least amount of work. *Strictly Come Dancing* isn't like *Celebrity Big Brother*, where everyone jockeys for position to see who can get paid the most – whether you stay for twelve weeks after your initial month of rehearsals (like Rachel Stevens) or one week (like me), you still get paid the same fixed amount. For the people who get into it and are keen, there's the chance to go on tour and do all the spin-offs, but the only spin-off there was likely to be for me was having the piss taken out of me everywhere I went. For the rest of my life.

Obviously I was lucky to be in a position to earn so much money for one job, but, looking back, I think it was a mistake for me to do it. I'd been led to believe it was fun and that everybody mucked in and had a laugh, but for me it was nerve-wracking.

My partner, Flavia, had got through to the final the year before with Matt D'Angelo, and I think she was expecting it to be (in terms of our *EastEnders* characters, at least) like son, like father. It means so much to the professionals to stay on the show as long as they can, and Flavia did try her hardest with me.

Arlene Phillips was nice – she'd actually worked with me before, on *A Clockwork Orange* – but the strange thing about the judges who really slaughter you is that they think they can come up to you afterwards and everything's gonna be all right. Totally demoralizing people is just part of the game to them. I think the BBC see it like that too, but I don't. And John Sergeant didn't either – that's why he left when he did, because he'd had enough of their personal attacks, and wanted to get his resignation in first.

I got called 'common' by that Australian twat with the double-barrelled name. Obviously that was my opportunity. If I'd wanted to stay another week and do my jive (which would have suited me better than the waltz) then when the time came to talk to the camera and everyone else made their impassioned pleas, I could have said, 'Listen, all you common people out there, vote for me, because he's calling you common as well.' But I didn't. I just said, 'OK, fair enough.' It wasn't my cup of tea, and the sooner I was out of there the better.

It was odd, being a celeb on one of those shows. I could see why other people were doing it, but my motives were wrong: the rationale was more fiscal than artistic, and you never do yourself too many favours when that's the case. I'd probably got a bit too caught up in the whole money thing after the *Outlaws* debacle – especially with the credit crunch looming – so it was probably good to get it out of my system.

I enjoy the bullshit that goes with the business, in a funny sort of way. I play a lot of charity golf now. You're always given three 'normals' (the bloke who was Jesus of Nazareth, Robert Powell, that's his phrase – though I doubt if the actual Jesus would use that kind of terminology). They pay a generous sum of money – say, £700 – between them, and you play as a team. The best two scores on each hole count, and they add them all up to find the best group at the end of the day. If you come second (like I did the other week) you might win a John Lewis voucher for £75.

At the end of the day, everyone's a winner. You give your time and have a nice round of golf, and a bit of money goes to a good cause (the charity I do it for is called Sparks, which pays for medical research into children's diseases). Robert Powell plays a lot, as it goes: I suppose the idea of a round of golf with the Messiah is a big draw. The last round I had, one of the punters was an importer of fruit, but I often seem to end up playing with scaffolders who worked on the new Wembley Stadium. I remember this one guy telling me that once you get a contract off the government you can virtually print your own money, which I found very reassuring.

In terms of the charity-golf circuit, I'm probably more famous now than I've ever been. People will regale me with plotlines of *EastEnders* in far greater detail than I knew them even when I was in it, and then insist they don't actually watch the show. So my plan to do something more mainstream did work at one level, but it's brought me a new set of fans who only know me from Albert Square, so I've got my *Quadrophenia* fans and my *EastEnders* fans, and never the twain shall meet. Now Act I and Act II are pretty much done and dusted, I'd like to do something in Act III that could bring 'em all together.

This business has a tendency to use you for what it wants, and you have to sort of fight against that and go with it at the same time. A few years ago, I did a one-off TV drama with Dawn French called *Sex and Chocolate*, where I played a skinhead who was very kind but never seemed to stop crying. After that, I suddenly started getting cast as quiet, downtrodden fathers the whole time. And now, since I was a policeman in *Waking the Dead*, everyone's happy casting me as a copper. That's how I ended up in *New Tricks* and *Poirot*, playing two more of our flat-footed friends. Luckily being Jack 'the Hat' McVitie in *The Long Firm* has helped maintain my credibility in London's criminal underworld.

I've done plays where I've been Scottish, Greek, all sorts – but people don't necessarily want that. They prefer to pigeonhole you as doing just one kind of work. When you're younger, that annoys you, but as you get older you begin to realize that you can use it to your advantage. You can earn your keep being typecast to enable you to be a bit choosier in other areas.

I turned down a couple more of Shakespeare's clowns recently – I'm hanging on for Iago, now. That's one challenge I'm definitely ready for. And hopefully there are a few other big parts waiting just around the corner for me as well. I was about to sign up for six months as Eddie Carbone in a touring production of Arthur Miller's *A View from the Bridge* last autumn, but they lost the financial backing at the last minute. That would have been a hard part, as he's a very dark character, but it would have definitely been worth the effort.

There's nothing like that feeling you get as an actor when you're in a brilliant play, with a good house in, and your performance is spot on. You can feel the audience listening. A laugh will come at exactly the right moment, and you'll know you've got 'em.

It's the same when you're improvising – but then you get that feeling from the other actors as well. I think the best improvisation I ever did was playing twins in a Les Blair TV film called *Bad Behaviour.* Stephen Rea and Sinead Cusack had a house in Kentish Town, and I was going to be both of their builders. One of the twins was decent and hard-working, and the other was just after a few quid, but Stephen and Sinead didn't know that yet.

I'd spent ages practising on my own with two chairs, jumping back and forth between them, going, 'All right, Ray?' 'How's Roy?' Then we did this improvisation where I knocked on their door, went in, looked around to price up the job, then sneaked out of the side window, knocked on the front door again and went through the whole process a second time with a slightly different emphasis. It was brilliant – they were so confused. They had no idea I was playing twins; they just thought I was some lunatic who kept climbing out of the window.

Now that I'm looking back on it, I think doing twins in a Les Blair film could be the crime that got me excommunicated by Mike Leigh. I remember someone telling me that because he'd had twins in one of his films, he thought we'd ripped him off. On the one hand, that's obviously a bit ridiculous – you can't really copyright the idea of twins, can you? You'd certainly have to pay Shakespeare a few royalties. On the other, I can kind of see where Mike was coming from.

You've got to protect your territory in this business. I watched a programme on the Cambridge Footlights the other night, and by the end of it I was fuming. I knew that lot were a bit of a mafia, but I didn't realize how widespread they were. Some of those people shouldn't be in showbiz – they should be in the House of Lords.

Obviously it would be wrong to tar them all with the same brush. Stephen Fry, for example, is a good mate of mine. He's always been a super-nice bloke, fiercely intelligent with it, and just generally someone who really knows the score. And anyway, who's to say Tony Slattery and Clive Anderson don't sit around sometimes and have a good moan about me, Kathy Burke, Dexter Fletcher and the guy out of Spandau? 'Fucking hell, this Anna Scher mob get everywhere.'

I don't know why that Footlights programme angered me so much, really. Maybe because it was on the same night that Liverpool had cheated Chelsea to get Lampard sent off. I'd had a few cans of lager and the best part of a bottle of red wine while I was watching the match, then I had a little snooze and woke up to the *South Bank Show* Footlights special. So it wasn't so much the booze that got to me, as a heady cocktail of righteous class rage and football-inspired anti-Scouse sentiment.

It was a good job there weren't any Scouse Footlighters, or my wrath might really have got the better of me. You can't fault those Cambridge boys on that score: they try really hard to keep the Scousers out. Nice work, Footlights, I'm proud of you.

EPILOGUE: 'HAS YOUR FILM BEEN ON TELLY YET?'

It's difficult to know how to react when four geezers – all in their forties – park their scooters and walk up to you in their fishtail parkas going, 'You changed my life. If it weren't for you, we wouldn't have all this.' There's not much else you can say but, 'All right, mate, thanks a lot for that.' It's a lovely thing in one way, but it's kind of a burden in another. Especially when you know that the next thing they'll probably say is, 'We've seen you on that *EastEnders*, but you'll always be Jimmy to us.'

In March of 2008, we did a thirtieth-anniversary *Quadrophenia* reunion. This guy who does a lot of *Star Trek* events put everyone (except Sting) up in a hotel in Brighton, and the punters paid for a package deal where they got a dinner, a late-night screening of the film, and some autographed photos. Trevor Laird and I hung about together signing a few pictures, and there was even talk of putting a band together for the occasion.

Spider – Gary Shail – had done a bit of record-producing, and Toyah was into it. We'd had a little bit of a falling out in the late seventies, but we get on really well now – she sometimes sends me text messages about how plastic surgery has given her the arse of a fourteen-year-old porn star. We'd have had a bit of fun for an hour, but in the end we realized that me, Toyah and Gary Shail playing mod covers as a power-trio is probably something that should only ever happen on a closed set.

The mood of that whole weekend was quite elegiac enough, without us adding to it. Obviously groups of mods turned up from all over the country. At one point about thirty of them came down the promenade on their scooters, and I went out and sort of saluted them – just as it started snowing.

Quadrophenia has always had that kind of cult feel about it. In the pictures that come with the original album there's a shot of a mod kneeling to pay homage to the Who outside the Hammersmith Odeon. On one level, that's just Pete Townshend having a laugh at himself, but on another, I think he'd almost had a vision of the religious element that definitely exists in rock 'n' roll.

A religion starts off as a few people in a cave and ends up with all the souvenir sellers in St Peter's Square. Music and films have kind of gone the same way, now, really. The iconography of it all has built up to the extent that it's holding the whole thing back. In the seventies, things happened, then other things happened. You couldn't get everything any time you wanted on DVD or video or illegal download.

When a film like *Quadrophenia* came out, you either went to see it when it was in the cinema, or you had to wait till it came on telly. 'Has your film been on telly yet?' If I had a pound for every time I'd been asked that, I wouldn't need to worry about repeat fees. But now everyone's got the bonus double-pack DVD version, and it gets passed down from man to son, from son to boy and from boy to baby. The whole thing's become a lot more industrialized, but it's also lost a bit of its mystery. That's why I don't mind that my daughter's never seen *Quadrophenia*.

I know she's proud of me and the things I've done, but I think she just sensed from a really early age that she didn't need the baggage. A lot of children of well-known people can get quite weighed down by it, but she never has been: she's managed to be normal, and I'm proud of her for that, too.

Last year, a touring stage-musical version of *Quadrophenia* opened in Plymouth, and Pete Townshend asked me to go down for the opening night. The main kid didn't half look like me. I've got a great picture of the two of us together – maybe he'll take the monkey off my back.

Tim Roth's son was in that production as well. First I had Tim Roth being a mod, now it's his son's turn. You'll be relieved to hear he's got his father's grimace. (I worked with Ray Winstone's daughter, Jaime, on *Poirot* last year, too. She's another chip off the old block).

Obviously Pete had again put back in all the metaphysical stuff that Roddam took out. They had four different actors playing Jimmy, to bring out the idea of the four different personalities. It did get a bit confusing sometimes, trying to work out which was which. But then I'm the last person to complain about that, as I've had that problem a few times myself.

Sometimes, when I wake up in the morning thinking, 'Why the fuck did I do that?' after Caroline Quentin's had to stop me having a go at someone at the Baftas, I wonder if maybe I never really got Jimmy out of my system. Usually I'm quite affable, but there's something driving me to do things sometimes – it's like there's a bit of him left in me. Those four personalities are floating around inside, and sometimes one of them kicks in and I go a bit mad. Presumably that was partly why they cast me in the role in the first place – because they saw that in me.

Even though the opening night went really well, Pete Townshend didn't go to the party afterwards. I did, but I could see why he gave it a miss – especially as he hasn't had a drink in fifteen years. When I have a spell off the booze, the last thing I want to do is go to a party.

I remember years and years ago I'd done a play with this old actor who was a bit of a cynic, and, because I was young and didn't yet know the ropes, I asked if I could have his number when the show was over. He said, 'Why bother? You ain't gonna ring me. We don't do that.' It seemed a bit harsh at the time, but over the years I've realized he was right. Of course you pal up with people when you're doing a job together, but when it ends you just move on.

That suits me fine, really, because I enjoy being with people, but I can be a bit of a moody fucker as well, and sometimes I just need to be on my own. When I think of some of the most interesting parts I've played – Jimmy in *Quadrophenia*, Mark in *Meantime*, Alex in *A Clockwork Orange* . . . Oskar in Gunther Grass's *The Tin Drum* (which I did for Radio 4), he's another one – they've definitely got something in common. It's almost as if they're participants and narrators at the same time. They're outsiders who are also in the middle of things. None of them look at things dead straight, either – they're all coming at life from slightly off to one side – so I guess there must be some of that in me as well.

I suppose my 'Parklife' character is another one of those narrator/participants. When I came on stage for Blur's two big shows in Hyde Park in the summer of 2009, I did a couple of lines of dialogue from *Quadrophenia*, just to get the crowd going. At Glastonbury, I'd gone on cold and it took everyone a little while to get into it, so I'd worked out that if you give them a couple of the old lines then you get a close-up on the big screen, and they know what's coming. If you're not going to let the side down as a fifty-year-old part-time pop star, you've got to learn to give yourself a bit of an entrance.

I only knew the Blur reunion was gonna happen when Damon asked me if I wanted to do it in the Fox & Pheasant pub before a Chelsea game. But I didn't know how well it was going to go, with Graham and Alex both playing really well, Dave holding it all together, and Damon really feeling it emotionally. The previous few times I'd gone on stage with them, everyone just seemed a bit embarrassed by it all. They were having to look for ways of making things work, which is how we ended up doing 'Parklife' acoustically. This time everyone just got on with it: it was the real thing.

Being on tour with that band now is a completely different ballgame to what it used to be, though. It's all pretty steady and supportive in the backstage area. You wouldn't have wanted little kids running about in the dressing rooms with the amount of carnage that was going on in the old days, but nowadays Graham and Damon have got their daughters, Pepper and Missy, Alex has three kids he road-tests his cheese on, and Dave's got his political career to think about, so he's not going to get up to too much mischief.

By the time you've thrown in the wives and the ex-wives, it's quite a family affair. The mums and dads are always there too – but then again, they always were. He's got a lovely mum and dad, Damon, and so have Graham and Alex. I never met Dave's, but I assume they were all right too, 'cos he is.

The funny thing is, even though there are a lot of sisters around as well, I've never met anybody's brother. In fact I think I saw in an article once that none of Blur have got a male sibling – they sort of fulfil that role for each other, and that's why they're so good at pressing each other's buttons when they have an argument. Obviously I ain't got any brothers either – they must have had a sense of that, and sniffed me out to join the gang.

When I think about what it means to really be a part of something – to really belong somewhere – it always comes back to London for me. Damon was saying a few words at Hyde Park about what that place meant to him, and how it was the inspiration for 'Parklife', but then I came in with the 'Knees Up Mother Brown'.

Sometimes disrupting the flow is the best way to keep things moving. That's how it works when people come up with their own bits of language, too. One thing I've always loved about London (and I know it happens in other places as well, but there's a particular way it works here which I think is unique to this city) is that someone's always got a better phrase than you.

That's what gives a place its character – the way people talk. I do fret for the lingo sometimes. I worry that maybe one day Cockney is just gonna kind of bite the dust. But with London being such a multicultural city, maybe a new kind of creole will develop.

The key point about evolution – and Charles Darwin would back me up on this, if he was still around – is that you can't predict which direction it's moving in. You never remember a block of flats being built once it's finished, do you? When you're walking around town, and one day the Astoria's there, and the next it's just a great big hole in the ground, you forget how it used to look straight away: it just ain't there no more.

The same thing can happen to whole communities, if the people doing the planning aren't careful. Shortly after I left King's Cross for Stoke Newington, one of the big, recently vacated blocks was completely turned over to Asian families. The council didn't make any attempt to integrate them, they just bunged them all in together, and my old primary school went from being more or less completely white to more than 50 per cent Asian, virtually overnight.

The people who make those kinds of decisions are very rarely the ones who have to live with the consequences, and that kind of drastic change isn't really fair on anyone. The pre-existing population are bound to struggle with something they'd probably have been fine with had it been done with a bit more care. The new kids who've come in will probably be OK, because they're all going to learn English at school. But their mums and dads have got no real incentive to put down any roots, because it's much easier just to try to maintain the social structures they've brought with them.

When I go back to King's Cross now, though – twenty years on – it all seems to have worked out all right. It's amazing how that place has managed to become a home to people, despite all the forces that seemed to be conspiring to make that impossible.

I suppose that shouldn't really surprise me though. The first thing that any random person would know about me is probably that I'm a Londoner, but I'm only second generation, after all. My Uncle Bob – my mum's brother – he came down here before I was born, and he still talks with a Geordie accent and supports Newcastle and Arsenal at the same time (which is obviously much easier now they're not in the same division).

That's the great thing about London, to me: it welcomes you in without you noticing, and lets you make your own decision as to how much you want to belong there. Acting's a bit like that as well.

ACKNOWLEDGEMENTS

Thanks to Ben Thompson, for listening to me drone on for hours and hours and doing such a good job. To Michael Hallett, and all at Emptage Hallett, for their help with this project; to Kerri Sharp, Katherine Stanton and Emma Harrow at Simon & Schuster, for bringing the book together; Jan Stevens, for stopping me sounding like a big head; Damon for being one of my favourite people, and the Cromer Aroma, in perpetuity.

PICTURE CREDITS

INDEX

(the initials PD in subentries refer to Phil Daniels)